THE HISTORY BEHIND
GAME OF
THRONES
THE NORTH REMEMBERS

For my parents, who always kept good books around to stoke my imagination. And for Mr Paul Brown, my high school history teacher at Donald A. Wilson Secondary School in Whitby, Canada, who lifted history off the page and made it fun.

'A story gives delight to read
Though it be fabulous indeed.
Then should a story that is true,
And told in skilful manner too,
Give pleasure that is full twofold.'

- John Barbour, *The Bruce*

THE HISTORY BEHIND
GAME OF
THRONES
THE NORTH REMEMBERS

DAVID C. WEINCZOK

PEN & SWORD
HISTORY

AN IMPRINT OF PEN & SWORD BOOKS LTD.
YORKSHIRE – PHILADELPHIA

First published in Great Britain in 2019 by
PEN AND SWORD HISTORY
An imprint of
Pen & Sword Books Ltd
Yorkshire – Philadelphia

ISBN 978 1 52674 900 0

A CIP catalogue record for this book is available from the British Library.

Typeset in Times New Roman 11.5/14 by
Aura Technology and Software Services, India
Printed and bound in the UK by TJ International

Pen & Sword Books Limited incorporates the imprints of Atlas, Archaeology,
Aviation, Discovery, Family History, Fiction, History, Maritime, Military, Military
Classics, Politics, Select, Transport, True Crime, Air World, Frontline Publishing,
Leo Cooper, Remember When, Seaforth Publishing, The Praetorian Press,
Wharncliffe Local History, Wharncliffe Transport, Wharncliffe True Crime and
White Owl.

For a complete list of Pen & Sword titles please contact
PEN & SWORD BOOKS LIMITED
47 Church Street, Barnsley, South Yorkshire, S70 2AS, England
E-mail: enquiries@pen-and-sword.co.uk
Website: www.pen-and-sword.co.uk

Or
PEN AND SWORD BOOKS
1950 Lawrence Rd, Havertown, PA 19083, USA
E-mail: Uspen-and-sword@casematepublishers.com
Website: www.penandswordbooks.com

Contents

PART THREE: PLAYERS OF THE GAME

PART FOUR: THE WHEELS OF WAR

Contents

Introduction

Never underestimate the power of a story. When the very first story was told, perhaps about some great hunt or a land of plenty and promise over the farthest hill, the world of the people who heard it became a grander place. They passed the story on to their children and their children's children, and eventually some of them found the courage to seek out the truth of it. Whether or not they succeeded is immaterial. The point is that they went searching.

When we fill our world with stories it becomes impossible to be bored. Certainly not in Scotland, the nation whose history this book is dedicated to. Walking the streets of Edinburgh, even if for the thousandth time, is to be immersed in an epic for the ages. The indomitable castle and scene of the Black Dinner looms over it all, the rock upon which countless armies have crashed. And what of the peak of Arthur's Seat, that mighty lion in repose, that reminds all who look upon Edinburgh – even from many miles away – that Scotland's story is one of the primordial clash between ice, fire and stone? Can we get closer to the Starks than by sitting astride the bewitching branches of the yew tree growing within the courtyard of Craigmillar Castle, the real-life Winterfell? How many of the students of the University of Edinburgh who drink and study in the nearby Meadows are aware that, had they been on that very spot 2,000 years ago, they would have witnessed Agricola's legions marching north to take the fight to the Caledonians beyond the Antonine Wall? Stories – and history is, after all, a collection of stories – are ultimately tools for understanding and forging connections to our own world. One of the greatest legacies of *Game of Thrones* is how it has got millions of people across the world thinking about and enjoying history. It may be the history of a world that happens to not in fact exist, but as this book will argue, George R.R. Martin built it around a framework firmly rooted in real events, individuals and concepts.

Introduction

In telling the story of *A Song of Ice and Fire*, George R.R. Martin has set innumerable people across the globe upon their own journeys of curiosity and wonder, and that alone makes it an invaluable tool for educators and storytellers. Some may begrudge the idea of learning Scottish or any other sort of history through the lens of popular culture. An all too common complaint about tourists in Scotland, for instance, is that they are 'just' here because they watched films like *Braveheart* or *Highlander*. Yet such complaints warrant no attention, for there is a long and proud tradition of popular culture setting the world's sights on Scotland's story. If we somehow found ourselves in the 1810s rather than the 2010s, we would be impatiently waiting for the release of the next *Waverley* novel by Walter Scott rather than Martin's *The Winds of Winter*. The release of *Ivanhoe* in 1819, a mere one year after *Rob Roy*, was met with intense speculation and rabid enthusiasm. Many a Romantic would be compelled by these and other novels to meander through the medieval streets of Edinburgh or study the ruins of Craignethan Castle, which became Tillietudlem Castle in Scott's *Old Mortality*, in the hope of coming closer to the essence of the tales they loved.

Fictional stories have also given some historic sites a new lease of life. Craignethan underwent a conservation programme in the nineteenth century as a result of renewed interest due to Scott's writings, and Doune Castle north of Stirling went from a beautiful but obscure ruinous keep to a beloved place of pilgrimage for pop culture devotees, having been used as a filming location for *Monty Python and the Holy Grail*, the television series *Outlander* and, not least, for the pilot episode of *Game of Thrones* where the Starks welcomed King Robert Baratheon and the Lannisters to Winterfell. At many historic locations in Scotland where the architecture has begun to crumble or the prestige of a place has long since receded, the telling of stories has restored them to their former glory and beyond.

A great pub quiz could be based around the superficial similarities between the histories of Westeros and our own world. Knowing that there is a region in the north-west Highlands called Wester Ross, or that the noble houses of Stark and Lannister sound an awful lot like the houses of York and Lancaster from the Wars of the Roses, would surely earn you some points in it. It is also fun to know trivia about the cast, for example that Rose Leslie, who plays Ygritte, is in fact part of an aristocratic Scottish family who own Wardhill Castle in Aberdeenshire, or that Rory McCann, who plays Sandor Clegane, was once the kilted and shirtless star of adverts for Scott's Porage Oats, a popular brand of Scottish porridge. Yet to think that the historical parallels and Scottish connections go *only* skin deep not only deprives you of much more interesting and useful knowledge, it vastly underestimates the extent to which George R.R. Martin has taken pains to create a fantastical world that not only reflects real history but actually enhances our understanding and appreciation of it. History done wrong can be a dreadful slog; throw in a few dragons and ice zombies, however, and suddenly a history lesson can become a global phenomenon.

What, then, does it mean to say that this book reveals the 'history behind *Game of Thrones*'? George R.R. Martin is not shy about being playful with sources of historical inspiration. It is easy to imagine him giving a spirited wink upon writing in *Fire and Blood* that the 'Dance of the Dragons' is 'the flowery name bestowed upon the savage internecine struggle for the Iron Throne of Westeros between two rival branches of House Targaryen', a subtle but unmistakable nod to the fifteenth-century Wars of the Roses that so informed *A Song of Ice and Fire*.[1] This book is similarly playful with the concept of historical inspiration and parallels, and deploys two main types of comparisons. The first type is the direct equivalency. Martin drew on a dizzying variety of eras, world cultures, folkloric traditions and medieval sources while forging the links in his literary chain, and though Scottish history is but one ingredient in his complex recipe, there are several cases where we can say with certainty that an event or person in Scottish history directly inspired an event or character in *Game of Thrones*. These include the Black Dinner at Edinburgh Castle in 1440, which provided the basis for the Red Wedding, and the forceful personality of Edward I of England, 'Hammer of the Scots', as the template for Tywin Lannister. There are also cases where geographical terms are taken directly from Scotland and infused into Westeros, such as the names of several of the Iron Islands, and where real archaeological terms such as *crannog* or *cairn* are applied to Westerosi locations.

The true value of *Game of Thrones* as a lesson in Scottish history and history in general is not found in direct equivalences, however entertaining they may be to highlight. Instead, take a look around the world of *Game of Thrones* – what do you see, beyond the various factions' heraldry and the stones that they build their power upon? You see a world in which the primordial whims of fire, ice and stone have created natural battlefields upon which nations have been made and broken time and time again. You see a world where no matter who sits upon the throne, it is the common people who suffer the brutalities of war while the heralds sing songs of great and noble deeds performed by jumped-up killers in shining armour. You see a world where morality and tradition have somehow conspired to make, paraphrasing Tyrion Lannister, the killing of ten men at a dinner a more ignoble act than killing 10,000 in battle. This is the second kind of comparison: a *thematic* one, where glimpses of the workings of the great wheel of Westerosi history, politics, beliefs and conventions reflect, and allow us to better comprehend, our own. Take, for instance, the comparison of Scotland's King Robert the Bruce to Westeros' King Robert Baratheon in Part Three. Sure, both of those characters were kings who happen to share the same initials, but what drove them to reach the heights they attained? What common factors ultimately defined their legacies? And what was it about their respective worlds that shaped them into the legends they became? These are the questions that really get us somewhere, and which prove equally useful when contemplating a historic site as when we sit around and debate the motivations of each character in microscopic detail after each episode of *Game of Thrones*.

As the title implies, and given that Scotland is the northernmost nation of the British Isles, this book's allegiance is primarily to the North of Westeros. We will be spending a great deal of time by the hearth fire of the Starks of Winterfell, raiding mainland shores alongside the ironborn and revelling in the frigid freedom of the wildlings beyond the Wall. We will wade through the bogs of the Neck and stand upon the shores of the River Trident, where Robert Baratheon won his crown with a well-placed swing of his war hammer. The lands to the south of the Trident's watery tendrils are outside our domain, though we will briefly walk the streets of King's Landing – albeit during the most terrible moment in that festering city's history. Similarly there are historical eras that we will return to again and again, while others will only be mentioned in passing. There is nothing to be gained from discussing, say, the impact of industrialization on Scotland in this book because the process of industrialization has yet to touch Westeros – and at the going rate of technological advancement in *Game of Thrones*, it may take 10,000 more years before some maester in Oldtown figures out how to harness steam to fuel the royal navy or tries to revive dragon eggs with electric currents. The earliest events that concern us are ancient in the extreme, going back over 300 million years, and we will spend a great deal of time in the ancient through to the high medieval periods (roughly 5,000 BCE until the late fourteenth century), with periodic check-ins on the early modern era. By the sixteenth century, which reflects the apex of technological achievement in Westeros, our journey mostly comes to an end, though a handful of historical episodes spanning into the seventeenth and eighteenth centuries will be reckoned with.

Knowing the stories of our past, and how our favourite fictional tales interwove them into their narratives, turns a simple visit to a castle, battlefield, museum or locale – or indeed, just the act of opening a book or turning on a television show – into an imaginative and informative odyssey. Whatever else may have changed about human society in the thousands of years since the ancient peoples of Argyll etched their enigmatic cup-and-ring marks on their rocky canvases, the allure of seeking the truth behind a good story has not diminished one bit. Long after the *Game of Thrones* finale fades to black and the last lines of *A Song of Ice and Fire* are written, its inspirations and parallels in Scottish history will remain for us to explore. It is a boundless extended universe in our own backyard. We may not be able to join the Night's Watch, but we can walk along the edge of the world at the Antonine Wall. We can climb the wintery mountains of the far north into the Queen of Winter's grasp, and enter the den of the old gods at Dunino. Find the old ford of the Bannock Burn at Milton and it is possible to stand in the precise spot where Robert the Bruce smote Henry de Bohun with a vengeful blow of his axe, just as Robert Baratheon struck down Rhaegar Targaryen with his hammer in the waters of the Trident. 'We read fantasy to find the colours again,' wrote George R.R. Martin in his short rumination, 'On Fantasy'.[2] If Martin is correct in this – and I wholeheartedly believe that he is – then it is my sincere hope that upon completing this book and venturing back into the realm of Westeros, both it and our own world will be just a little more colourful.

- Edinburgh, February 2019

PART I

THE LAND ITSELF

Chapter 1

Nature's Crucible: Stirling, The Neck & the Twins

Geography is so often the paper upon which history is written. We may determine the precise words that are recorded, yet in some cases the raw materials were provided long before any of us could possibly leave a mark. More specifically, geography creates crucibles. There are the places which, through a quite indifferent convergence of phenomena such as volcanic activity, glaciation and the rise and fall of sea levels over many millennia, become landscapes where history seems bound to be made. Think of the Hot Gates of Thermopylae, which made it possible for the Spartans and their allies to hold, however briefly, against the overwhelming numbers of Xerxes' army; or the Golden Horn of Constantinople, a brooch clasping East and West together that became a civilizational flashpoint for over 1,000 years; or the mountain passes of Switzerland, which allowed the cantons to endure amidst the tumultuous sea of medieval European politics crashing in from all sides. Then there is Stirling. If ever a place was destined to be a crucible, it is Stirling.

The hint is in the name. Stirling in Gaelic is *Sruileagh*, meaning a place of battle or strife. Until the nineteenth century, which saw major leaps forward in transportation technology and land management, any significant armed force wanting to invade the north of Scotland from the south, or vice versa, had no choice but to pass through the eye of the needle at Stirling. To understand why, we need a map.

Matthew Paris, a thirteenth-century English chronicler and Benedictine monk at St Albans Abbey, mapped Britain as he knew it. Of all the great rivers that intersect the island in Paris' rendering, there is one glaring peculiarity. It is a change so radical that you could easily wonder if you were looking at some quasi-fantastical version of Britain after all. About three-quarters of the way up there is a massive rift in the land, the south separated from the north by a watery tendril spanned at its narrowest point by a single bridge. It is the focal point of the whole map, a place unlike any other shown. Long before the battle that would make it a household name, Matthew Paris already knew that Stirling Bridge was the key to the north.

The split was seen as so definitive that many classical commentators regarded the lands beyond the Scottish Sea as an entirely separate island from Britain. Tacitus observed that, once Rome had fixed its frontier at the narrow neck between the firths of Forth and Clyde, the 'enemy', possibly referring to the Maeatae who inhabited the region around Stirling and the Trossachs, had been 'pushed back, as if into a different island'.[1] This view was echoed over 1,000 years later in Walter Bower's *Scotichronicon*, which went so far as to say that, if not for a thicket-laden morass a mere 22 miles wide, the rivers Clyde and Forth would touch and sever the land entirely.[2] It was even common for medieval sources to refer to the Forth-Clyde line as the 'Scottish Sea'.

This was more of a symbolic analysis than a literal one. It was known, for instance, that the River Forth was fordable not far upstream from Stirling Bridge, an option that was open to and yet declined by English forces under John de Warenne and Hugh de Cressingham at the Battle of Stirling Bridge in 1297. It was also possible for small, mobile warbands to circumvent the bridge by weaving through the hills to the west of Stirling, yet this was not an option for any sizeable force. From the mid-fourteenth century, English armies, having learned repeated lessons about the cost of facing the Scots at Stirling, preferred to sail across the Scottish Sea and land in Fife or Angus. Still, raising a fleet is expensive at the best of times. For all practical purposes, Stirling remained the key to Scotland until 4 March 1890, the day that the Forth Bridge, now one of Scotland's six UNESCO World Heritage Sites, opened – the first time a structure had spanned the Scottish Sea.

The Land Protects Its Own

Game of Thrones' Balon Greyjoy may have commanded the mighty Iron Fleet, but that would only get the ironborn as far as the shores of mainland Westeros. Ships alone could do little to actually conquer the North, and even less to hold it. This was the main stumbling block in

Balon's plot to declare himself King of the Iron Islands and wrest control of the North from the Starks. He could launch endless raids of the sort that the ironborn had plagued mainlanders with for thousands of years, and perhaps even seize a castle or two, but as soon as the strength of the North coalesced against the ironborn they would be forced to return to the waves. Unless, of course, they could hold the narrows of the Neck and trap Robb Stark and Roose Bolton's armies in the south. Then the kraken could strangle the wolf into submission.

The North had, until Aegon's Conquest brought Torrhen Stark to his knees, the ability to retain its independence from the other six kingdoms thanks more to the geography of the Neck than to any boasts about 'northern valour'.[3] Before an invader could come within a sword's swing of a northman they had to do battle with the land itself, whose bogs and beasts foiled even the mighty Andals time and time again. It could take upwards of twelve days to run the gauntlet of the Neck, plenty of time for a multitude of hazards – including quicksand, lizard-lions, hidden pools and the stealthy Crannogmen – to prove your undoing.[4] The geography of the Neck provides such a staunch defence for its inhabitants that they see no need to build castles or maintain armies, as do the other realms of Westeros. 'Our land,' boasts Meera Reed rightly, 'protects its own.'[5]

There was a time when the Neck was no more waterlogged than the Riverlands to the south. So much of Westeros' identity is tied up in its island status that it is all too easy to forget that it was not always so. The First Men, who wrested control of the land from the Children of the Forest, did not arrive in Westeros by boat – they simply walked. Westeros and Essos were once linked by a land bridge called the Arm of Dorne. The First Men wielded bronze weapons and rode horses, giving them a major advantage over the Children, who had neither.[6] But the Children did possess the gift of magic, and a great ritual was held – some say on the Isle of Faces, others say in the Children's Tower of Moat Cailin – to call forth the elements and drive the invaders back across the Arm. 'The Hammer of the Waters', the maesters call it. A great deluge shattered the Arm of Dorne into splinters that we now call the Stepstones, but the south was not the only place that felt the Hammer. Waters inundated much of Westeros, and when they at last receded the festering swamps of the Neck were their legacy.[7]

There is another theory, however, that frames the creation of the Neck in terms that prehistoric Britons would have been all too familiar with from tales passed down by their ancestors. In *The Song of the Sea: How the Lands Were Severed*, Archmaester Cassander argues that it was not the Hammer of the Waters that flooded the Neck but a much more gradual process caused by centuries of warm temperatures that melted much of the ice in the Shivering Sea.[8] Our own history reinforces Cassander's theory. So much of Britain's idea of itself is, like Westeros, caught up in its island status – 'that sceptred Isle', protected by the 'splendid isolation' provided by the English Channel, and so forth (though the Saxons, Normans and Norse clearly were not at all bothered by it). Just as Eddard Stark told Robert Baratheon that 'Even a million Dothraki are no threat to the realm, as long as they remain on the other side of the Narrow Sea',[9] so too was the island of Britain spared the worst ravages of the wars that utterly consumed continental Europe. Yet in 9,000 BCE, Britons could make no such boast, for Britain was not an island but a peninsula of Europe accessible over a chalk land bridge between Dover and Calais. The Thames and Rhine fed into the North Sea basin, the resulting lake lapping up against the Anglian ice sheet.[10] Eventually, like a tub without an overflow drain, the waters burst over the chalk bridge. The people on the south side found life continued much as before, but those on the north were now fated to be an island people, with profound consequences for the shared history of both. This was no great cataclysm but an almost imperceptible process that unfolded over centuries. What was once a dry land bridge gradually became a bog, and the footsteps of people making the crossing sunk ever deeper into the muck as the years progressed. By 6,000-5,500 BCE, the transformation of Britain into an island was complete, and a wall of water greater than any structure humanity could hope to raise became its people's best defence.[11] In a fascinating instance of people copying nature's example, on 6 May 1994, Eurotunnel opened, which made it possible to cross from Calais to Dover without setting sail for the first time in 8,000 years.

If ever there was an ally of the Scots against invaders, it too was the land. While it may be only a fraction of the size of the Neck and lack lizard-lions (though not midges, which if not as deadly are at least as damnable), the landscape of Stirling was almost as challenging. The River Forth serpentines in great arcs through Stirling, passing almost within bowshot of the castle and ever ready to flood its banks. The Ochil Hills, rising abruptly from the hinterland of Clackmannanshire, flank Stirling from the east. To the west lie the Touch and Gargunnock Hills, less impressive than the Ochils but every bit as much an obstacle to a large force burdened with wagons, supplies, horses and camp followers. The convergence of hills on Stirling is obvious to modern visitors, particularly from the walls of Stirling Castle or from atop the iconic Wallace Monument on the other side of the Forth. The land resembles a corridor, with the walls closing in narrower and narrower until they reach a focal point at the castle crag. What is not obvious, however, is how much tighter the land's grasp was until very recently.

After the retreat of the ice from Scotland approximately 13,500 years ago, the low-lying ground around Stirling Castle rock, known as the Carse, was a part of the sea. Remains of whales up to 25 metres long have been discovered in the soils of this alluvial floodplain,[12] and the ancient coastline is clearly visible in the form of a ridge running from central Stirling to St Ninian's and on to Balquhidderock. With the silting up of the Forth estuary around 6,500 years ago and the gradual lowering of sea levels, the Carse became a middle ground between the firm soils atop the ridge and the tidal waters of the River Forth. Deep peat beds formed atop a base of clay, and the Carse was left riddled with streams, recorded in medieval chronicles as *pows*.[13] The Carse, while not a swamp, forced anyone seeking easy passage through Stirling onto the higher ground to the west and directly within sight of the mighty castle. Otherwise an almighty logistical headache was in order. For instance, having been forced into the Carse by pits akin to minefields laid by Robert the Bruce upon the higher, dryer ground, the English at Bannockburn had no choice but to spend hours tearing down the roofs and doors of local houses to create makeshift bridges to carry them over the soggy ground. Nature had given a blessing to Stirling's future defenders and a curse to its attackers – a barrier utterly inhospitable to the panoplies of large-scale warfare. It is a choke point on a national scale. Walter of Guisborough, a fourteenth-century chronicler, concluded correctly that, 'There was, indeed, no better place in all the land to deliver the English into the hands of the Scots, and so many into the power of so few.'[14]

Stirling & Moat Cailin: The Keys To The Kingdom

Returning to Westeros, if the Neck is, in Balon Greyjoy's own words, the 'key to the kingdom',[15] then Moat Cailin is the padlock. The first time we set eyes on Moat Cailin, from the perspective of Theon (in his new guise as Reek) on a mission from Ramsay Bolton, it is a graveyard of armies. Dead northmen are half-sunk into the bogs that creep right up to the castle's walls, and the perilously narrow causeway that leads to the gates is pockmarked by corpses and abandoned siege equipment. The castle itself is built atop a large mound, possibly a motte formed by a combination of glacial deposits and manpower not unlike the one at Ruthven Barracks near Kingussie in the Scottish Highlands. There is no way around without boats that does not end in a squalid death, with the semi-ruinous skeleton of the castle plugging the only passage 'like a cork in a bottle'.[16] Moat Cailin is a serious contender for the title of most strategically important castle in Westeros, and the amount of blood spilled in its name over its 10,000-year history – by First Men, the Marsh King, the Andals, ironborn and more – is a testament to that.

Of the thousands of castles across Scotland, Stirling is the most strategically vital of them all. The formula is simple. Control the river crossing and you control the flow of people and armies through the gateway of Scotland. Control the castle, which stands sentinel atop a volcanic crag and dominates the landscape, and you control the crossing. For this reason, more nation-defining battles have been fought for Stirling and its castle than for anywhere else in Scotland.

Looking out from the castle's ramparts, elevated by the volcanic crag and tail on which the royal fortress was built, the story of Scotland unfolds before you. To the north-west rise the mountains of the Highland Line – Ben Lomond, Ben Ledi, Stuc a'Chroin and Ben Vorlich – in whose shadows the Romans fought bloody wars against the Maeatae in the early third century. Much nearer is Stirling Bridge, where Wallace and Moray's spearmen trapped the English army in a loop of the River Forth on 11 September 1297. With the noose tightened, all the Scots had to do was push towards the bridge and river until there was no one left to push against. One year later, on 22 July 1298, Wallace would be routed by the Hammer of the Scots, Edward I, at the Battle of Falkirk a few miles to the south. Also to the south, and visible to the naked eye, a saltire flies proudly at the site where Robert the Bruce raised his standard at the Battle of Bannockburn, fought on 23 and 24 June 1314. Stirling Castle itself changed hands no less than eleven times during the Wars of Independence,[17] of which the battles of Stirling Bridge, Falkirk and Bannockburn were major parts. Not far from Bannockburn is the Sauchie Burn, where King James III was killed in the chaotic aftermath of a battle against his own son on 11 June 1488. High in the Ochil Hills to the north-east was fought one of the great 'what if' battles of Scottish history, the Battle of Sheriffmuir, on 13 November 1715. Had the Jacobites not hesitated when on the brink of victory there, they could very possibly have won the war and radically altered the history of Britain. A survey of the land around Stirling is nothing less than a crash course in the martial history of Scotland.

A Bridge To Cross At Any Cost

Moat Cailin may fulfil the parallel of a castle guarding a vital crossing, yet that alone does not quite equal the strategic value of Stirling. To do that takes two Westerosi castles. We must, like Robb Stark, reckon with The Twins. Seeking to strike a killing blow to the Lannisters by invading the Westerlands, Robb – named by his bannermen the King in the North – was faced with an unenviable dilemma. He could take his Northern army on a detour that would add hundreds of miles to their time-sensitive march, or come to terms with the Lord of the Crossing, the odious Walder Frey, and cross his bridge. Looking at a map of Westeros, it is clear that Robb had little choice. Frey's bridge had to be crossed at any cost, though few could have imagined that doing so would set in motion the chain of events that would culminate with the Red Wedding.

Six hundred years before that fateful decision was made, a Frey also looked at a map. He saw a land of rivers, with the mighty Trident choking the lands just south of the Neck like a collar.[18] Knowing the strategic value of the Riverlands, and that there would be no shortage of armies seeking to march through them to and from the North, opportunism – the foremost quality of the Freys – took care of the rest. By reading the land, the Freys established themselves as one of the most disproportionately influential and vexing families of Westeros.

Spanning the Green Fork of the Trident was no mean feat, and it took the Freys three generations to establish a small timber bridge. This sounds a lot like Stirling Bridge, which was a relatively small timber structure at the time of William Wallace and Andrew Moray's renowned stand there in September 1297. This bridge was possibly destroyed during the battle, and timber remnants were identified in 1905 about

200ft upstream from the picturesque stone bridge that has spanned the River Forth since the late fifteenth or early sixteenth centuries. Back at the Twins, timber castles soon followed on both banks, allowing the Freys to charge tolls and enrich themselves by exploiting geography before anyone else could. On reflection, it is quite remarkable that none of the ancient families of the Riverlands thought to do the same before the Freys, given that castles like Moat Cailin already dominated strategic choke points in Westeros over 9,000 years before the Twins were built.

As the years passed and the tolls flowed in, the Freys were able to recast both the bridge and the castles in stone. The narrow timber bridge became a broad avenue to rival the Kingsroad, with space enough for two wagons to cross side by side.[19] A third castle, the Water Tower, was built in the middle and bristled with arrow slits, crenellations and other delightful features like murder holes (more on those nasty pieces of work later). While Stirling Bridge certainly never had anything like that, Stirling Castle served just as well.

In the case of both Westeros' Moat Cailin and Scotland's Stirling Castle, both are exceedingly powerful fortifications. Stirling is much less worse for wear, having been magnificently maintained and in some places restored, whereas Moat Cailin belongs to no house and so has no one to mend the many cracks that have formed. Their true power and importance, however, is not in their thick walls, high towers or even the people charged to defend them. They are ultimately both the keys to their respective kingdoms because the forces of nature made them so long before their first stones were laid.

Chapter 2

Rocks of the Ages:
Dumbarton & Casterly

A Song of Ice and Fire would be a cracking title for a book on Scottish geology. The mountains, glens, lochs, castle crags and coastlines that make up so much of Scotland's iconic imagery are all thanks to the epic battle between those two elements. The rending and reforging of the earth's crust through volcanic activity over 300 million years ago was a chaotic process, yet, as with the Doom of Valyria, it also held the seeds of creation. Though entirely inhospitable to all but the most elementary and resilient life forms, the volcanic landscape of prehistory forged not only the glens, lochs and isles for which Scotland is so famous, but the literal bedrock on which the nation's greatest fortress-builders would raise their walls. They may not have understood the processes that created the volcanic plugs and crags that their power rested upon, but the early rulers of the land we call Scotland certainly knew that building their strongholds upon them would make quite an impression. Find an outcrop of rock in Scotland, or better yet an extinct volcano, and you have likely found a seat of power.

Some of these volcanoes became plugged when a portion of magma cooled enough to seal the vent through which it had previously been escaping. Over tens of millions of years, the volcanoes themselves eroded away while the extremely tough basalt or dolerite of the plugs better weathered the elements. The retreat of the glaciers some 12,000 years ago[1] sometimes transformed these plugs into 'crag and tail' formations, with some of the most prominent examples being Edinburgh Castle rock, Stirling Castle rock, nearby Abbey Craig and the Minto Crags in the Scottish Borders. They resemble giant stone ramps sloping upwards to a sheer terminus.

The resident of Edinburgh is constantly aware of this phenomenon. If not for the great volcano whose carcass Castle Rock inhabits, the earliest locals would never have intuited this as the place to build their stronghold. From a high place, perhaps from the ramparts of Edinburgh Castle or the summit of Arthur's Seat (itself a volcanic plug shaped like a lion in repose), you can establish a pattern of prehistoric settlement in the Lothians with the naked eye. Simply scan the horizon for a large bump and you'll have found a hill fort or ancient capital. Along the coast rises North Berwick Law, a plug that from certain angles appears so perfectly triangular that, the first time I saw it from a distance, I wondered when Scotland had gotten around to building its own great pyramid. Due south-west from North Berwick is Traprain Law, shaped like a leviathan's back breaking the surface of the sea. It was likely the capital of the Votadini, the people who lived between the two Roman walls, and it yielded the greatest horde of Roman silver ever found outside the boundaries of the Roman Empire. To the south are the Pentland Hills, home to the remains of Castlelaw Hill Fort and a remarkably well-preserved souterrain, an Iron Age underground tunnel used for storage, which you can still clamber into. To the west is Corstorphine Hill, where a hillfort and cup-and-ring rock art have been discovered, and beyond that lays Stirling, another place defined by the lay of the land. All of these settlements would have had beacon fires, and if an enemy – such as the Roman legions or later the Angles – were approaching from the south the entire country would know about it in a matter of hours. When you know what to look for, the land can be read just as a book, though one you can proceed to walk through the pages of.

All of those are within one swathe of the Lowlands. Extend the range to the rest of Scotland and the number of settlements and fortifications built upon the ruins of volcanoes and the leavings of glaciers is beyond reckoning. You can see why, if a Scot says that they're going for a walk up 'the Rock', there are any number of places they might be intending to go. When a denizen of Westeros refers to 'the Rock', however, there is only one place they can possibly mean: Casterly Rock, seat of House Lannister and the greatest fortress in the Seven Kingdoms.

The Lion's Den: Casterly Rock

More mountain than castle, Casterly Rock is a single, massive stone spire – a monolithic promontory, to be geologically precise – two leagues across and, it is reckoned, three times higher than the Hightower of Oldtown or even the Wall.[2] Its might is inseparable from that of House Lannister, whose wealth is founded upon the rich veins of gold and silver that course through the seemingly endless tunnels that permeate the Rock. Like Arthur's Seat in Edinburgh, Casterly Rock strikes the form of a lion in repose, particularly in the low light of evening when the Sunset Sea lives up to its name.[3] Perhaps that is where the Lannisters got the inspiration for their lion sigil. In fact, the Rock is so mighty that the castle built atop the Rock is almost superfluous; with an internal harbour and innumerable deep caverns every bit as strong as modern bomb shelters offering refuge for its residents in times of crisis, not even dragon-flame can threaten Casterly Rock.[4] Though it would seem that the Rock is vulnerable to attack from the likes of the Iron Fleet, it has never been taken by storm, with the reivers of the iron islands – ever gnashing and nipping at the Westerlands – preferring to hit softer targets like Lannisport. Compliments of Tyrion Lannister, however, who grew up a son of the Rock, we eventually learn that no castle is truly impregnable if the attackers are willing to get their hands dirty.

No one knows when the first person – if indeed it was a person – made their home upon or within the Rock. It has been used since at least the time of the Children of the Forest and the First Men, giving it one of the longest recorded histories of any fortification in Westeros. At some point over the intervening millennia, the Casterlys, lords of the Rock before it was taken from them by Lann the Clever, built a ringfort atop its peak and began to convert the caverns below into spacious halls.[5] The Rock has been a seat of power ever since, without which the Lannisters would be no more than bit players in the game of thrones.

Undeniably, the closest real-world parallel to Casterly Rock is found not in Scotland but Gibraltar. A quick glimpse at images of the two side by side leave no room for doubt as to what primarily fuelled Martin's imagination in this case. The Rock of Gibraltar, also known simply as The Rock, is one of the Seven Natural Wonders of the World. It guards the narrow neck that spills from the Mediterranean into the Atlantic Ocean. It is easy to see how Phoenician and Greek sailors would have thought themselves to be rounding, to borrow a phrase from Melisandre, one of the hinges of the world[6] as they passed it. At a peak of 1,396ft, it is still not as grand as Casterly Rock, which stands at over 2,000ft, though it is imposing enough that classical texts called it, epically in the purest sense, the Pillar of Hercules. Defying belief, the Moors built a castle atop The Rock which appears, like the fortifications of Casterly Rock, as little more than a blemish or small growth on the gargantuan peak. The Rock of Gibraltar is also riddled with over 30 miles of tunnels constructed between the eighteenth and twentieth centuries, but there is no gold to be found within them.

The Rock of the Britons

While I am fairly sure that no one will have ever made this recommendation before, if you cannot make it to the sunlit south of Spain to see the Rock of Gibraltar, then Scotland's River Clyde is the next best thing. Not for the sun, of course, which is as elusive on the Clyde as it is in the rest of Scotland, but for that other great Rock – *Dùn Breatann*, the 'Fort of the Britons', known today as Dumbarton Rock. The volcanic plug of Dumbarton juts out into the water like a defiant exclamation point, commanding attention for miles around. From certain angles it, too, resembles a lion in repose, though perhaps with its twin peaks and central cleft that give the Rock the form of a capital 'M', a camel would be the closer silhouette to match. It is difficult to contemplate a better site for defence. It is approachable from only one direction, north, on the landward side along a relatively narrow peninsula which is interrupted abruptly by the sheer face of Dumbarton's cliffs. Elsewhere, the Rock mostly plunges directly into the waters of the Clyde, and where it does not it is guarded by walls that snake along the crag so congruously that from even a short distance away it is difficult to tell which stones were shaped by masons and which were crafted by the primordial volcanic forge.

Despite Edinburgh and Stirling claiming the lion's share of the limelight when it comes to fortresses built upon volcanic plugs, Dumbarton Rock can boast a tale longer in the telling than any other fortified site in Britain. Known during the early historic period as *Alt Clut*, the 'Rock of the Clyde', it possibly appears in records as early as the second-century works of the Greco-Roman polymath Claudius Ptolemy, who made note of the settlement of Alauna, meaning 'headland' or 'spur', at the approximate location of Dumbarton.[7] Bede, writing from his lifelong abode at the monastery of St Peter in Jarrow, England, in the early eighth century, referred to the Rock as *civitas Brettonum munitissima*, meaning roughly 'the very well fortified city of the Britons'.[8] Clearly this was no mere local hub but a place that international chroniclers felt was worthy of note.

The twin peaks of the Rock are known as White Tower Crag and the Beak, and upon the easterly White Tower Crag Iron Age people established a hillfort of which no visible trace remains. From its summit, the residents of the Rock would have witnessed some of the most transformative events in Scottish history, some to their benefit and others resulting in calamity. They would have heard the sound of hammers and strange military drills as the Romans raised the western extremity of their Antonine Wall at Old Kilpatrick, a short paddle upstream. Some say that the Rock even played host to Merlin, a character whose historical origins likely lie in the south of Scotland. By the middle of the fifth century, the Rock had become the capital of the powerful independent Kingdom of Strathclyde, the longest-lived Brythonic domain within what was known in Welsh as *Y Hen Ogledd*, 'the Old North'.[9] At this time the waters around Dumbarton would have swelled with ships coming and going from its port, and the Rock would have been one of a handful of centres in Scotland that were approaching something like metropolitanism.

And then the Vikings came. Led by the infamous Ivar the Boneless and Olaf the White, the Norse King of Dublin, the fury of the Norse crashed upon the Rock in 870. As many as 200 longships carrying more than 5,000 Vikings surrounded and besieged the Rock, but even with such a force the Norse were unable to storm the fortress. Viking patience must have been sorely tested as the siege dragged on four months, with the Rock seeming little worse for wear. Unfortunately, Dumbarton Rock did not ultimately prove as unconquerable as Casterly Rock. The end came quietly. It did not arrive with a dramatic breach in the walls, a sneak attack in the night or a traitor opening the gates, as so many other sieges did. It ended when the well inside the Rock dried up[10] and the defenders, already starved and without hope of salvation, had no choice but to give up their home or die miserably upon it. How many might have chosen the latter had they known the fate that awaited them? The Norse pillaged the Rock and took away all the spoils they could carry in their longships, the most valuable of which by far were the thousands of people, described in the *Annals of Ulster* as a 'great prey of Angles and Britons and Picts',[11] pressed into slavery and sold at the lucrative Dublin slave markets. So despoiled, the Rock disappeared from the historical record until the thirteenth century, when it would rise from the ashes and become a linchpin of the Kingdom of Scotland.

Children of the Rock

While most of Dumbarton's residents were packed on to Norse longships to live out their days as slaves to the highest bidder, some were able to make a getaway. The *Welsh Annals* of 890 record how some survivors made their way to Gwynedd as refugees, where they were made welcome amongst their Brythonic brethren who had similarly faced the wrath of both Viking and Saxon.[12] If there is any truth to the idea that a nation is not at heart a place but a people, then we can say that the nation of Strathclyde did not die but merely moved house and blended in with the neighbours – a comforting thought.

Though it disappeared from the records for two centuries after the Viking assault, it emerged again in the Middle Ages as one of the most strategically and politically vital strongholds in Scotland. For instance, it was not, as the film *Braveheart* would have you believe, Robert the Bruce who betrayed William Wallace to the English but John 'the False' Menteith, who served as Dumbarton's governor and delivered Wallace to the English to face gruesome execution. The price of betraying a man who became a national hero is steep, however, and now Menteith is remembered solely for his treachery. A reminder of it decorates the guardhouse that plugs the cleft between the two peaks of the Rock. Look closely at the line of its roof and you will spot a grotesque face, twisted and appearing to be in dumb agony, staring back at you – the visage of Menteith, set in stone for posterity to mock. As late as the mid-sixteenth century, Dumbarton Rock was still considered to be the 'key of the north'[13] by no less than Henry VIII, who of course sought (and failed) to conquer it. It was the last piece of Scotland that the young Mary, Queen of Scots stood upon before embarking for France at the age of 6 for her ill-fated marriage to the Dauphin, Francis.

Perhaps Dumbarton's most enduring legacy, however, is the number of other Dumbartons it spawned across the globe. Dumbarton Rock would have been one of the last landmarks of home for the tens of thousands of Scots that were shipped down the Clyde and on to the four corners of the British Empire. They would not soon forget it. There are now places called Dumbarton in Canada, the United States, Australia and New Zealand, and one hopes that school children growing up in those offshoots of the Rock are taught the illustrious history of their home town's namesake. For they are the children of the Rock.

Chapter 3

The Isles

A World Apart?

The Isles are where the elements go to dance. Sea and sky and stone swirl together, often harmoniously, sometimes furiously, rarely predictably. In the ethereal light that so often accompanies a Hebridean sunrise or sunset, the boundaries between the land and the waters that lash it seem to dissipate. Instead of a battle of elements it becomes a chorus. Standing upon the prehistoric and long-abandoned rocky ramparts of forts like Dùn Morbhaidh on the Isle of Coll or Dun Sgùrabhal on Barra, both of which watch over the boundless western horizon, it is perhaps easier here than anywhere else to feel time's immutability.

Our modern fascination with Scotland's Isles is largely due to our perception of them as remote. Residents of urban Scotland speak often and wistfully of 'getting away from it all' and taking a trip beyond the reach of mobile phone reception to havens like Jura or Harris. On a recent expedition to Colonsay, within thirty minutes of docking at the port of Scalasaig I overheard two conversations between locals that seemed to sum it all up. 'All money does is buy you a better class of misery,' said one, a sentiment you'll never hear on the streets of Edinburgh. Within moments another resident provoked a hearty debate by boldly stating: 'This sea kelp brouhaha has got the whole island in a froth.' Simple living and sea kelp scandals; that, to my urban twenty-first-century ears, sounded like the very definition of a world apart.

As it turns out, this is a very new way of thinking about the Isles, and much has changed – quite radically in many cases and places – in merely the last century. Had I gone to Colonsay in 1917 rather than 2017, for instance, I would not have been able to understand the musings of the locals because they would have been expressed in Gaelic, not

English. We must once again challenge our preconceived notions by examining the map a little differently than we are used to. Imagine a Scotland without motorways, train lines, cycle paths or roads, and the idea of travelling overland becomes far more daunting than going in even a rudimentary vessel by sea. Until the early eighteenth century, when General Wade began constructing a network of simple roads into the Highlands as a means to dominate them, this was the reality for most Scots. The moment that we view waterways – seas, firths, lochs and rivers – as highways rather than boundaries is the moment that we can begin to understand the world that the Gaels and Norse of the Isles inhabited. For the people of the west, the compass was not centred on Scone, the ancient inauguration site of the Kings of Scots, or the pre-eminent royal castle of Stirling, but firmly in the Irish and North Seas. Events in Antrim, the Isle of Man and even Scandinavia were of far greater concern to the Islesmen than those unfolding in Perthshire or the Lothians.

With a good wind and a strong crew at the oars, a vessel departing Norway in the ninth century could reach Shetland, 180 nautical miles away, within two days.[1] From there, they could make the relatively small skip over to Orkney, and then on to Caithness and Sutherland on the mainland. Sailing west then south from Orkney around Cape Wrath, it would only take another day to reach the Hebrides, themselves being stepping stones to the Irish Sea and the shores of Ireland, Wales, Cornwall, Brittany, the Basque country and beyond.[2] These sea routes, far more efficient than any form of overland travel until well into the nineteenth century, meant that the world of the Isles – a term here applied to the Hebrides as well as Orkney and Shetland, given their interconnectedness – was not one of remoteness and isolation. Instead, the Isles are the north-westernmost nodes in a network linking Scandinavia to Britain, Britain to Northern Europe, Northern Europe to the Mediterranean, the Mediterranean to Byzantium, and Byzantium to Mesopotamia as far as the great city of Baghdad, where one could find slaves from Britain and Ireland sold to the caliphs by the Norse through an international racket. Since humanity first reached the rocky west coast and the Isles, the waterways that force modern roads to embark on vast detours were never the barriers we think of them as; they were express routes whose destinations were as limitless as the courage of the captains that sailed them.

In Amongst The Machair

When first laying eyes on the shores of the Isles, the sage words of *The Lord of the Rings*' Bilbo Baggins seem most apt for them: 'Like butter that has been scraped over too much bread.'[3] The thin, patchy soils are regularly breached by the rock beneath, as though the grasses were little more than blemishes on a stony foundation. The Lewisian Gneiss that makes up this foundation in the Outer Hebrides is some of the oldest stone in the world, bearing much in common with the Laurentian Range of North America where many Hebrideans were sent to settle during the Highland Clearances.[4] What soil there is on most of the Isles is shallow, acidic and suitable only for grazing sheep and cutting peat, with the Orkney mainland and Islay – famous for its whisky and the barley that goes into it – being notable exceptions. Hunting and fishing, therefore, were essential for survival, with diets augmented by grazing animals like goats and sheep.

Elsewhere, the machair, one of Europe's rarest habitats and unique to the west of Scotland and Ireland, provides an almost surreal transition from sea to land. Machair, a Gaelic term meaning a fertile, low-lying, grassy plain, is created by the lime-rich shell sands of the beaches being blown inland. The result is a magnificent gradient. Starting from the turquoise-silver waters which make Hebridean beaches the aesthetic equal of any Caribbean counterparts, waves lap up against exposed rock and sand dunes that can rise well over 30ft high. The dunes develop a green fuzz of grass that thickens with each stride inland, until the grass completely overtakes the sand. The final layer on this unusual cake is the cultivated, flower-rich fields that are often a literal stone's throw from the dunes. From vivid blue water to golden-white sands to green grass and a symphony of wildflowers, the machair makes a rainbow of the shores.

Another immediately noticeable feature of the Western and Northern Isles is their near-total lack of trees. Orkney is perhaps most famous for this, with hardly a tree on the whole archipelago. While much of Scotland was stripped of forest in order to build the vessels of the Royal Navy in the shipyards of Glasgow, the 'Second City of the Empire', the Isles have been deforested since at least the early Iron Age. On a grand tour of the Isles in the late eighteenth century, James Boswell and Samuel Johnson observed that the only fuel widely used was peat,[5] with the only available timber being the driftwood that would perchance wash ashore, sometimes from as far away as the Americas, carried across the ocean by the Gulf Stream. Nearly 1,000 years before Boswell and Johnson, when the Norse drove their longships onto their beguiling beaches, the Isles looked much as they do today.[6]

The Iron Islands

The Iron Islands, so named not due to any abundance of metals but for the constitutions of their inhabitants, latch on to Westeros' western shore. They are not as far north as you might expect, aligned not with the frozen shores of the North but with the middle ground of the Neck. The isles off the west coast of Scotland are much further to the north, in relative terms, than the Iron Islands are to Westeros. If the position of the Iron Islands accurately mimicked the position of the Outer Hebrides, for instance, they would not be parallel with the Neck but significantly further north, with Torrhen's Square or even Winterfell.

While the climate on the Iron Islands is bracing to say the least, with seemingly relentless winds and the damp chill of the ocean biting into every holdfast and through the thickest padded coats, life is not so hard here as it is beyond the Wall or even in the mountains beyond Winterfell. The sea, home to the Drowned God and immediately accessible to the vast majority of ironborn, is always bountiful. Were it not, according to *The World of Ice and Fire*, famine would decimate the islands every winter.[7] That the ironborn have endured at least as long as the First Men, and perhaps even longer, is proof that they're doing something right.

There are two main island groupings. The nearest group to Westeros has thirty-one islands, though only seven sustain populations of more than a few hundred. Many of their names have obvious real-world inspirations. Two of the most significant, for instance, are called Great Wyk and Old Wyk. While Wyk may be a modification of the Old Norse *vík* (an inlet or bay), from which the term Viking is possibly derived,[8] it is also phonetically identical to a major settlement in Caithness, Wick, aptly named for the Vikings that conquered the area. Near Wick there are two castles that would do any ironborn proud. The spartan clifftop castle of Old Wick clings to the heights of a storm-wracked cliff, and just up the coast is Castle Sinclair-Girnigoe, which is as close to *Game of Thrones'* castle of Pyke – built perilously on a series of sea stacks linked by rope bridges – as it is possible to get. Another of the greater Iron Islands is Orkmont, which is surely a nod to the Orkney Isles, where the Norse established a mighty earldom based first at the Brough of Birsay and then at Kirkwall with its magnificent St Magnus Cathedral. Finally, the Iron Island of Harlaw shares its name with both an area within the Pentland Hills near Edinburgh and, more evocatively, the Battle of Harlaw fought on 24 July 1411 between Alexander Stewart, Earl of Mar, and Donald of Islay, Lord of the Isles, near Inverurie. The other major Iron Islands of Blacktyde, Pyke and Saltcliffe have no exact equivalents in Scotland, but, by evoking salt, battle and the tides, are wonderfully phonesthemic.

In terms of quantity, the Iron Islands are humbled by the Isles of Scotland, which number more than 500. Thirty-two are large enough to support considerable populations. Mull or Skye, for instance, fostered multiple competing factions and continue to sustain people in their thousands. Then there are isles like Kerrera or Eigg, which can be traversed on foot in a single afternoon. Some are far smaller yet, and we'll visit those lonely bastions shortly.

Harlaw and Great Wyk are the largest and most populous of the Iron Islands, with Pebbleton on Great Wyk boasting a population of several thousand who are almost universally engaged in reaping the harvest of the sea. Any ironborn who lives too far from the sea is treated with suspicion, such as those toiling in the inland mines of the Hardstone Hills run by Gorold Goodbrother. Some of those folk even go their whole lives without tasting sea water, a baffling oddity that causes the drowned priest Aemon Damphair to scoff, 'Small wonder that such folk are crabbed and queer.'[9]

Resource scarcity is an issue for the ironborn in much the same way as it was for the Islesmen. The ironborn tell their tales around driftwood fires not because it burns any better than other types of wood, but because it's the only wood they have. Islands such as Old Wyk are almost entirely mountainous, and nothing can be grown on them aside from the sparse grasses that feed grazing beasts – there is nothing quite like the Hebrides' fertile machair explicitly mentioned in the Iron Islands. These grasses are insufficient for even medium-sized horses, however, and a good rider in the Iron Islands is harder to find than a home without damp. Even the lords of the ironborn – much like their real-world Orcadian, Shetlandic and

Hebridean counterparts – ride garrons and ponies.[10] The ironborn have converted that poverty into a prideful scorn of the mounts of mainland knights. Aemon Damphair weighed in on this matter with characteristic dismissiveness, saying that horses are, 'creatures from the green lands and helped to make men weak'.[11] The Isles of Scotland are entirely the same in this regard even to this day, something that distinguishes them most of all from the Scottish Lowlands but also from Ireland, where many young men took up arms as javelin-hurling horseboys.[12] The lack of fertile land and the limitations imposed by it were major motivators for both Vikings – and to a lesser extent their Norse-Gaelic descendants – and ironborn to take to the waves and carve, rather than sow, their path to greatness.[13]

A Network of Stone & Ships

To experience first-hand what held the watery realm of the Lords of the Isles together across a seemingly fragmented landscape, we must set sail. The harbour at Oban, known as the gateway to the Isles, is the beginning of the gauntlet that I have come to call Scotland's castle corridor, the perfect illustration of the Lordship's authority.

The first lesson is immediate. Standing guard at the entry to Oban is the ancient seat of the MacDougalls,[14] Dunollie Castle. Its gaunt tower is being slowly conquered by ivy and erosion, such that the castle appears to be incrementally reintegrating itself into the rocky promontory on which it is built. Fittingly, on the grounds of the castle is a stone depicting a war galley, the successor to the *birlinn* longships favoured by the early Norse-Gaels. With Dunollie at our backs we are faced with three possibilities. Sailing south to Islay, perhaps to convene at the Lordship's capital of Finlaggan, would take us past the Isle of Kerrera, where Alexander II died while campaigning against the Norse. It is a wondrous island, the haunches of its hills rising and falling whimsically towards stony beaches. Just out of sight at the very southern tip of Kerrera is Gylen Castle, a solitary tower clinging to a crag and looking every inch the fantastical, fairytale tower. In fact, a brief glimpse of a castle in the Vale of Arryn shown in Season 5, Episode 1 while Robert Arryn trains under Littlefinger's watch bears a striking resemblance to Gylen in both its form and location.[15]

Heading north also appeals, for it would bring us to the gates of the other great MacDougall castle of Dunstaffnage, its uncompromising, tight-fitted curtain wall resembling a tortoise withdrawn into its impenetrable shell. Stories even tell of the Stone of Destiny being held at Dunstaffnage before making its way to Scone, though the mists veiling such legends obscure any attempt at getting to the absolute truth of them. Beyond Dunstaffnage lay Loch Linnhe, punctuated by the unparalleled heights of the mountain of Ben Nevis looming over Fort William, and Lochaber. En route we could disembark on the Isle of Lismore, an island halfway to everywhere which was once home to a great cathedral where the Lords of the Isles convened. The 2,000-year-old stone walls of Tirefour Broch guard Lismore's east coast, while the much-ruined castles of Achadun and Coeffin watch the west. The latter's crumbling corners distinctly resemble a crooked crown or perhaps a giant's hand emerging from the rock and slowly curling its withered fingers into a fist. From Castle Coeffin the beacon fires of Glensanda Castle, that lonely watchman on Morvern, could easily be seen across the loch.

Enticing as they are, neither south or north are our destinations. Our way is west, through the Sound of Mull, flanked on each side by quintessentially rugged Highland landscapes. About half an hour's sailing from Oban, one of Scotland's most spectacular sights appears off the port side. At first it seems small up against the mountains of Mull, yet as the ferry crawls towards it, the majesty of Duart Castle invariably causes every jaw on board to hit the deck. It is perched, like the eagles that roam the island, on a cliff overlooking the sea, roaring defiance at the elements that have battered it for over 700 years. The revered seat of the MacLeans of Duart is at least on a par with the far better-known Eilean Donan Castle that appears on postcards and shortbread tins the world over, not only in terms of its beauty but also its remarkable legacy as a castle rebuilt from ruins by imagineers in the early twentieth century.

The next two hours of the voyage are best spent criss-crossing the deck as castles and sheltered bays, perfect for anchoring a fleet of *birlinns* ready to strike at a moment's notice, appear on all sides one after the other. Rushing from port side to starboard, you get the distinct sense that the strongholds of the castle corridor are tracking you, like a series of CCTV cameras on a lonely road, as you proceed through their realm. Ardtornish Castle on the starboard side is the next in line, a hall house and favoured residence of the Lord of the Isles himself that is now home to naught but sheep and the grasses they graze on. Aros Castle on Mull reveals itself soon after, though while it can see you with ease, a good set of binoculars is required to glimpse its fragmentary remnants from on board.

Beyond Aros, the land on each side gets rougher, particularly to the north with the almost lunar landscape of Ardnamurchan coming into view. Yet the castles do not abate. Caisteal nan Con, the Castle of the Hounds, appears on the starboard side not long before Mingary Castle, the seat of Clan MacRuari. After passing under their watchful eyes, the open sea beckons as both Mull and Ardnamurchan Point reach their furthest extent and give way to the sea. Strange forms can be spotted in the distance, such as the Treshnish Isles to the south. One of them, Bac Mòr, is known as the Dutchman's Cap for its uncanny resemblance to a pilgrim's hat from the right angle. The Small Isles to the north, especially Rùm, appear from a distance like pods of rocky leviathans breaching the surface.

Despite crossing a large swathe of open water on the next leg of the journey, the Isles are never out of view. Upon realizing that, it is easy to see how an islesman would think nothing of a day's trip from Lewis to Colonsay, or from Mull to Islay, or even from the tip of Kintyre to Barra, our ultimate destination. The world of the Isles is at once as vast as the horizon and as small as a chessboard, its pieces moving with ease in their ships from square to square. The castle corridor comes to a climactic end at the aptly named Castlebay in Barra. There, Kisimul Castle – that lonely light to which we'll soon return – guards the edge of the world. Only a scattering of archipelagos like St Kilda interrupt the expanse of ocean separating the Outer Hebrides from the Americas. From the start of the castle corridor to the end, there was hardly a single moment when our vessel was not within sight of a castle's walls and a good anchorage from which longships could spring at a moment's notice. Ships and stones – a 'perfect symbiosis' to which we'll return when discussing the Lords of the Isles – is the thread that wove the west together.[16]

The strongholds of the Iron Islands serve an identical role. All ironborn castles save one, Hammerhorn Castle, are built by the sea as a means to police waterways and offer safe anchorage for the Iron Fleet. Pyke, where the Lord of the Iron Islands sits on the Seastone Chair, is the most spectacular example. It was built thousands of years ago on a rocky promontory jutting out into the Sunset Sea, though erosion eventually turned that promontory into three separate sea stacks upon which the castle's isolated towers are precariously perched. The towers of Pyke are connected by rope bridges, and as the elements eat away at the stacks they cause parts of Pyke to crumble away. The ironborn, stubbornly and ingeniously, have simply modified the masonry to accommodate the changing space.[17] Like the other great castles of the Iron Islands, including Ten Towers, Greygarden and the Tower of Gilmmering, Pyke has quick access to a harbour so that packs of sea wolves in their longships can be assembled with haste. Even if the Iron Fleet was defeated, like it was during Balon Greyjoy's rebellion against King Robert, attacking Pyke was a logistical nightmare and doing so would exact a terrible price for even the mightiest host. The world of the ironborn pivots around the symbiosis of castles and ships, just like that of the Lords of the Isles. As ever in *Game of Thrones*, they simply take that principle to new heights.

So much so, in fact, that at first glance the castle of Pyke upon its stacks seems architecturally impossible. As ever, Scotland rises to the challenge. The aforementioned Gylen Castle on the Isle of Kerrera is in the right spirit, though even better examples are found in coastal Caithness, an area intimately linked with the powerful Norse Earldom of Orkney. These include Castle Sinclair-Girnigoe, Bucholly Castle and Keiss Castle, all built on narrow juts of land flanked on every side but one by high cliffs. Sinclair-Girnigoe in particular is the closest match to Pyke; its walls morph directly into the seaside cliffs, a sea stack stands nearby and the castle is only accessible across a bridge, which could be retracted to completely isolate it from the mainland. Another real-life bastion comes to mind, but we must leave the Isles for a moment and travel to Scotland's east coast to behold it – Dunnottar Castle. Though mainland nobles, the Keiths, raised the castle we see today, the great stone platform they built on has been fortified since earliest times. The geological marvel of Dunnottar was formed 400 million years ago,[18] its shape evoking the great promontory fort of the Fist of the First Men north of Westeros' Wall. Cliffs surround the promontory on three sides, and over the years many prisoners fell to their deaths into the churning sea while attempting to climb to freedom. There is only one way in or out of Dunnottar, an extremely narrow defile that exposes you on all sides to the teeth of the fortress. Such is Dunnottar's might and majesty that in 2013 it made the top ten shortlist for the mantle of Eighth Wonder of the World. When the haar, a thick sea mist, rolls in and veils the fortress in fog, it seems a castle of dreams.

If you pass through the gate and walk out to the edge of the promontory, gaze north along the coast. Less than half a mile away an even more improbable fort comes into view, though despite its proximity to iconic Dunnottar it is scarcely visited save by the birds. Dunnicaer is a completely isolated sea stack rising sheer over 100ft from waters on all sides. Despite seeming like an impossible location for any kind of human settlement, symbol stones were discovered atop it in the nineteenth century. In 2016, researchers from the University of Aberdeen uncovered evidence that the vertiginous stack was the site of one of Scotland's earliest Pictish forts, dating from the third or fourth century.[19] While it was inhabited it was likely a promontory that had yet to be severed, but it is easy to imagine slivers of the rock giving way to the winds and waves over the years and the occupants adapting until conquered by them at last. When pressed to the limits of their creativity and necessity, the people of ancient Scotland were more than capable of making homes from places we can hardly fathom. If the Picts could fortify Dunnicaer, and the Lords of the Isles construct their castles on the clifftops, then the spindly towers and sea stacks of Pyke seem within the realm of possibility after all.

The Light At The End Of The World

The Iron Islands are considered by most Westerosi to be the very definition of rugged and remote, yet there are places that even the ironborn think of as teetering on the edge of the earth. Thousands of years ago, a crew from Great Wyk was blown far off their intended course. After eight desperate days, they arrived at a cluster of thirteen islands that were little more than rocks rising abruptly from the Sunset Sea. They clung to those rocks and made them home, though most could only support a single household. Their captain, taking the name Farwynd, managed to scrape together the archipelago's meagre resources to build a tower and a beacon light, and ever since the Lonely Light has been the final bastion of the known world in the west.[20] Few have followed in their wake, though rumours abound of the strangeness of the people there;

selkies, they call them, half man and half seal. Some even say they can change their skins and become spotted whales, the Westerosi equivalent of orcas.[21]

Approaching the scattered islands lying off of Scotland's north-west coast, it's easy to imagine why such tales are told. Many modern Scots can go their whole lives without hearing of places like Sula Sgeir, 40 miles north of Lewis, or the uninhabited North Rona. Just off the coast of the north-west Highlands are a set of four islands known as the Summer Isles, a name shared by a chain of tropical pirate havens south-west of Westeros. Far from being havens, these different sets of distant isles are some of the most rugged and isolated places in Europe. Sula Sgeir, just 150 metres wide at its broadest, has only a tiny lighthouse that receives a constant battering from waves, a true lonely light holding fast against the ceaseless storms. Some of these miniscule islands were home to early Christian hermits seeking the utmost ends of the earth on which to live out their extreme asceticism. A number of them even have ancient standing stones, evidence that thousands of years ago these barely perceptible specks on the map were not only explored but inhabited, though most could only support a handful of families at best. Another of these marvels, Handa Island, was abandoned after the 1848 potato famine. Prior to that calamity, seven families called the island home and, like the more famous St Kilda and in a move that would do the ironborn proud, had their own 'queen' and 'parliament'.

None of these lonely isles can boast of a castle like Westeros' Lonely Light has, however. For that you must go to Barra, an ethereal island at the southern tip of the Outer Hebrides. There is a castle here like no other in Scotland, defiant as the tides that lap against its salt-stained walls. Kisimul Castle rises straight out of the waters of the aptly named Castlebay, its diamond shape and towerhouse giving it the appearance of a stout ship. What better form for a castle of the sea kings to take? For 1,000 years Kisimul has been the seat of Clan MacNeil of Barra, in whose blood runs the story of the Isles – a fusion of Scots, Norse and Irish. Despite their location far from the mainland, the MacNeils are no strangers to the annals of Scottish history, having led men into battle against the last Vikings at Largs in 1263 and alongside Robert the Bruce at Bannockburn in 1314.[22]

Unlike the Farwynds of the Lonely Light, no one believes the MacNeils to be skinchangers. Tradition has, however, passed down some tales of their medieval chieftains' eccentricities. It is supremely amusing to imagine the spectacle that supposedly occurred each day at Kisimul. Once the MacNeil chieftain had his midday meal, a herald would ascend the tower of Kisimul, play a flourish with his trumpet and declare, 'Hear, ye people, and listen, ye nations! The MacNeil of Barra having finished his dinner, all the princes of the earth are at liberty to dine!'[23] MacNeil family legend goes so far as to say that during the Biblical flood their chieftain refused Noah's offer of a space on the Ark because he had a boat of his own to see his clan through it.[24] Being one of the most distant sea lords in the known world would, in fairness, endow you with more than a little mystique.

Chapter 4

North *versus* South?

In some parts of Scotland, the difference between north and south is clear to behold. The Isle of Arran in the Firth of Clyde is known as 'Scotland in miniature' for just this reason. Its southern end, from Lamlash on the east shore to Machrie Moor with its magnificent standing stones on the west shore, is mostly rolling hills and river valleys. Look to the north and a great stone spearhead rises up nearly 900 metres – Goatfell, Arran's tallest mountain. Its razor peak is easily visible from the prehistoric henge at Cairnpapple Hill over 80 miles away in the middle of the country. The sudden division between north and south is the product of the Highland Boundary Fault which slices Scotland in two between Highlands and Lowlands. It is a wall of stone, whittled by the retreating glaciers of the last Ice Age.

If one was to ride north from Winterfell you would see much the same progression, albeit a little more gradual than on Arran. The one major difference is in scale. While both the North of Westeros and Scotland occupy approximately a third of the overall land masses that they are a part of, you could ride a horse across even the widest part of Scotland in a matter of a few days, while it takes over a week just to reach the Wall from Winterfell. The land beyond the Wall is even more inflated, reckoned to be approximately the same size as Canada.[1] After three days on the Kingsroad having departed Winterfell, the farms become less numerous and less robust in tandem with the quality of the soils. A dense forest covers much of the land, and hills of flint grow taller and more jagged with each mile until their snow-capped peaks scrape the clouds.[2] Yet there is another divide in the land, one that even more accurately reflects Scotland's geography. While the journey north from Winterfell to the Wall results in ever more rugged terrain overall, the most noticeable difference is actually on the east-west axis rather than north-south. The imposing sight of flint hills and their rocky summits capped

28

by watchtowers looms to the west of the Kingsroad, while to the east the land flattens into gently rolling plains, criss-crossed by swift rivers and dotted with farms and walled homesteads.[3] If one was to be blindfolded and taken along the Kingsroad, spun around so as to be disoriented and then asked, based upon the lay of the land, which direction was north, there is a good chance you would in fact point to the west.

The same experiment could be conducted in much of Scotland and produce the same result. It is so natural, given the historical boundaries established in Britain such as Hadrian's Wall, to view the north-south axis as the definitive split. That the Highlands are in the north and the Lowlands are in the south seems like such an obvious concept as to not bear investigating. A closer look challenges this assumption. The Highland Line, after all, does not bisect Scotland horizontally but diagonally, from south-west to north-east. What truly makes the Highlands the Highlands and the Lowlands the Lowlands is the type of lifestyle that has historically been possible in each as determined by the ruggedness of the land and the fertility of the soils. For instance, despite being at the extreme northern tip of the Scottish mainland, the landscape of Caithness, with its flat plains and fertile farmland, has far more in common with the topography of the Lothians in the south than with the mountains of Highland regions like Lochaber or Ross. Much of the Borders in Scotland's extreme south, on the other hand, can be just as rugged and rough-hewn as the wildest Highland glen. While the Isle of Arran may be a perfect example of the traditionally held north-south dichotomy, the entire island is considerably further south than Scotland's largest city, Glasgow. In contrast, if you align just about any two roughly parallel points, one on the west coast and the other on the east, the difference will be startlingly clear. No one could possibly mistake Oban for St Andrews, Fort William for Montrose or Applecross for Aberdeen. Scotland as a whole may be much more rugged than virtually all of England, but within Scotland itself the north-south division does not hold up nearly so well.

The idea that the north equates to toughness and the south equates to softness runs deep in Westeros and the British Isles. It is a sentiment summed up well by Ser Rodrik Cassel, Winterfell's master-at-arms, when Bran dispatched him to retake Torrhen's Square from what they believed was a Lannister attack. 'Won't take long, my lord,' Ser Rodrik said overconfidently. 'Southerners don't do well up here.'[4] In Westeros the arrival of winter is received in the south as a fearful cataclysm. Northerners, on the other hand, seem to greet its arrival with a sense of grim yet stalwart fatalism reminiscent of the determined look upon the faces of Edinburgh residents when the winter winds slice like scythes through the narrow corridors of the Old Town. Jon Snow sees winter's arrival as a necessary evil that makes it possible to appreciate the warmth of summer, in much the same way as the prospect of death has a habit of making us value life while it lasts. 'Without the cold, a man cannot appreciate the fire in his hearth,' he says. 'Let the south have its sun, flowers, and affectations. We Northerners have home.'[5] Whether this amounts to wisdom or masochism is entirely in the eye of the beholder.

Along with that hardiness come perceptions of barbarism, which will be further explored in Part III. We encounter this prejudice straight away in *Game of Thrones*. Reacting to the discovery of the butchered wildlings at the start of the very first episode, Waymar Royce, as former southern lordling, says derisively, 'What do you expect, they're savages. One lot steals a goat from another lot, before you know it they're ripping each other to pieces.'[6] This entire book could easily be filled by similar descriptions of the Scots by the English, and of the Scots' ancestors by the Greeks and Romans. Following the Battle of Falkirk, for instance, one English poem barked that 'The Filthy Scots attack England like a pig rising up against the valour of the lion.'[7] Never mind that England at the time occupied much of Scotland, had slain many of its people and despoiled much of its countryside – how dare those filthy Scots take up arms against our noble cause?

This attitude was not exclusive to Anglo-Scottish relations. Historically, the Scots are just as adept at putting each other down. The cultural divide between Highlands and Lowlands may seem eternal, yet until the fourteenth century there was little aside from language that truly separated them. The first explicit mention of major character differences between Highlanders and Lowlanders comes from John of Fordun's late-fourteenth century *Cronica Gentis Scotorum*, in which he described the Highlands as 'savage and untamed' while the Lowlands were 'civilised and domestic'[8]. Only sixty years prior, many a Highlander laid down their lives to aid Robert the Bruce's claim to the throne of Scotland and proudly fought alongside their Lowland cousins in pivotal engagements like the Battle of Bannockburn. Perhaps the increasing assertiveness of the Isles as a semi-autonomous domain had something to do with this significant cooling of relations. The Lowland perception of Highland barbarism only hardened with time, to the point where Lowland lairds and royal representatives spoke of exterminating Highland clans such as the MacDonalds of Glencoe with the same coolness that one describes the culling of deer.

The farce of this is that it's all relative. One man's north is another man's south. Winterfell certainly regards itself as the heart of the North, but to the Free Folk, Winterfell is just another southern city full of kneelers. Ask a Thenn from the Frostfang Mountains what they think of the rest of the Free Folk, however, and they're likely to deride them as southern softies. If there are people living beyond the Thenns in the Lands of Always Winter, they surely continue the trend.

Scots, too, pride themselves on being the northernmost peoples of Britain, with all the ruggedness and fortitude that tends to represent. Yet to a Viking, Scotland was a positively balmy southern paradise. One of the most northerly regions of mainland Scotland, for instance, is Sutherland, and many Scots go their whole lives without setting foot that far north. Yet the hint is in the name. Sutherland was given that name, Southern Land, by the Norse based on its position relative to Norway, Shetland and Orkney.[9] To the Norse, the fact that over nine-tenths of Britain lay to the south of Sutherland was immaterial. In their world, Scotland was obviously a southern realm.

If not for the building of the Wall, could we still call the peoples beyond it 'wildlings'? Or, like the mountain clans north of Winterfell with their endless feuds and bottomless hospitality, would they merely be seen as eccentric extensions of the realm rather than as beasts who threaten to devour it? This will not be the first occasion where the wise words of Ygritte will be evoked to sum it up best. After Jon claims that the wildlings are the bane of the North and that all they do is raid and ravage the innocent, good and respectable Stark lands, she skewers the arbitrariness of it all like an arrow through the eye of a rabbit at 200 yards: 'They're not your lands! We've been here the whole time. You lot came along and just put up a big wall and said it was yours!'[10] The North, both in Westeros and our own world, may seem like an immovably fixed point, but perhaps it's a state of mind after all.

PART II

STORIES OF THE STONES

Chapter 5

No Ruined Stones

'There are plenty of ruined buildings in the world but no ruined stones.'

- Hugh MacDiarmid, *On A Raised Beach*[1]

Samwell Tarly would make a fantastic archaeologist. Enthusiasm, after all, is half the battle. Upon taking his first steps on the Fist of First Men, an ancient hillfort beyond the Wall, Sam's curiosity and sense of wonder is irrepressible. 'Think of how old this place is!' he proclaims to his decidedly less keen Brothers of the Night's Watch. 'Thousands and thousands of years ago the First Men stood here, where we're standing, all through the Long Night. What do you think they were like, the First Men?'[2]

Those are precisely the sorts of questions that arise walking through the fields and hills of Scotland. They may seem like lonely landscapes at first, but when you know what to look for there is hardly a view in Scotland that does not take in archaeology spanning centuries or more. One of my favourite examples, because it is close to home and can be explored impulsively whenever the mood strikes, is the area around Crichton in Midlothian. Driving (or cycling, as I do) through Crichton without prior knowledge of what is hidden there, it seems like a beautifully situated but otherwise average rural hilltop village. Its best-known attraction by far is Crichton Castle, a medieval fortification with links to the story of the infamous Black Dinner that inspired *Game of Thrones'* Red Wedding (see Part V for that bloody tale). But how many people know that Crichton is also home to Pegasus? Just a mile from the gates of the castle is Crichton souterrain, an Iron Age subterranean passageway. Getting inside it means crawling almost on hands and knees, but that's all part of the fun. Deep within the dark passageway, some of the stones are marked with scratches and grooves, but one stands out from the rest. On the ceiling of the souterrain is the worn but unmistakable image of a Pegasus. What is such a winged wonder doing in this forgotten lair that never sees the sun? It likely came from a Roman fort built nearby in the first century, though that fort's precise location is still to be discovered. Perhaps it was upon the ridge that overlooks the souterrain a few hundred yards to the south. If you ascend that ridge you will then glance the ruins of Fala Luggie Tower, a medieval towerhouse, and just beyond it the heights of Soutra Hill, home to not only one of the best-surviving stretches of Roman road in Scotland but also to the remains of a medieval super-hospital that once treated thousands of patients. Take care if you visit – lethal hemlock, used in the delicate blending of medieval anaesthetics but known locally as 'deid man's oatmeal', can still be found growing on the site. You could continue in this fashion, hopping from one archaeological wonder to the next, for as long and as far as you cared to. It has been said of the once mighty Caledonian Forest that blanketed the land when the Romans arrived, that a squirrel could leap from treetop to treetop all the way from the east coast to the west and never once touch the ground; so, too, could someone with a keen eye go from historic site to historic site across the length and breadth of the land.

One of the reasons that Westeros feels so historically 'alive' is that evidence of its ancient and complex past is scattered throughout the landscape in much the same way. Ruined castles stand alongside occupied ones, houses of the living are within sight of houses of the dead and many of the monuments in the countryside are being slowly reclaimed by the elements in a way that convincingly conveys the inexorable passage of time. Many fantasy worlds touch upon the theme of lost civilizations and dilapidated grandeur, but while Westeros has Old Valyria as a prime example of this trope it also has innumerable smaller instances that go almost without mention, in much the same way that most people would pass through Crichton without remarking on its hidden history. In the spirit of Sam at the Fist of the First Men, let us then take a brief tour of the types of ancient monuments found in the north of Westeros that can also be found if you are lucky enough to live in or visit Scotland. We will start with the oldest and conclude with the 'newest'.

Standing Stones

Samwell Tarly is treated to a two-for-one wonder at the Fist of the First Men. Atop the lofty crags of that ancient hillfort stand something even older and more mysterious: standing stones. They are immovable

35

in the face of the howling winds, unfazed by the lethal cold and more ancient than perhaps anything other than the Children of the Forest themselves. They are far from the only ones of their kind in Westeros, though it is worth noting that this particular stone arrangement is well beyond the Wall and may well even predate it. The execution ground where Ned Stark takes the head of the Night's Watchman is set within a standing stone circle, and Bran's vision of the creation of the Night King by the Children also takes place within a standing stone spiral, with their sacrificial victim tied to one of the stones as an offering to some unknowable and unspeakable power.[3]

Standing stones are clearly amongst the oldest and most revered monuments in Westeros, and so too with the standing stones of Scotland. Such is the iconic status of locations like the Ring of Brodgar in Orkney or the Callanish Stones on Lewis that they have become inseparable from many people's conceptions of Scottish history. Too right. Approaching a set of standing stones, like those tucked away in the trees just off the road at Kingarth on the Isle of Bute, is like being a voyeur to a secret assembly of the arcane. Even if you are entirely committed to a rationalist's view of the world, it is impossible to enter a stone circle without the distinct sense that you have stepped into something greater than yourself. Given that many of Scotland's standing stones, such as the megaliths of Orkney's Stones of Stenness, date from as long as 5,400 years ago and have witnessed innumerable human lifetimes, dramas, joys and tragedies, that lingering feeling is only apt.[4]

By the fifth millennium BCE, stone arrangements such as circles and henges could be found throughout Britain and Ireland.[5] The most famous of them is undoubtedly Stonehenge, though recent research has postulated that Stonehenge was in fact inspired by much older incarnations such as those at the heart of Neolithic Orkney. Yet again, the north proves itself to be the preserve of the ancient, and rather than being the place where technologies and fashions were last to arrive, the far north may well be the crucible that created them. Stone circles like the Ring of Brodgar were not built all at once but over many phases, with its henge spanning over 300ft and requiring some 80,000 hours of labour to construct.[6] In many cases, not all of the stones at such sites survive. Brodgar, awe-inspiring as it is, used to be doubly so as only thirty-six of up to sixty original stones are left standing. One of the most regrettable losses at the Ness of Brodgar was the destruction of the Odin Stone by a farmer in 1814. Its most notable feature was a hole bored straight through the middle of it, through which young lovers would link their arms and vow their eternal love for each other. The number of other such romances lost to the ravages of time and man cannot be known.

Barrows & Cairns

In the North the halls of the dead are just as grand as those of the living, only instead of being contained within castle walls, they are laid out under the open sky for all who pass to behold. Grassy knolls, nearly indistinguishable to the untrained eye from the sedimentary mounds deposited in great numbers across the land by retreating glaciers, line the Kingsroad. Robert Baratheon does not seem impressed. 'Have we ridden onto a graveyard?' he asks his old friend, Ned Stark. 'There are barrows everywhere in the north, Your Grace,' Stark answers. 'This land is old.'[7]

These are the barrows in which the noble dead of the First Men are interred. In days of old, it was not the Starks who ruled the north but the Barrow Kings, based at Barrowtown where The Great Barrow was raised thousands of years before anyone thought to record the creation of such monuments. So, too, in Orkney, where the greatest of Scotland's monuments to the dead are found. They date from around 5,000 years ago – substantially older, to use that tried and true historical yardstick, than the Great Pyramids of Giza. In Scotland they are not called barrows, which is an English term, but cairns. From the Orkney 'mainland', the largest of the Orkney Isles, a small ferry transports you across the Eynhallow Sound to the Isle of Rousay. Turn west from the small jetty and follow the setting sun and you will come upon a landscape that tells more than 7,000 years of stories. Abandoned nineteenth-century crofts stand alongside Iron Age brochs, round stone towers that bear an uncanny resemblance to the cooling towers of nuclear power plants. This is the Westness Walk, known as the 'Egypt of the North' for the dazzling diversity of archaeological sites it cradles. Here it is easy to wonder if you have not slipped into some fantasy realm after all, for the many cairns that line the walk bear peculiar and unforgettable names like Taversöe Tuick, Blackhammer Cairn and the Knowe of Yarso. The grandest of all is Midhowe Chambered Cairn. At over 100ft long, it is amongst the largest Neolithic monuments in Europe. The remains of at least twenty-five individuals were found within, and the internal space is divided by stone slabs into stalls for a little privacy in the afterlife. Taversöe Tuick is modest by comparison, but is also the one that requires the steadiest nerves to explore. Inside that ancient mound one must descend a ladder into a second, unlit subterranean chamber to be alone with the Old Gods in the house of the dead. Blackhammer Cairn is only slightly less daunting. The only way inside is by a rusted sliding metal hatch that is tucked into the hillside, not unlike the entrance to a Hobbit hole. Closing that hatch behind you as you slip under the ground is a test of mettle if ever there was one.

Undoubtedly the greatest of the mounds is Maeshowe in the heart of Neolithic Orkney at the Ness of Brodgar, one of Northern Europe's most awe-inspiring and significant ongoing archaeological sites.[8] Here a ceremonial landscape that we are only beginning to understand converges on the great mound of Maeshowe and the stone sentinels of the adjacent Ring of Brodgar. All the land seems to conspire to accentuate the Ness, for the waters of an inland lake converge upon a narrow strip of land punctuated by the silhouettes of standing stones as tall as giants. For several weeks before and after each winter solstice, Maeshowe puts on a show for the ages. The tomb was so precisely aligned by the genius of the ancients that the setting sun's rays illuminate the low, 10-metre-long passage into the depths of the chamber. The observations that made this phenomenon possible must have been calculated over the course of many generations, and the spectacle is every bit as wondrous now as it was to those who first witnessed it. A webcam has been set up within Maeshowe so that with every solstice the modern world can witness its luminous dance.

Another kind of cairn is introduced to the world of Westeros almost immediately upon us entering it. In the very first episode, *Winter is Coming*, while Ned Stark prepares to execute the Brother of the Night's Watch who fled the White Walkers, a rider is seen passing by a memorial cairn. These are different from cairns like Midhowe or Blackhammer, for while they often commemorate the dead they do not contain them. Some have no relation to the dead at all – you will find at least one cairn atop almost every mountain peak and deep within every hidden valley pass in Scotland, simply meant as waymarkers. The tradition is to add a stone to them as you pass, thereby forming a communion with others who have come before you. The cairn that the *Game of Thrones* rider passes is most like those built at the site of battlefields in the nineteenth century, the most famous of which is the cairn that stands upon the sombre field of Culloden Moor near Inverness where the Jacobites made their last stand on 16 April 1746. This tradition is followed in Westeros, too, with similar stone cairns erected by northmen upon the battlefield of the Whispering Wood where Robb Stark defeated and captured Jaime Lannister.[9] For anyone who lives in a part of the world where such stones were raised, their inclusion in the series was a brilliant way of blending the fantastical with the familiar.

Cup & Ring Marks

When Jon Snow revealed the ancient carvings of the Children of the Forest beneath Dragonstone to a sceptical Daenerys, it was one of the single greatest 'a-ha!' moments in all of *Game of Thrones*, and not just for what it reveals about the plot.[10] Alongside startlingly detailed depictions of White Walkers (which it must be said looked like they were hastily drawn by a production intern that very morning rather than by any ancient peoples) was something altogether more realistic. We have been tantalized by the mysterious meaning of the spiral symbol that has repeatedly shown up in the series, and here we seem to see its earliest incarnations. Upon the walls of the cavern are carved myriad designs, many of them taking the form of circles within circles with lines bisecting them. It seems the Children of the Forest, like Bronze Age Scots, were also fond of cup-and-ring marks.

Sometime between 3,000 and 2,000 BCE, ancient artisans pecked patterns with pointed tools into the large stone outcrops that flow down the Argyll hillsides.[11] Some are smaller than a fist, while others span nearly a metre in diameter. In their centre is a concave groove, hence the 'cup', that often traps the morning dew and rains that trickle down the slopes like a miniature reservoir. These cups are surrounded by rings, sometimes only two or three but occasionally as many as seven, that give the whole design the appearance of a radiating target. Almost always, one side of the rings is left open, such that a sort of corridor leads into the centre of the rings. The fact that some of Scotland's best-preserved cairns, such as the Clava Cairns or the many examples found nearby Achnabreck throughout Kilmartin Glen, have precisely the same design when viewed from the air – a ring of stone penetrated by an open channel leading into a ritualized central space – cannot be an accident.

One of the finest collections of cup-and-ring marks is at Achnabreck, not far from the hillfort of Dunadd with its stone-incised footprint and the hundreds of prehistoric monuments in Kilmartin Glen. Several huge areas of exposed rock, stretched across the hills like an artist's canvas, bear at least 323 carvings, from classic cup-and-rings to double and triple spirals and cups interlinked by zigzag lines like a connect-the-dots puzzle.[12] Their true meaning faded with the names of their makers. Archaeologists have noted that the vast majority of cup-and-ring marks face towards waterways, and their bisecting lateral grooves invariably follow the slope of the hills.[13] Their shallow grooves are difficult to discern at midday as the sun hangs directly above the rocks. With the arrival of the soft evening light, however, and especially in the winter when the northern sun never rises high, they come to life and can be seen vividly from a distance. Were they meant as maps, readable only to those who knew when to look for them? Were they representations of unknown entities guarding or keeping watch over landscapes that interwove earth and sea? Some have, inevitably, suggested that they are celestial maps, which does not fit the available evidence any more than the flippant theory that they are merely graffiti done by bored Bronze Age teenagers.[14]

We should not be too dismissive of such notions, however – very recently a series of twelve pits at Warren Field in the grounds of Crathes Castle in Aberdeenshire were discovered that archaeologists have heralded as the world's oldest calendar system dating from an astonishing 10,000 years ago, with the pits seeming to track the phases of the moon. Millennia before the far more 'advanced' Egyptians or Mesopotamians had worked out similar systems, the ancient peoples of Scotland, so long dismissed as barbarians at the edge of reason and the world, had begun to unravel the secrets of the skies. With such discoveries coming to light, who can say for sure what message the enigmatic rings of Achnabreck were meant to convey? Thus far they have proven every bit as mysterious as the markings in the Dragonstone cave, though it can safely be predicted that the secret of *Game of Thrones'* cup-and-rings marks will be revealed long before those of their Argyll counterparts.

Crannogs

We see little of the Crannogmen who dwell in the shifting swamps of the Neck, but even less of their namesakes which are just as peculiar. Perfectly accommodating the Crannogmen's almost amphibious lifestyle, crannogs are thatched dwellings perched upon timber stilts over bodies of water. We know that crannogs were used as dwellings by the earliest inhabitants of Westeros, the Children of the Forest, and that the Crannogmen are rumoured, because of their slight stature and elusive nature, to have intermarried with the Children and so inherited their architectural legacy.[15] Thus the Crannogmen can avoid the lizard-lions that stalk the swamps, and sustain themselves by fishing directly off the side of their homes. It's the perfect arrangement for a society that thrives neither on the land, like the Starks, or on the sea, like the Greyjoys, but along the murky lines between the two.

The first time you see a Scottish crannog you are likely to think that you have somehow been whisked away to some Polynesian atoll (if not for the temperature and lack of palm trees). Extending well out over the water of lochs, and in a handful of cases seasides, crannogs bear a striking resemblance to the iconic bungalows of Bora Bora. Sadly there are no complete original crannogs, as their timbers have rotted away in the more than 2,000 years since the majority of them were built. The only opportunity for us to appreciate them in their pristine glory is at the Scottish Crannog Centre on Loch Tay, deep within Highland Perthshire. There, within a recreated crannog, Iron Age society is brought to life in vivid, sensory detail, with craftspeople leading workshops and storytellers gathering guests around the crannog's central hearth. Its wattle walls and 16-metre-long timber walkway may look like they are several thousand miles out of place, but crannogs were common dwellings in Scotland from around the fourth century BCE up until, incredibly in some cases, the eighteenth century, when they were used as refuges by survivors of the killing field of Culloden.[16] Their predecessors were the lake villages that appeared in mainland Europe earlier in the first millennium BCE, in which a large log raft was fixed to the floor of a body of water and used as a platform for a palisaded structure.[17] Ancient Scots seem to have taken up this practice with exceptional enthusiasm. Hundreds of crannogs have been identified in Scotland and Ireland, yet another example of the intensive and prehistoric connections between those two nations, yet only one has thus far been identified in Wales and none whatsoever exist in England, not even in the Fens of East Anglia, whose defiant medieval inhabitants almost certainly also inspired Martin's Crannogmen[18].

Building a crannog was a massive undertaking. Experts at the Crannog Centre estimate that at a minimum it would require 1,000 trees to build a single crannog, and there are eighteen crannogs along Loch Tay alone.[19] Crannogs were clearly not the product of an impoverished and primitive people but of a society that was able to leverage a tremendous amount of labour and resources. The precise reason why such monumental efforts were taken is not known – was there some danger upon the land that they wished to escape? Was there a spiritual component to living at the boundary of land and water, like the bogs and pools that the Celts worshipped as divine portals? As with cup-and-ring marks, we shall probably never know precisely what motivated their creators, but that does not stop us from marvelling at their ingenuity and creativity.

Chapter 6

The Walls at the Edge of the World

Walk far enough down the stony spine of Edinburgh's Royal Mile and you will pass The World's End. You would be forgiven for not noticing it. It seems a baffling name for a pub in the middle of a city on a street that shows no sign of the imminent end of civilization. Yet this was where Edinburgh ended and something else began: the Canongate, not quite another world but another town, or *burgh*, with its own identity and policies. The Netherbow Port, a twin-towered gatehouse comprising part of Edinburgh's city walls, regulated the flow of people between the two towns. Though the gate has long since disappeared, portions of the old town walls can still be traced, for instance by standing in front of The World's End and looking down to the end of St Mary's Street, or by trekking to the nearby Grassmarket and climbing the steps of the picture-perfect Vennel. Dwarfed by the Old Town tenement buildings that the wall enclosed and reaching a maximum height of just under 25ft, at a physical level the town's wall was hardly comparable to Westeros' great wall of ice. Yet for many of the residents of Edinburgh, the world might as well have dropped off into an abyss beyond it. Considering the number of times the surrounding countryside was set ablaze by invaders, or the plague camps that proliferated outside them where the walking dead rotted away, you can hardly blame them.

Existential dread about what lay beyond has been a companion to every wall humanity has ever raised. Sometimes that dread could reach delirious heights. Writing during the sixth century about the long since defunct Hadrian's Wall, the Byzantine historian Procopius of Caesarea terrified readers with his account of the land beyond the wall:

> '[C]ountless snakes and serpents and every other kind of wild creature occupy this area as their own ... if any man crosses this wall and goes to the other side, he dies

43

straightaway, being quite unable to support the pestilential air of that region, and wild animals, likewise, which go there are instantly met and taken by death.'[1]

There is an extraordinary moment in the *Game of Thrones* season three episode *The Climb* where Procopius' alarmist vision seems to be borne out.[2] After an arduous and nearly fatal scaling of the Wall as part of an expedition sent by Mance Rayder, Jon and Ygritte, breathless from the climb, stand together awestruck at the top of the world. Ygritte at first looks back to the land she was leaving behind. The North – the True North – appears a barren menace, with black clouds tumbling above a sea of brooding mountain peaks. The earth is completely frozen, with not a spot of green grass or life to be seen aside from the Haunted Forest, whose name does not exactly imply safety. Snowdrifts accumulate at the base of the Wall as though it were a bastion against the creeping cold itself rather than the wildlings left to freeze in it. It is a land, not unlike *The Lord of the Rings*' Mordor, that proclaims with every facet of its being that humanity has no place amongst it. 'Every shadow seemed darker,' Jon observed, 'every sound more ominous.'[3] Then, for the first time in her life, Ygritte looks south of the Wall. Within a few hundred yards of its southern face, the snows and permafrost give way to green fields, and though there are mountains here, too, they are dappled in sunlight and seem to hold the land in an embrace rather than in oppressive thraldom. The air itself is different – more like a cool kiss than a frigid barrage. South of the Wall is a land that bears the promise of safety, growth and hope; looking north, in contrast, once can only shiver and despair.

Life on one side and death on the other; that instinctive dichotomy looms in the minds of men whenever they look upon a wall, and it is precisely the feeling that George R.R. Martin sought to capture with the Wall of Westeros. Fittingly, as the Wall is the very first thing that we see in the pilot episode of *Game of Thrones*, it is also where Martin's long adventure through Westeros began. While visiting a friend in England in 1981, he stopped at Hadrian's Wall, built in the early second century to cut off the ravenous north of Brittania from the Roman-dominated south. Standing, as Tyrion one day would, upon the edge of the world, Martin attempted to fathom the feelings of a legionary plucked from the coasts of Libya or the lush vineyards of Tuscany and placed at the remotest, wildest, most unknown corner of Rome's empire. 'The Wall predates anything else,' he said in a 2014 interview with *Rolling Stone*. 'We know that there were Scots beyond the hills, but they didn't know that … . It was the sense of this barrier against dark forces – it planted something in me.'[4] That seed germinated in his imagination and grew into the 700ft-high, 300-mile-long Wall in Westeros. Even Procopius, for all his hyperbole, could hardly have conjured such a frightful wonder.

The Roman Walls

It takes not one but two historical walls to even begin to measure up to such a behemoth, and we'll pass through each in turn on our way into the wild north. Most readers will be aware of Hadrian's Wall, the much romanticized stone frontier in the very north of England upon which George R.R. Martin stood and kept an eye out for marauding Scots. It has been immortalized in poetry, film, television and lore such that if someone in the Western world says they're going 'beyond the wall', you can be almost certain that they're talking about a trip across Hadrian's frontier.

Hadrian visited Britain in 122 CE to assess the situation facing the remotest corner of his empire. Recognizing the threat from the northern tribes and the need to consolidate what had already been gained, he ordered the construction of the wall, which would take fourteen years to complete. Hadrian's Wall spans the north of England from the Solway to the Tyne, a distance of 73 miles. It is as though the Romans bejewelled the land with a great stone necklace, with Scotland as the head. A common misconception is that Hadrian's Wall marks the border between Scotland and England. However, when it was built there was no such thing as either nation, and though the wall comes very close to the border at its western extremity it lies entirely within the boundaries of what is now England. On average, Hadrian's Wall stood 20ft high, scarcely the height of a single flight of the zigzag steps ascending Westeros' Wall. Still, what it lacked in height it made up for in style. Its entire length was lime-washed a dazzling white, making it visible from many miles distant.[5] That flourish lent a certain symmetry to Roman Britain. The first sight to greet the legionaries upon landing in the extreme south was the famous White Cliffs of Dover, a great wall crafted by nature, and by applying lime wash to the length of Hadrian's Wall, the White Cliffs' majesty was mirrored in the distant north. That observation is most likely the product of poetic hindsight rather than of Hadrian's original intentions, though given that emperor's extraordinary character and dynamism I would not entirely put the notion past him.

The wall was composed of lime-bonded stone and infilled with Roman concrete, an exceptionally durable concoction that in many Roman ruins still survives relatively unscathed after 2,000 years or more. The peoples to the north of Hadrian's Wall, like the Scots who followed them, were not inclined towards large-scale siegecraft and so had nothing with which they could hope to break through it. Any attempt to storm the wall by force would need to go over it, a daunting prospect given the discipline of the men defending it and the myriad obstacles, such as earthen ditches and pits filled with wooden spikes known as *lilia*, that turned the task of even reaching the wall into a deadly obstacle course. The wall's main strength was in its interconnectedness. Without being able to effectively communicate and send reinforcements to beleaguered sections, the wall was in danger of being overrun by a concentration of force at a single point. This is a major weakness of Westeros' Wall – despite being an almost impossibly robust structure, it does little good if there is no one around to patrol and defend it against climbers.

Initially Hadrian's Wall had eleven forts along it, each capable of housing 1,000 auxiliaries and built within a half day's ride of each other. Between these larger forts were 'mile forts', built, you guessed it, at each Roman mile, and between each mile fort were two watch towers.[6] The watch towers would not be able to stand long against a concerted assault, but that was not their purpose. They were meant to raise the alarm so that troops from the nearby mile forts could rush to whatever point was in danger, secure in the knowledge that not far away a large group of reinforcements was mobilizing at the major forts. Organization, as ever, proved Rome's greatest asset. While there were no distinct orders like the Rangers, Stewards and Builders of the Westerosi Wall, those subdivisions reflect the fact that while not fighting, the legionaries and auxiliaries were labouring. It took a vast amount of manpower to build Hadrian's Wall in the first place, with 18,000 men housed in temporary camps during the construction process.[7] There were almost unfathomable logistical operations needed to support this endeavour, and many of the Romans present at the emerging frontier would have spent far more of their day with a hammer or sack of grain in hand than a *gladius*.

On the south side of the wall was the *Vallum*, a wide earthen ditch. While the main threat undoubtedly came from the north, the Romans were all too familiar with the rebelliousness of Celtic tribes to trust entirely those living to the south of it. The *Vallum* created a no man's land between the occupiers and the occupied, and over time it was developed to channel traffic towards points of control. Before the construction of the *Vallum*, people could choose to pass through the wall at as many as seventy-six gates along its length; the *Vallum* was bisected by only sixteen crossing points, making it far easier for Rome to police its great boundary.[8] The word 'frontier' was earlier applied to Hadrian's Wall, and that is in fact the best word to describe it. Despite how we think about Hadrian's Wall, it was not some unyielding barricade meant to stop anything and everything beyond it from getting through, as the Wall in Westeros is. For all its strength and imposing grandeur, Hadrian's Wall served that most quintessential of Roman functions: a bureaucratic one.[9] The best way to think about Hadrian's Wall is as a heavily militarized hard border between modern nations, such as the one that shall hopefully never rise again along the border of the Republic of Ireland and Northern Ireland. In building Hadrian's Wall, Rome did not seek to stop the flow of humanity – only to control and, even better, to tax it.[10] In this sense, the logic underpinning Hadrian's Wall was not so different from that of the town walls of Edinburgh that opened this chapter, albeit on a much larger scale. It's not as exciting as keeping White Walkers and half-mad wildlings at bay, but it is a lot more profitable, and that is what empires are all about.

Almost immediately following the death of Emperor Hadrian in July 138 CE, his namesake wall was seconded by an even more daring venture.[11] One hundred miles north of the line between the Solway and Tyne is the Forth-Clyde isthmus, the great choke point that, by entirely natural means, effectively severed the north of Scotland from the south (as described in-depth in Part One: Nature's Crucible). Taking advantage of the foundations that nature had already provided, Rome established perhaps the most audacious and over-ambitious frontier in all the empire: the Antonine Wall.

'We walk beneath one of the hinges of the world,' says Melisandre to Jon as they pass through the gated tunnel under the Wall.[12] I wonder how many of the children playing on the steep grassy slopes lining the yard of Callendar House in Falkirk realize that they, too, tread upon one of the great physical and psychological hinges of history? Though never as grand as its counterpart 100 miles to the south, the Antonine Wall was the true final frontier of the Roman Empire in Britain. It does not have nearly the number of adoring fans as Hadrian's' Wall, for the Antonine Wall was built of turf and timber and no actual stretch of wall survives for photographers to fawn over. What does remain are earthen ramparts, faint impressions of buildings such as barracks and bathhouses, and artefacts in glass cases in museums. The finest surviving sections are to be found, from east to west, on the grounds of Kinneil House, Callendar House, Rough Castle, Watling Lodge and Bearsden.

At 37 miles long, the Antonine Wall is almost precisely half the length of Hadrian's Wall. It had a stone base typically about 14ft wide, onto which soil was compacted and topped with turf to a height of around 10ft – hence why the ramparts blend so seamlessly into the landscape today.[13] In front of the wall was a large ditch called the 'upcast', and at Rough Castle in Falkirk there is a surviving patch of the deadly *lilia* pits intended to skewer or at least stall any attackers. There were no towers along the Antonine Wall like there were upon Hadrian's, but there were seventeen forts of varying sizes (just two shy of the number of castles along Westeros' Wall). The largest was Mumrills, which covered 6½ acres, and on the other side of the scale were the forty-odd fortlets which measured as little as 70ft by 60ft – small enough that a javelin could be hurled from one side to the other.[14] Some 6,000 men were set to work to construct the wall, a much easier task than building Hadrian's Wall but still no mean feat, especially given the hostility of the local Maeatae tribe and the inescapable damp which no doubt resulted in many chafes, blisters and sniffles.[15]

Though George R.R. Martin was primarily inspired by Hadrian's Wall rather than the Antonine Wall, it seems a suspiciously specific coincidence that the shape of Westeros' Wall precisely matches that of the Antonine Wall. Running eastward from Castle Black to Eastwatch-by-the-Sea, Westeros' Wall is straight as an arrow, with any geographical obstacles giving way to it rather than the other way around. Head west from Castle Black, however, and the Wall begins, imperceptibly at first, to curve and bend as it traverses the Frostfang Mountains.[16] The western extremity of the Wall does not, in fact, extend all the way to the sea, but terminates at a gorge along the Milkwater River that is nearly as high and insurmountable as the Wall itself. Even Bran the Builder, the giants and whoever else had a hand in building the Wall had no choice but to relent to geography's imposition. This echoes precisely the layout of the Antonine Wall, which runs almost perfectly straight from its eastern end until it reaches the River Kelvin at Balmuildy. There, even Roman engineering could not prevail over the forces of nature, and the Antonine Wall proceeds west in a zigzagging pattern until it reaches the Clyde at Old Kilpatrick in the shadow of Dumbarton Rock. At one point along its western stretch, at Croy Hill, there is an 80ft section with no wall at all. A great jut of rock rises so precipitously in the wall's path that the Romans simply built up to either side of it, turning it into a part of the defences.[17] Whether this perfect mirroring of the Wall in *Game of Thrones* is indeed a coincidence, or if Martin snuck in a research trip to the Antonine Wall, too, will have to be settled some day.

By 180 CE, Rome's priorities lay elsewhere and the Antonine Wall was abandoned and dismantled a mere twenty years after it was constructed. The Roman Empire had at last found a frontier that it could not afford to push, and the limits of alleged civilization were once again set at Hadrian's Wall.[18] The expression on the face of the first person to pass from the north through the Antonine Wall's abandoned forts must have been something to behold. The wall did not, however, disappear entirely from the scene like a stage prop during the intermission of a play.[19] The Roman emperor Septimius Severus, along with his sons Caracalla and Geta, pushed beyond it in the early third century in a last attempt to tame the north. Several large forts were built well beyond the Antonine Wall and there was some limited success against the Maeatae, but eventually, like everyone who had tried before him, the emperor was forced to fall back and merely hold the Forth-Clyde line against the inevitable. After Septimius' final, futile push, no Roman force would ever again march beyond the Antonine Wall. Of all the historians who have written on the subject of Rome's failed campaigns of conquest in Scotland, none put the essence of struggle so well as Qhorin Halfhand of the Night's Watch when he taught Jon Snow a valuable lesson: 'We're at war. We've always been at war. It's never going to end because we're not fighting an enemy, we're fighting the North and it's not going anywhere.'[20]

The Land Between the Walls

So far we have briefly passed through two frontiers of the Roman Empire, but what about those caught in the middle? Sandwiched between the Caledonian north beyond the Antonine Wall and Romanized Britain south of Hadrian's Wall was the *intervallum*, or 'land between the walls'.[21] The roots of Roman civilization may have spread into the *intervallum*, as evidenced by hoards of goods such as at Traprain Law in East Lothian that demonstrate intensive contact and trading relationships between the legions and the locals, but those roots ultimately failed to take hold. Ptolemy records four main tribes within the *intervallum*: the Novantae, with a likely base around Whithorn; the Votadini, who occupied Traprain Law and Edinburgh (called *Din Eidyn* in the native Brythonic); the Selgovae around Kirkcudbright; and the Damnonii, who were the precursors to the Kingdom of Strathclyde.[22] How much of a hierarchical relationship there was between the people of the *intervallum* and their nominal Roman overlords is up for debate, but for most people day-to-day life under Roman occupation was likely little different than it was before.

While the imposition of Rome was not as intrusive or oppressive in the *intervallum* as along, say, the Germanic frontier, traces of the would-be conquerors were everywhere to be found. The *intervallum* was heavily fortified, with somewhere in the neighbourhood of fifty forts and other military installations dotted across southern Scotland, hosting a total strength of approximately 21,000 legionaries and auxiliaries.[23] With the construction of these forts and the endless procession of Roman soldiers through the valleys, the people of the *intervallum* must have felt as though their land was being recast in Rome's likeness. And yet, aside from the odd discovery like the bathhouse at Bearsden along the Antonine Wall, there were no villas, *civitas* or other forms of civil infrastructure anywhere to be found. The occupation of the *intervallum*, and indeed all parts of Scotland that fell within Rome's tenuous grasp, was entirely military. This cannot have failed to raise the ire of the locals, who probably adopted an attitude something like the classic proverb, 'When the great lord passes, the peasant bows deeply and silently farts.'

The exception to the lack of infrastructure built by Rome in the *intervallum* was the one thing that no true Roman went anywhere without: a good road to march along. Westeros may have the Kingsroad, but from the glimpses we get it is a paltry thing next to what the Romans made; and whereas the Kingsroad peters out into little more than a dirt path once it gets north of Winterfell, the Roman roads maintain their integrity all the way up to, and in one case beyond, the Antonine Wall. A service road called the Military Way ran parallel to the Antonine Wall some 40-50ft from its southern face, allowing troops and supplies to be hurried from point to point as required. Roman roads are wonders in themselves, more often than not straight as the flight of an arrow and paved so well that some original sections throughout Europe are still walkable today.

The Walls at the Edge of the World

The Romans built two main roads into Scotland, one in the west and another in the east. The western route ran north from Carlisle (then called Luguvalium) and wove through Annandale up to the Antonine Wall at the Clyde. The eastern branch, known as Dere Street, ran from York (then Eburacum) through the deep valleys of the Borders into the Lothians. One of the best surviving stretches of Dere Street can be found on Soutra Hill, 20 miles south of Edinburgh. Though the paving has long since vanished, the outline of the road is clear to behold, and the sheer width of it – about 30ft, easily wide enough for several large carriages to pass by each other without cutting it too close – is almost unbelieveable.[24] These were no mere single-track paths like those still found in parts of the Highlands but *bona fide* highways that were so efficient and well-planned that many of our modern motorways or trunk roads, such as the A7 and A68, were built virtually over the top of them.[25] There is a certain irony to them in that sense. Though they were intended to be merely the first phase of the victory of Rome over the barbarians of the north, they are now one of the only tangible reminders of their failure.

There are lessons to be had in the ruins left in Rome's wake. Every wall that has ever been built, from the first walled cities of Mesopotamia to the Great Wall of China and the Theodosian Walls of Constantinople, failed in their one and only task. More often than not, they actively empower the very forces they were meant to keep at bay. Thinking of Hadrian's Wall and the Antonine Wall, for instance, the peoples to the north of them had spent their entire histories until then quarrelling with each other in loose confederations, one consuming the other and then in turn being consumed, like the Ouroboros serpent eating its own tail. With the raising of the walls, however, the hegemony of Rome loomed so large before them all that the tribes achieved what was never possible before: unification.[26] A compelling case is made by the passing of the wildlings through the Wall by invitation of Jon Snow. After thousands of years of attempting to storm it by the sword, the gates of Castle Black swing open to them in what Martin presents as a moment of triumph – albeit an uneasy one – rather than defeat. It is a liberation, not a calamity, and the two factions whose entire lives had hitherto been defined by which side of the Wall they stood on are all, together, the stronger for it. At the time of writing, part of the Wall of Westeros has come crashing down. We should have expected nothing else. If history tells us anything, it is that the walls we build, whether on our lands or in our minds, are without exception found wanting.

Chapter 7

Castles: Towers of Power

Castles dominate the opening credits of *Game of Thrones* for good reason. They are not just places where events happen, they are often *why* events happen. Westeros' castles are the ancient and revered seats of noble houses, whose identities are inextricably linked to them – what, after all, are the Lannisters without Casterly Rock or the Starks without Winterfell? They are the focal points of every major military campaign, and the mere possession of a castle, even symbolically, is viewed as a crucial step in what Littlefinger calls 'climbing the ladder'. Castles act as mirrors held up to the motivations and follies of their architects. Whether an indictment of hubris in the form of cursed Harrenhal, an echo of a revered and distant past like of the Broken Tower in Winterfell or a modest towerhouse like the multitude sprouted up in the Riverlands, Martin's castles are as individual and fully developed as his characters. They are therefore worth getting to know quite well.

The Makings Of A Castle

Almost everyone could, if asked, picture a castle in their mind's eye, but would any two peoples' creations look the same? While someone steeped in Romantic literature may imagine a Walter Scott-style crumbling ruin astride a glistening loch, people reared on Disney may picture a spiralling confection made of 100 turrets reaching up to impossible heights. Westeros, as it happens, has both of those types and everything in between, but the question remains: what is the common thread that links these vastly different visions? It's simple enough to list the components of a castle – towers, walls, arrow slits, gatehouses and the like – yet any one of these things alone, and even all of them together, do not necessarily make a castle. So what does?

Instead of getting caught up in definitions which will inevitably have more exceptions than rules, it's best to think in terms of broad guidelines. Any time I arrive at a site described as a castle, I ask three basic questions of it to work out where on the spectrum it lies. First, when was it built? It will be shown soon why that is a more complex question than it seems, but if a structure in Scotland has a recorded history dating between the late eleventh and early seventeenth centuries, that puts it within the range of when 'genuine' castles were built. Second, does it balance domestic and wartime functions? A castle has to be both a home for a laird or lady and their household, and serve some military purpose. There is no tried and true ratio to go by, or even a foolproof way to quantify these factors, but both have to be present to some degree. If a site is purely military, like Fort George near Inverness, which was built in the wake of the final Jacobite Rising of 1745-46, then it cannot be a castle; if it is purely domestic, with no practical way of being defended, like the marvellous Hopetoun House to the west of Edinburgh, it also cannot be a castle. Third and finally, if it has castellated features – things that we expect a castle to have, such as those towers and arrow slits mentioned above – do they actually contribute to the building's defence or are they just for show? Charles McKean suggested borrowing the helpful French term *château* to refer to buildings that present castellated architecture at face value but do so purely symbolically and not functionally.[1] Taken together, these three checks will generally sort the *bona fide* castles from the many styles of Scottish architecture that emulate them.

It can be very easy for us to visit castles and come away thinking of them as barely fit for human habitation, with their bare walls, draughty corridors and lack of lighting. What we must remember is that ruinous castles are like the skeletons of beached whales – the essential form is there, but most of what made it what is was has long since been plundered or rotted away. Tapestries, wall hangings, floor coverings, timber beams, fixtures and all the little touches added by people no less inclined to comfort than we are must usually be added in our mind's eye. Harren the Black, who was burned out of Harrenhal by Aegon the Conqueror on his dragon, seems to have forgotten this. Harren had shrugged off Aegon's threat to unleash the dragon Balerion against the castle since, he boasted, 'stone does not burn'[2] The wooden floors and ceilings, victuals, straw, wool, grain and countless other goods stored within burned very well, however, and the impregnable stone walls of Harrenhal turned into an oven that cooked alive the last of Harren's line inside. It's a rather grim way to learn a lesson about the realities of keeping up a castle, though it's one no resident of Westeros shall soon forget.

In addition to their practical function as homes and fortifications, castles were potent symbols of power. They remained so from their first appearance in Britain in the eleventh century until the seventeenth century and, at a more mnemonic level, endure as such even into our own time.[3] The mere act of building one was a statement of wealth, authority and exclusivity, and the medieval barons who raised them often did so with the express intention of declaring, loud and clear, and quite literally in stone, their ambitions. The term 'architectural theatrics' has been used to neatly sum up this ostentatious display of power. Baronial castles like Tantallon or Sinclair-Girnigoe were, and remain, every bit as impressive and imposing as anything the royals could build, a fact that regularly roused their ire.

Of course, any discussion about power has to ask the question, power of who over whom? Norman knights may have built motte-and-bailey castles to establish themselves in Scotland's frontier zones, but that didn't mean the locals had to like it. To those inside a castle, its main function might be security, yet the broader pattern of early castle construction was one of aggression and expansion by the nascent Kingdom of Scotland.[4] A twelfth-century Scot living in the traditional heartland of the kingdom, perhaps along the Tay or in central Fife, would have very different feelings about castles than a Gael in Argyll. Where castles first rose up on their earthen mounds in Scotland, they were, to say the least, not loved at first sight.[5] This made castles targets. Following the capture of Scottish king William the Lion at Alnwick in 1174, for example, assaults were launched by the men of Galloway against the many timber castles that had sprouted up in the south-west. Castles, not just in Scotland but the world over, are inseparable from the aggressive expansion of kingdoms and the consolidation of baronial and royal power.

This is clearly also the case in Westeros. One of the many fascinating insights about Westerosi castles in *The World of Ice and Fire* is that the great castles of the land, such as Casterly Rock or Winterfell, began their lives as the high seats of nascent noble families. In time, they incorporated – that is to say, conquered and subdued – wider lands and minor estates to become the powerhouses and hubs of activity that they are in *Game of Thrones*.[6] Winterfell did not become the heart of the North by mistake; it became that only after millennia of warfare against rivals such as the ancient Barrow Kings of Barrowtown and the Boltons of the Dreadfort.

The North being predominantly under the authority of Winterfell may seem like a monolithic and eternal concept to us now, yet it was only one of several power centres vying for supremacy north of the Neck.

Given their symbolic, administrative and martial advantages, castles were the focus of nearly every major military campaign throughout the medieval and early modern eras.[7] They were absolutely pivotal in the many attempts by English armies to subjugate Scotland, for they served as bastions of relative security in an openly hostile land. In the countryside, an occupying force is almost always at a disadvantage, but a few soldiers could exercise control over a considerable area from inside a castle. Castle garrisons were tiny relative to the populations they were meant to dominate, with a typical English garrison in Scotland comprised of around 130 soldiers including mounted men-at-arms and archers.[8] Scotland's castles were targeted by and integrated into Edward I's war machine so thoroughly upon his invasion in 1296 that while travelling leisurely from Dunbar in the south to Elgin in the north, he only had to spend one night out of dozens camping 'under canvas'.[9] The most significant regional castles, such as Bothwell and Caerlaverock, were made into administrative centres from which men like Aymer de Valence and Robert Clifford, respectively, were to govern the newly conquered territories. Robert the Bruce, too, knew how vital castles were to controlling the land. That is why, instead of stretching his forces out too thinly to occupy the castles he reclaimed one by one from English garrisons, he had the vast majority of them slighted – that is, not completely destroyed but reduced enough that they wouldn't be a threat to anyone for the foreseeable future. If Bruce could not use Scotland's castles to his advantage, he was certainly not about to let his enemies get any use from them, either.

Castle Types In Scotland & Westeros

The variety of castellated architecture in *Game of Thrones* imbues Westeros with a sense of historical depth, speaking of changing technologies, resources, belief systems and geopolitical priorities over a tremendous span of time. Unlike in many more conventional fantasy realms, not every castle in Westeros is a massive, fairytale-like flight of fancy with a prince or princess waiting within. The Eyrie is perhaps the closest that Westeros has to the Disney ideal, with its many similarities to Germany's iconic Neuschwanstein. Wander the North in particular and you will find everything from rudimentary timber halls built by the minor nobility to royal and baronial castles sprawling over many acres.

With only a few exceptions, every kind of castle that can be found in Scotland can be found in Westeros. The Seven Kingdoms have not yet had the opportunity to develop country houses, *châteaux* or Jacobean mansions such as Scotland's Fyvie Castle. Nor is there explicit mention of castles of enclosure, the kind of early stone castle built by the Norse and Norse-Gaels along the western seaboard and northern isles. The castles of the ironborn, the culture which most closely resembles the Norse-Gaels, seem to simply be rougher versions of mainland castles. That leaves three broad categories of castle to compare between Scotland and Westeros: the early timber castle, the towerhouse and major baronial and royal castles.

The first European castles were built not of stone, which has become so synonymous with the idea of what a castle is, but of timber and earth. Unfortunately, timber rots and soil erodes, so there is not a single surviving example of an original, unmodified timber castle anywhere to be found. Interpreting these sites therefore requires a great deal of imagination, or the talents of a reconstruction artist. Even the best-preserved of them, such as the great earthwork rising up at the confluence of the rivers Don and Urie known as the Bass of Inverurie, go relatively unregarded. A first-time visitor to what remains of Scotland's early timber castles could well wonder if they have arrived at the wrong place, for all that is left now is the mound that such castles used to perch upon. That is where we get the name for this type of castle, commonly known as mottes, derived from *motta*, meaning a clod of earth.[10] There were many different kinds of timber castle, but the archetypal and most widely known variety was the motte-and-bailey, which consisted of a timber structure, either a tower or hall-house, atop an earthen mound (the motte) and ancillary buildings enclosed within a connected lower, broader area (the bailey).

Not all timber castles were motte-and-baileys. As Simon Forder argues, the term is actually far more applicable to developments in England and Wales, where indigenous aristocracies were replaced on a far larger scale by William the Conqueror's followers after 1066 than they were in Scotland.[11] These incoming knights were the builders of the first true motte-and-bailey castles throughout Britain, yet they arrived in a landscape already densely packed with fortified sites. Hillforts, ringforts, crannogs, duns, hall-houses and other fortified dwellings were and would remain vastly more numerous than motte-and-bailey castles in Scotland.[12] In fact of 331 sites containing the term 'motte' in the online Canmore database maintained by the Royal Commission on the Ancient and Historical Monuments of Scotland, only forty include any mention of a bailey.[13] Sites like duns and hall-houses have left little to us after more than 1,000 years of weathering, such that the faint traces of ditches, mounds and foundations are often difficult to appreciate without aerial photography or a dusting of snow to emphasize them.

An average timber castle in the late eleventh and twelfth centuries could be constructed from scratch by a workforce of around fifty in a little over a month. In areas where security was a matter of urgency, that speediness was very appealing to their builders. A survey of motte-and-bailey castles around Scotland demonstrated that where the crown's authority was most secure, there was little need for building timber castles.[14] Angus, Fife and Perthshire have relatively few such sites, while the majority of the more than 300 so far identified in Scotland are concentrated in areas such as Moray and Dumfries and Galloway, frontier zones between the nascent Kingdom of Scotland and the Norse and Gaelic domains.

If the North of Westeros is a place where the old ways endure, then it is only fitting that it also has the best examples of the oldest real-world style of castle. Timber castles were common in Westeros after the coming of the First Men, with many of the grand baronial castles that are now home to mighty houses having begun as modest timber works. Most famously, Aegon the Conqueror built the humbly named Aegonfort, described explicitly as a motte-and-bailey castle, immediately upon landing in Westeros where the Red Keep now stands.[15] This is very reminiscent of how William the Conqueror brought a pre-fabricated wooden castle with him across the English Channel from Normandy to Pevensey, which was up and running within a single day of his landing in England.[16] Other early timber fortifications are also mentioned. For instance, Winterfell possibly began as a series of ringforts that joined together over time. There are no castles beyond the Wall, but Craster's Keep is a very crude example of the duns and fortified farmsteads that were popular during the Iron Age and early medieval period.

The best surviving example of a motte-and-bailey castle in Westeros is undoubtedly Deepwood Motte, the seat of House Glover. It is located about 300 miles north-west of Winterfell, deep, as the name implies, within the Wolfswood. It is the tallest structure on its side of the northern mountains and follows the classic motte-and-bailey prototype, albeit scaled up in classic

Martin fashion, with a 50ft-high timber watch tower capping a conical earthen mound with its top flattened. It is widely derided, perhaps because of the relative primitiveness of its construction, with Theon dismissing Deepwood Motte as nothing more than 'a wooden pisspot on a hill'.[17] Here again, even from the perspective of the ironborn who are looked down upon by most of Westeros, is a clear sense that the further north one goes in Westeros the less refined the architecture, and the people, become. Yet there was a time in our own history when such castles were seen alongside the mounted knight as the ultimate expressions of a new and advanced military order.

Examples of timber castles in Westeros: Deepwood Motte, Moat Cailin, The Aegonfort (now the Red Keep)

Examples of timber castles in Scotland: Bass of Inverurie, Duffus Castle, Motte of Urr

Having spent a great deal of time thinking about what makes a castle and the different forms they take, I was delighted by a particular exchange between Jon and Ygritte in *A Storm of Swords*. Passing by the crumbling remains of a modest stone tower several storeys high, Ygritte is awestruck. Having come from beyond the Wall, where there is not even a single motte-and-bailey castle, she wonders aloud why anyone would be fool enough to abandon such a mighty stronghold. Jon smirks. 'It's only a towerhouse,' he says. 'Some little lordling lived there once, with his family and a few sworn men. When raiders came he would light a beacon from the roof.'[18] With that slightly condescending reply, Jon Snow perfectly summed up the essence of the Scottish towerhouse.

Towerhouses are the castellated equivalent of the big house in a modern suburban community. They may look impressive, and extensive security measures may dissuade all but the most determined burglars, but if the Army turns up with some high-powered weapons then they won't be delayed from getting in for very long. Towerhouses are best thought of as being defensible rather than defensive;[19] they are capable of putting up stout resistance to a degree, but are not great fortresses that dominate an area or the strategic lynchpins of the nation like Bothwell or Stirling castles. There are a few notable exceptions, such as Borthwick Castle south of Edinburgh, whose walls are so thick that it was used as recently as the Second World War to keep vital documents and artefacts safe from bombings, or Neidpath Castle near Peebles, which allegedly held out against Cromwell's canons for longer than any other castle in the south of Scotland. In Westeros, the Frey towers of the Twins are exceptional in this regard. Towerhouses are typically three or four storeys high and, as the name implies, consist of a single tower. That is not to say they stood alone. The towerhouse was almost never self-sufficient and required ancillary buildings such as stables, smithies, accommodation for guards and mercenaries (the latter of which you don't want sleeping under your own roof), brewhouses and other domestic buildings. Any time you see a small square or rectangular slot in the outer wall of a tower, it is likely a put-hole marking where a timber building used to adjoin the stone tower, hinting at a far more bustling past than the present state of most towerhouses belie.

The greatest concentration of towerhouses are found in areas like the Scottish Borders, which suffered hundreds of years of perpetual warfare on both a grand and localized level, resulting in an environment of destabilization and fear. The phrase 'every man's home is his castle' is perhaps more true in the Borders than anywhere else in Britain, where they are so numerous that when standing on the roof or battlements of one towerhouse, you can more often than not spot one or more other towers with the naked eye. Legislation passed in 1535 demanded that anyone dwelling in the Borders whose land was valued at more than £100 (Scots) build a barmkin, a small enclosing wall, and a stone tower.[20] Those whose lands were valued at less than £100 were instructed to build peels, a sort of fortified farmhouse with its entrance above ground level so that access can be severed with a retractable ladder. If the king or a mighty nobleman came knocking then the average towerhouse, and certainly peels and barmkins, would not offer much by way of resistance. Yet for the majority of day-to-day threats, mostly on account of raiders and bandits, they were more often than not up to the task.

Towerhouses also seem to be the most common type of castle in the Riverlands of Westeros, an area which has seen more warfare and turbulence than any other in the Seven Kingdoms.[21] An account of an attack on a towerhouse there reads precisely the same as a great many attempts on towerhouses in the Scottish Borders. Ser Roger Hogg, owner of one such tower, tells Jaime Lannister how Amory Lorch, a Lannister captain, slaughtered a great many of his livestock before trying to roast Ser Hogg out from his holdfast by setting fire to the doorway. This was a very common tactic employed by Scottish and English Border Reivers.

'My walls are solid stone and eight feet thick, though,' boasted Ser Hogg, 'so after his fire burned out he rode off bored.'[22] Sitting tight and waiting out the storm was the best bet for the residents of a towerhouse, and more often than not the aggressors would decide that it wasn't worth the time and effort after all and move on to easier pickings. Even the thickness of Ser Hogg's walls matches the average thickness of the walls of Scottish towerhouses, which were typically in the range of 5-10ft.[23] Ser Hogg's name will never be spoken of with reverence in the taverns of Westeros like that of Brynden 'the Blackfish' Tully, and his castle will, like its appearance in *A Feast for Crows*, merit only the most fleeting mention in the maester's histories. Yet his tower and the hundreds more just like it dotted across Westeros and Scotland, are far more representative of the norm than the great seats of the high and mighty such as Riverrun.

Examples of towerhouses in Westeros: Sow's Horn, The Twins

Examples of towerhouses in Scotland: Neidpath Castle, Smailholm Tower, Crathes Castle

When castles come up in conversation, a long-since rotted motte-and-bailey or humble towerhouse is likely not what springs to mind. Instead our imaginations are dominated by grand curtain walls bristling with arrow slits and crenellations, gatehouses flanked by towers and a great keep where the laird or king hold court. These were the kind of castles built by Scotland and Westeros' leading families, wealthiest barons and mightiest warlords, often functioning as regional capitals, or *caputs*, to which more minor castles and lairds are in deference. In Scotland, these include castles like Edinburgh, Stirling, Urquhart, Dunnottar or Caerlaverock; in Westeros, these are Winterfell, Casterly Rock, the Red Keep, Riverrun, the Eyrie or Highgarden. All these places are inextricably intertwined with the fates of their respective realms and reflective of the ambitions of the nobles that inhabit them. They stand as testaments in stone to the tremendous wealth, authority, pomp and pride of Scotland's leading nobility in the thirteenth and fourteenth centuries.[24]

This was a radical departure from the castle-building of the late eleventh and twelfth centuries. No longer were a flurry of timber castles being raised upon the kingdom's fringe; greater beasts were now stirring. The majority of major stone castles in Scotland that still stand and draw visitors today were built during what is often called the 'golden age' of castle construction, lasting from the early thirteenth century until the outbreak of the Wars of Independence in 1296.[25] The thirteenth century was, at last in relative terms, a peaceful and prosperous time in much of Scotland. Reasonably friendly relations with England, the consolidation of royal power into the north and west and the rule of competent kings meant that resources could be dedicated to building stone castles over years and decades rather than months. This may at first seem paradoxical; however, castles on the scale of those built in Scotland, indeed throughout Britain and Europe, in the thirteenth century required a tremendous investment of money, manpower and time – all three things most readily available in times of peace.

The results speak for themselves. There are well over 100 major baronial castles in Scotland. They run the gamut from elegant symphonies in stone like Dirleton Castle near North Berwick or Drummond Castle near Crieff to what some refer to as 'sod off' castles, such as Ravenscraig in Kirkcaldy or Dunstaffnage Castle near Oban, whose brooding and combative stance is seemingly channelled into every aspect of their architecture. Many of them are managed by national heritage organizations such as Historic Environment Scotland and require a fee to enter, while others lay completely open and are the domain of local schoolchildren who let their imaginations run wild through their crumbling halls. Though the great (and terrible) founders of Scotland's mightiest castles would likely be aghast at the prospect of a procession of strangers rooting through their old bedchambers or of children playing in the dungeons their enemies once rotted in, we nonetheless have them to thank for building some of the most awe-inspiring monuments to our evolving heritage.

Examples of major stone castles in Westeros: Casterly Rock, Winterfell, Riverrun

Examples of major stone castles in Scotland: Bothwell Castle, Dunnottar Castle, Stirling Castle

Scaling up the Walls

Aside from the Wall, there is no better example of Martin's governing rule of using history as a basis for fantasy, which is to mash it all together and 'turn it up to eleven', than his castles. Despite its many wonders, our history has nothing that can quite match the soaring turrets of the Red Keep, the monstrous bulk of Harrenhal or the perilousness of the Eyrie. Scotland's largest castles, such as Edinburgh, Stirling, Urquhart or Bothwell, would scarcely fill even a quarter of Winterfell. Even the far larger castles built by Edward I in Wales, such as Beaumaris and Harlech, are dwarfed by scale of the major baronial castles of Westeros. To get anywhere remotely close we need to turn to walled towns such as France's Carcassonne or the Theodosian Walls of Constantinople – neither of which are castles, but walled cities and towns.

The ultimate expression of this scaling-up is, of course, Harrenhal, a castle so absurdly huge that it is too big to succeed. Theoretically, it is invincible. Winterfell could fit seven times over inside Harrenhal's gargantuan walls, and its godswood alone covers 20 acres. Its defences are so massive that Jaime Lannister, a man not unused to huge castles given his birthplace of Casterly Rock, noted with near disbelief that he passed under twelve murder holes – gaps that defenders can drop heated substances and heavy objects down through – within a single gateway.[26] In a Scottish castle, two or three would be considered overkill. With five towers, each larger than most entire castles, and masonry so strong that no trebuchet could make more than a scuff on the ramparts,[27] Harrenhal is the ultimate expression of might.

As a narrative device, Harrenhal is not so much a place as a shorthand for hubris, a sort of Tower of Babel for the Seven Kingdoms. It is cruelty and human ambition cast in stone, a monumental indictment of the ultimate futility of arms races – a theme that George R.R. Martin, with his well-documented leaning toward pacifism, no doubt sought to deliberately emphasize. Black Harren, the builder of Harrenhal, sought to build a castle to end all castles, only to be ended himself by a hitherto unimaginable weapon of even greater power in the form of Aegon the Conqueror's dragons. Harrenhal is a paradox, with the very thing that makes it powerful also being the seed of its undoing. Catelyn Stark knows as much, observing that, 'Even stretched to the end of your means you cannot fill and manage the whole castle.'[28] Many lords have learned this lesson well, for even if no dragons have descended on it since Balerion, the logistical nightmare of managing so large a place has consumed the resources, and even sanity, of every noble family that has attempted to tame it. Harrenhal does not just humble its occupants. It teaches us, as Martin is so often wont to do, that when subjected to the limitations imposed by the devil's advocate that is real history, many of the sky-scraping towers of our favourite fictional universes would come crashing down under their own weight.

While Westerosi castles may win out when it comes to scale, they are vastly outnumbered by their Scottish counterparts. Some 2,500 castles mark the Scottish landscape, ranging from vast baronial complexes that are still inhabited by the descendants of their founders to piles of moss-covered rubble obscured by stinging nettles and bracken. By comparison, a survey of the maps in *The World of Ice and Fire* labels just under 100 castles, ninety-six to be precise, in Westeros. There are some notable and surprising trends, such as Dorne being home to more castles than any other region with sixteen, and the Riverlands, a place of considerable riches and perpetual warfare, having the fewest with only six, on a par with the Iron Islands. If Westeros is roughly the size of the South American landmass, and also broadly feudal from top to bottom, these are paltry figures. For instance, there are well over 100 castles within a 25-mile radius of central Edinburgh, and Scotland is less than one half of 1 per cent the size of Westeros. Where did all the Westerosi castles go?

Martin likely and understandably left the majority of them undocumented. Definitive counts of castles in Scotland are notoriously hard to come by, with figures ranging from 750 (much too low) to over 3,000 (a touch too high). No physical map could make room for every broken tower and forgotten foundation. The Collins *Castles Map of Scotland*, for example, lists over 715 locations and, while very useful, is already overwhelming with less than a third of all sites accounted for. Martin has clearly chosen to take the approach of showcasing the most significant Westerosi castles while leaving the countless smaller towers, ruins and fortified homes for our imaginations to fill in.

The Complicated Lives Of Castles

'When was it built?' is one of the most deceptively complex questions you can ask about a castle. Take Edinburgh Castle, for instance. My usual attempt at an answer goes something like this: 'Well, there was a hill fort on the Rock 2,000 years ago, but it didn't become a castle until the twelfth century under David I, and that one was mostly destroyed by Robert the Bruce. David II built a huge tower, but that was destroyed, too, and construction ran on piecemeal from the late fourteenth century. The first gatehouse you encounter when visiting today is newer than Edinburgh's Georgian New Town, and the War Memorial in the castle's Crown Square is from the early twentieth century. So, depending on how you want to define it, sometime between the Iron Age and now.' By that point they're probably sorry they asked.

Most castles, especially major baronial and royal ones, are the Frankenstein's monsters of the ages, assembled from the leftovers of centuries of destruction, reconstruction and transformation. There is an old Scottish proverb that sums it up well. 'This is my grandfather's axe. My father gave it a new handle, and I gave it a new head.'[29] Nothing material from the original axe remains, and yet its provenance is unimpeachable. Let's take Crichton Castle, the home of William Crichton, who plotted the real-life version of *Game of Thrones'* Red Wedding known as the Black Dinner. On a tranquil terrace overlooking the River Tyne, his father, John de Crichton, built an imposing towerhouse in the late fourteenth or early fifteenth century. John's son, the aforementioned William, converted his inheritance into the courtyard castle that we see today and also established the nearby collegiate church. After the Crichtons had been blacklisted for their misdeeds, the castle changed hands until it fell into those of Frances Bothwell in 1581. Frances used his extensive travels throughout Europe as inspiration for architectural flourishes such as the stunning Italianate arcade, or *loggia*, with its diamond-pattern façade and the stable block with Moorish-style doorways. So, who built Crichton Castle? Was it John, because he was first to establish it? Or was it William, who gave it much of the form we appreciate today? Arguably, the castle's most notable surviving features were added by Frances, so what credit does he receive? The story of a castle's development is thus as nuanced as the lives of those who called them home.

Winterfell: King of Castles

To pass through the gates of Winterfell is to enrol in a masterclass in the evolution of castle architecture. The castle is sprawling yet intimate, the product not of one single vision but many different visions colliding, combining and reconfiguring over the centuries. It has its quirks, its strengths, its faults and its secrets that we may or may not ever be privy to. In *Game of Thrones*, Winterfell first reveals itself to us in a way that many Scots know well, obscured by a veil of fog across a soggy field. One look at it is all you need to know that it would take a mighty effort to get inside if the Starks barred the gates to you. Two huge curtain walls surround the castle complex, the inner one standing 80ft tall and the outer one 100ft,[30] as high as any tower in Scotland. These walls are separated by a wide moat, traversable at only four points and guarded by stout gatehouses with flanking towers. For millennia they have held against ironborn, rebellious lords, wildlings, Boltons and worse.[31] Timber hoardings extend from the castle's multitude of round towers, crenellations afford protection for archers on the battlements and there are precious few weak points such as windows in the monumental masonry for assailants to take advantage of. All physical evidence points to the residents of Winterfell being able to sleep soundly in their beds behind the ancient walls of the capital of the North.

And yet it is not invincible. Theon Greyjoy was able to take Winterfell with a single longship's worth of ironborn by launching a surprise attack when the majority of the castle's garrison left for Torrhen's Square, not unlike how James Douglas took Roxburgh Castle or how Thomas Randolph took Edinburgh. Even a behemoth like Winterfell can be vulnerable if caught by surprise or while undermanned. There is also one architectural gripe that must be raised. It turns out that Winterfell's most glaring weakness is betrayed by its name. Many of the towers that punctuate its great walls are round, with flat roofs capping them. Ask any architect working in a climate where snows are common and they will immediately see the fatal flaw in this: at the first significant snowfall, those roofs would collapse under the weight and turn the towers into ruins. Ironically, if Winterfell was a real castle, winter would be its undoing!

Despite Robert Baratheon's complaints about the cold, Winterfell is not short on comforts. If it were, the Starks – for all their spartanness – would have found somewhere else to call home. Thanks to the hot springs that attracted the first settlers to the area, Winterfell has hydraulic central heating of a kind unrivalled in medieval Scotland or Britain, more reminiscent of Roman and even Victorian baths. Sansa Stark says that this system is so effective that the glass gardens over the hot springs are as warm as the hottest day of summer even in the depths of winter.[32] Food can be grown throughout the year, a tremendous boon for both the castle's defenders in times of siege and the 15,000 or so residents of the seasonal winter town who raise their hovels against the castle's walls when the winds of winter begin to howl.

In addition to this remarkable system, Winterfell has many domestic and civic spaces, most notably the Great Hall, which can seat 500 for a feast. The godswood, the spiritual centre of the Starks' world, takes up 3 acres within the castle complex. Aside from moments such as when Ned sharpens his sword under the heart tree, which comes across as an act of prayer in itself, the godswood is entirely demilitarized. Winterfell's design clearly indicates an appreciation of the balance between martial and domestic features that real castles struck and takes us, accurately, away from the popular misconception that medieval castles were nothing but stationary war machines.

Legend tells of a single founding moment for Winterfell, its walls raised by Bran the Builder as if by mere command alone after the Long Night, a tidy creation myth not unlike the supposed founding of Rome by Romulus and Remus. Even from afar, however, it is clear that Winterfell was not built overnight. The chronicles tell a more complex tale, with some maesters suggesting that Winterfell began as a series of interlinked ringforts in the early days of the First Men.[33] This is supported by the fact that the ground beneath Winterfell's walls was never levelled, such that the castle incorporates the natural fluctuations in the soil and rock. If there was a single large construction phase, that would almost certainly not have been the case. To paraphrase Roose Bolton's observation about Winterfell, it's likely that no one intended to build a castle at all until one day someone looked up and realized they were in one.[34] There is also an abundance of evidence to be read, as at any historic site, in the stones themselves. The combination of both square and round towers, the varying type and quality of masonry and the way that the whole castle complex appears to emanate organically from a central core outwards are all clues hinting at a long process of growth and change.

Hand-in-hand with the slow pace of development is the existence of ruinous and abandoned areas within a still-functional castle. Winterfell wears its age as a badge of pride. A squat, round keep known as the First Tower lays abandoned at the very heart of the castle complex. It is likely the oldest stone structure in Winterfell, a relic on display like the prize object in a museum. Its exact vintage is unknown; one maester, Kennett, argued that round towers only started being built after the Andals invaded, meaning the First Tower cannot have been built by the founding First Men.[35] Whatever the case, there is something of the nineteenth-century Romantic in this preservation and idolization of the past. A less sentimental approach would have been to redevelop the First Tower as the centuries moved on, yet the choice to let it endure in the form that their ancestors knew was a powerful and deliberate way of fusing the Stark name with the land upon which they had built their legacy. The message that the First Tower sends is clear: we have been here for thousands of years, and shall be for thousands more; we are this land, and this land is us. Fantasy castles, especially those of fairy tales, are often presented as being in impeccable form, everything perfectly maintained and glimmering with ostentatious demonstrations of power in the present. The fact that Winterfell has wrinkles that can be read like the grizzled face of an old adventurer does not diminish its majesty; on the contrary, it elevates the castle from a spectacle into something imbued with the lifeblood of the past. 'What is dead may never die' may be ironborn words, yet in the First Tower the Starks have one of the most perfect representations of the power of continuity.

Other areas of Winterfell have been left to ruin, though more simply due to neglect or redundancy than sentimentality. The Broken Tower, from which Bran is pushed by Jaime Lannister, was struck by lightning a century-and-a-half before the events of *Game of Thrones*.[36] It was once the greatest tower in all Winterfell, yet its charred and crumbling remains were never repaired, with it now serving as a redoubt for pigeons and licentious lovers. This is not unusual and has plenty of historical precedents. The once-mighty donjon at Bothwell Castle was slighted by Andrew Murray, whose ancestral tower it was, in the 1330s to deny its strength to the English. When Archibald the Grim, bastard son of James 'the Black' Douglas, took over the castle he gave the donjon – once the castle's nucleus – over to his servants and moved himself and his wife, Joanna, into more comfortable accommodation in the south range. The donjon would never be repaired, and stands to this day split vertically in two like an artist's cross-section.

Craigmillar Castle: Winterfell In Miniature

Sadly there is no perfect equivalent to Winterfell in Scotland. Edinburgh Castle, due to its sheer scale and status as protector of the capital, is a tempting yet imperfect match. However, you need not travel far from it to find the best approximation of a castle like Winterfell that Scotland can offer. Craigmillar Castle, just 2 miles south of the city centre, is one of the best-preserved medieval castles in the country. Craigmillar is a courtyard castle built around a central L-plan tower. Long a well-kept secret that few visitors and even Edinburgh locals knew existed, it has recently catapulted to fame as a result of being used as a set for programmes and films including *Outlander* and *Outlaw King* – proving once again that stories can give historic sites a second lease of life. While this means that, unlike as recently as four or five years ago, you almost never have Craigmillar to yourself, the atmosphere and architectural dynamism of the castle deserves a turn in the spotlight. The best way to approach it is by way of the adjacent woodland, for this takes you along the same paths that were walked by Mary, Queen of Scots on the two occasions she stayed at Craigmillar Castle. The area is still known as 'Little France' as a result of Mary's presence along with French soldier and courtiers.

Craigmillar bristles with defensive features, from keyhole gunloops and functional machicolations to multiple strongpoints that can be defended independently of each other. Walking its walls and corridors feels a bit like a castellated Easter egg hunt, for you can check off almost every kind of defensive feature used in medieval castles by scouring the warren of neuks and crannies within – gunloops, arrow slits, machicolations, crenellations and more are all present. Entering the castle complex through a small gate in the outermost wall, you emerge into a sprawling courtyard that once would have sung with the sounds of smithies and stench of sweat and horses. A second curtain wall, older and mightier than the first,[37] still stands between you and the castle's central keep just like the twin walls of Winterfell (though not nearly so tall).

It is within the innermost layer of the castle that the Starks would feel most at home. A great wooden doorway leads into the inner sanctum, where a most unexpected sight greets you – the ancient and meandering branches of two yew trees growing straight out of the stony courtyard, flanking the doorway like a pair of guards. Yew trees can live for millennia, and while the exact date of their planting is not known with certainty, it is possible that they were familiar to Queen Mary in the 1560s. While not quite an equal to Winterfell's 3-acre godswood and its weirwood heart tree, the yews create an undeniable atmosphere of contemplation and ethereality. Children regularly scramble up their low-lying limbs, and as they do it is easy to picture Bran Stark happily doing the same while Robb and Jon practise archery in the courtyard, Sansa embroiders in the great hall and Arya chases cats through the main tower's many chambers and spiral stairways.

A striking feature of Winterfell is that there are domestic courtyards and building ranges emanating out in all directions from the ancient First Keep in the centre. Most real castles would have at least one range of outbuildings, but to have them surrounding the main tower on all sides is rare indeed – hence why Winterfell can feel more like a castellated city with multiple distinct areas rather than just a castle. This is also the case at Craigmillar. The central keep dates from the fourteenth century, while the machicolated inner curtain walls date from the fifteenth century. The outermost curtain wall was added a century later, and a domestic west range with private chambers, kitchens and a once-ornate hall capped it off in the seventeenth century. Craigmillar also did not lack for comforts. While it may not have had anything as luxurious as the glass gardens of Winterfell, you can still clearly discern the dried-up slopes of a fish pond shaped like a capital 'P' for the Preston family which was once the focal point for the castle's extensive grounds and gardens.[38] Hawking, archery and horse riding were popular pastimes for the nobility at Craigmillar, who used it to escape the din of the claustrophobic streets of nearby Edinburgh, known to Scots as 'Auld Reekie' (old smokey).

More vividly and atmospherically than perhaps any other Scottish castle, Craigmillar illustrates the way in which major landholders would add to their estates as the centuries and architectural trends progressed,[39] turning them from powerful yet simple towers into sprawling complexes that their founders could never have foreseen. Add to that the sheer fun of discovering every quirky corner of the castle and the distinctly fantastical feeling imbued by yew trees in the courtyard, and Craigmillar is the closest we can come to walking the walls of Winterfell.

PART III

PLAYERS OF THE GAME

Chapter 8

The Sea Kings: Islesmen & Ironborn

Vikings & the Old Way

Regaling each other with stories around driftwood fires, the ironborn long for the Old Way, a time when the very sound of waves struck terror into men's hearts.[1] It was a time when the ironborn were not mere Lords of the Iron Islands, but kings, and every captain with a ship was a monarch to their crew.[2] In *Game of Thrones*, Euron Greyjoy promises to return the Iron Islands to their former glories, and that promise gains him the Driftwood Crown at the Kingsmoot on the sacred island of Old Wyk. The desire to once again take to the waves as the unchained wolves of the sea is strong in the ironborn. Their future, in their blood-drenched dreams, is their past.

The ironborn may pine for the Old Way, but Svein Asleifarson of Orkney was out living it.[3] He spent each winter with his family and household in the warmth of his drinking hall, the largest in the Orkney Isles. After sowing his fields come the spring – something an ironborn would never stoop to, of course, for their words are 'We Do Not Sow' – he would set sail for the Hebrides and Ireland, rounding Cape Wrath to plunder jovially during what he called his 'spring-trip'. Having exerted himself and won many spoils, he would return home, reap the harvest and then depart for another round of raids on his 'autumn-trip'.[4]

Svein was a Viking. His yearly habits are related to us through the *Orkneyinga Saga*, composed by an unknown writer in Iceland sometime around 1200. For Svein, his spring and autumn trips, which are related in the *Orkneyinga Saga* with all the casualness of a bored child's account of what they did over the school holidays, were not the defining aspect of his identity but merely one part of it. Viking, after all, is not a noun but a verb. There is no 'Viking' tribe or nation but plenty of Scandinavians went a-viking. So much so, in fact, that Old English simply conflated all

Scandinavian raiders, whether Norwegians, Danes or those permanently settled in Orkney and Shetland by the late eighth century, as Vikings.[5]

Almost every account of the 'Viking Age', a term that has come to apply to the period between 793 and the Norman Conquest of 1066, begins with the infamous raid on Lindisfarne. The palpable fear behind the oft-cited refrain of shocked Christian monks – *A furore Normannorum libera nos, Domine*, 'From the fury of the Northmen deliver us, O Lord' – has immortalized the raid's place in the annals of world history. No less dramatic was the raid on Iona, the ancient heart of Celtic Christianity and the source of priceless illuminated manuscripts such as the *Book of Kells* only two years later. Iona would be ravaged again and again, with all the resident brethren slain in one especially violent episode in 806.[6] Similar violence engulfed the north and west coasts of Scotland, and soon enough would spread throughout the shores of the Irish Sea and wherever else a longship could disembark.

The arrival of the Vikings into the crucible of early medieval Scotland radically altered the political landscape. Not a single kingdom went unscarred; most would be destroyed or absorbed within a little over a century.[7] These included the Brythonic kingdom of Alt Clut based at Dumbarton Rock, as well as the Picts, whom Viking raiders and armies clashed with many times, with significant wins and losses on both sides. The crawl of Norse power across the Isles and mainland seemed inexorable, with both Caithness and Sutherland falling wholesale to them by the early ninth century. The Gaelic inhabitants of Scotland and Ireland did not call the invaders Vikings as we do, but *gall* – 'strangers'. The Outer Hebrides came under such total control of the northmen that the islands' name in Gaelic to this day is *Innse Gall*, the 'Islands of the Strangers'.[8] Soon, however, the strangers became a part of the family. Their legacy is plain to see, most notably in Shetland, where the Vikings established a major power centre at Jarlshof on the site of an earlier Pictish settlement; at the Brough of Birsay in Orkney, which became the seat of the powerful and sprawling medieval Earldom of Orkney; and in Lewis, which has the highest proportion of Norse place names in the Isles[9] and where the now world-famous Lewis chessmen were discovered in 1831. There was even a distinctive dialect called Norn spoken in Shetland, Orkney and Caithness until as recently as the nineteenth century, whose closest surviving linguistic relatives are Faroese, Icelandic and the Nynorsk of western Norway. What started as a scourge eventually became a permanently integrated feature of life in northern and western Scotland, and remains a part of many islanders' identities to this day.

The parallels between the ironborn and Vikings are well established and not exactly subtle; as stand-ins for real civilizations, they are perhaps the least altered of the major factions in *Game of Thrones*. Yet there are multiple phases to the story of the ironborn, and a closer look at their historical relationship with the rest of Westeros reveals an even closer match. Vikings of the eighth to the thirteenth centuries and ironborn prior to Aegon's Conquest would undoubtedly get along, but old ways are called that for a reason, and as the centuries progressed new ideas and identities emerged in both worlds. If we want the closest possible fit to the ironborn and their ambitions, we must turn not to the Vikings but to their estranged heirs, the Lords of the Isles.

There will be a lot of back and forth between Scotland's Isles and the Iron Islands ahead. So, for the sake of clarity, the terms the Isles and Islesmen always designate Scottish history, while Iron Islands and ironborn always relate to *Game of Thrones* history. One exception is the term King of the Isles, which was used by both the Norse and the ironborn.

In both Westeros and Scotland, the old ways of reiving and thrall-taking died along with a king. In Westeros, the Riverlands had been throttled for years by the iron fist of Harren Hoare, builder of the monstrous castle of Harrenhal. When Black Harren, as his deeds made him known, was roasted by Targaryen dragonflame during Aegon's Conquest, the ironborn hold on the Westerosi mainland turned to ash. What few ironborn survived the scourge trickled back to the sea like a drying stream with nothing left to do but to bend their swords into fishhooks.[10] In the years that followed, the ironborn would continue to terrorize the coasts and occasionally even the major settlements of the Westerlands under leaders like the Red Kraken, Dalton Greyjoy, who briefly restored the Old Ways, took salt wives and held an iron grip on the Sunset Sea while Westeros was consumed by the Dance of Dragons.[11] Yet such glimpses of past glories were brief, and the high water mark of ironborn power to date had long since been reached.

King Håkon IV of Norway also sought to relive the old days when his ancestors seized Shetland, Orkney, the Hebrides and the Isles by fire and sword. Things got off to a good start. In 1263, Håkon sailed with a mighty fleet of up to 200 ships to the west coast of Scotland, eager to strike a decisive blow to the Kingdom of Scotland. It was the first time that a Norse king had come in person to the Isles since 1102, and the great castles of Rothesay – where Norse warriors had hewn through the walls thirty years before – and Dunaverty fell to his host.[12] Despite these early victories, Håkon's forces were defeated, or at least repulsed, at the inconclusive Battle of Largs and were forced to limp back to safety in Orkney. Håkon died of illness in St Magnus Cathedral in Kirkwall and his successor, Magnus, ratified the Treaty of Perth in July 1266, ceding the Isle of Man and the Hebrides to Scotland.[13] So ended the Viking Age, not with a legendary siege or the clash of shield walls in the field, but with a tired, sick king dying in his bed and leaving a kingdom no longer willing to sacrifice its sons on Hebridean shores.

What is Dead May Never Die

As Norse influence gradually waned in the west in the century prior to the Treaty of Perth, a new power that was not wholly aligned with either Norway or Scotland emerged to fill the vacuum. Rather than rending the Isles neatly in two between Norse conquerors and the Gaelic inhabitants, the centuries-long tug of war produced a vibrant hybrid culture of Norse-Gaels. Perhaps no one embodied this better and more boldly than Somhairle mac Gillebride, or Somerled. In the Isles, the name of Somerled – meaning 'Summer Voyager'[14] – holds the same foundational status as Cináed (Kenneth) MacAlpin in Scotland or Harald Fairhair in Norway. He was the son of a Gaelic nobleman, Gillebride, and a Norse mother who is unfortunately unnamed in the annals, and three of the greatest clans in the west – MacDougall, MacRuari and MacDonald – trace their origins to him.[15] Coming to power in a land torn between two realms, Somerled opted not to continue down either path but to forge his, and his peoples', own.

Somerled, whose domains included Kintyre, much of mainland Argyll and Lorne, gained tremendous influence by marrying Ragnhild, daughter of Olaf the Red, Norse King of Man and the Isles.[16] Olaf was *Rí Innse Gall*, 'King of the Isles', a title used since the ninth century which had always been subservient to the King of Norway. When Olaf was killed by his nephews, his son, Godred, took the title, though he proved a loathsome and ineffectual leader. In a culture where individual prowess and charisma mattered far more than parentage, this was a fatal flaw. Norse lords approached Somerled to intervene and depose Godred, and he duly obliged by defeating Godred's navy at the evocatively named Battle of Epiphany in January 1156. This victory brought the isles of Mull, Jura and, most importantly, Islay into Somerled's domain. Somerled then assumed the mantle of *Rí Innse Gall*, and in doing so completely reinvented it. No longer would the King of the Isles answer to the King of Norway – Somerled embarked on an altogether new path, establishing a 'kingdom within a kingdom' that made its home in the fissure left by the quaking of the Kingdoms of Norway and Scotland.

Having thrown off the better part of the Norse yoke, his attention turned to the Kingdom of Scotland which was ever pressing westward. Somerled was not alone in this – a revolt by Fergus of Galloway in the south-west mainland of Scotland was borne of the same sense of defiance against the feudalizing Scottish state.[17] The Kingdom of Scotland was also expanding into Moray in the north, and taken altogether with events in Galloway and the Isles it is easy to see how the Gaelic and Norse-Gaelic world perceived an existential threat emanating from the royal power centres of Perth, Stirling and Dunfermline. Somerled decided to strike first, and led a large invasion up the Clyde into Renfrew in 1164 with forces assembled from the Hebrides, Argyll and even Vikings from Dublin.[18] For all the power of his personality, the fates did not side with Somerled, and he was killed in battle against a Scottish army led by Walter FitzAlan. His descendants, who would become the Lords of the Isles, ever looked back to *Somhairle Mor*, the 'Great Somerled', when they contemplated their ambitions.

Striking this middle way on the fluid edges of multiple kingdoms produced some very interesting results. Rather than belonging in spirit wholeheartedly to Norway or Scotland, the people of the Hebrides achieved a sort of balance. They could be Norse, Gael and even Scot at once, if not by blood then by political allegiance. A good example is Sir Duncan MacDougall, a thirteenth-century Lord of Argyll. He helped to lead the ferocious Norse assault on Scottish-held Rothesay Castle in 1230, yet only seven years later he travelled to Rome as a formal ambassador of the King of Scots to the pope.[19] Perhaps the better way to think of the Isles in the time of Somerled is not as a 'kingdom within a kingdom' after all, but as a kingdom whose circle of influence overlapped, like a Venn diagram, with a multitude of other kingdoms wherever the waves carried it.

Ambitions of Empire

By the late twelfth century, the relationship between the Isles and the mainland had settled into an almost predictable rhythm of conflict. The Isles would flare up, the King of Scots would decide that a punitive expedition was in order, a few clashes and chases through the lochs and glens would ensue and all sides would retire to lick their wounds. Alexander II led expeditions into Argyll aimed at dislodging the fledgling Norse hegemony in 1221 and 1222, each lasting several weeks.[20] It was enough to make the royal presence known and remind the Islesmen and their Norwegian overlords of his encroaching authority. The story of the eventual submission of the Isles is one of a thousand such small cuts inflicted on both sides, and brings us to the 'third phase' of the Isles' fate.

With the Norse threat an increasingly distant memory and the Isles fighting for a place in the new order, a new title came to prominence in the west. John of Islay, son of Aonghus Óg MacDonald, was the first to explicitly call himself *Dominus Insularum* – the Lord of the Isles. While it did not hold quite the same weight as Somerled's status, which asserted kingship rather than lordship, the Lord of the Isles was, from that day on, the premier title in the west. It is likely that the King of Scots regarded them as *reguli*, or sub-kings,[21] but they would scarcely dare to say that to their face. The Lords of the Isles thought of themselves as every bit the sovereign equals of not just the King of Scots but the kings of England, France and beyond.[22] With the MacDonalds reigning supreme in the Isles, it was only a matter of time until their Norse blood boiled up and they were drawn towards the mainland once again. The wealthy and vast Earldom of Ross was the real apple of the Lordship's eye, though the temptation to bite into it would ultimately prove to be the Lordship's Achilles' heel.[23] John's successors, Donald and Alexander, made major incursions into mainland Scotland, and the latter even succeeded in assuming control of the Earldom of Ross and the 'capital of the Highlands', Inverness. It was the high point of the Lordship of the Isles, with Alexander pushing its boundaries to its greatest ever extent, beyond even the realm of the great Somerled. It was a high place from which they would eventually fall.

The Greyjoys harboured similar ambitions over the Westerosi mainland, with the Riverlands and the North, in the absence of the bulk of Stark strength, becoming the springboard for a renewed ironborn empire.

Since the fall of Black Harren, the Greyjoys had ruled as Lord Reapers of Pyke, no longer kings but lords in the manner of the rest of the Seven Kingdoms after Aegon's Conquest. A people whose whole way of life is built upon reiving and the cult of the warrior will never take easily to peace. Several Greyjoys, most notably the Red Kraken, brought fire and sword to the mainland, only for the destruction to be paid back upon the Iron Islands with interest by the Lannisters. Resentment about the Iron Islands' former independent status seeped into the stones themselves, with ironborn children being raised lamenting the loss of a freedom their parents had never known. Balon Greyjoy was one such child, and he yearned above all to make mainlanders fear the sound of waves once again.[24] Only a crown, not a lordship, could do that, so after becoming Lord Reaper of Pyke, Euron put life into the ironborn mantra, 'what is dead may never die', and revived the Kingdom of the Iron Islands. We are told by the maesters that Balon's bid was not borne of any injury done to him or the ironborn by the Iron Throne, but of zealous ambition alone.[25]

The glory days were short-lived. Within a year the Baratheon storm had landed on Pyke, two of Balon's three sons were dead and the Iron Islands were once again reduced to tributary status to the crown.[26] The reign of the King of the Isles had ended in humiliation. Astonishingly, Robert Baratheon allowed Balon to keep his head, though it would no longer deign to sport a crown. Balon bent the knee and sent his surviving son, Theon, to be a ward – effectively a well-treated hostage – of Ned Stark at Winterfell. Despite this crushing defeat, it would not be long before Balon would again wage war against the mainland and claim a crown for himself, an act whose consequences are still being played out at the time of writing. It must be said that despite the seeming futility of his efforts, if anyone in Westeros can claim to embody the spirit of the Scottish king Robert the Bruce's maxim, 'if at first you do not succeed, try, try and try again', it is Balon Greyjoy.

The Sinking of the Lordship

The fourth and final Lord of the Isles, John of Islay II, inherited a realm whose power and reach easily overshadowed that of Somerled himself. His lands included all the Hebrides, Lochaber, Garmoran, Kincardine, parts of Buchan, Ayrshire, Knapdale and Kintyre, and upon becoming

Earl of Ross he could also claim the largest castle in the Highlands, Urquhart, and the sheriffdoms of Inverness and Nairn.[27] The Westerosi equivalent would be if the Greyjoys had managed to capture not just Winterfell and some minor castles like Deepwood Motte, as they did, but half of the entire North as well as large swathes of the Riverlands, the Neck and lands beyond the Wall. John's was an unparalleled height of power and reach, but in the end it only meant that he had farther to fall. Having started his reign as one of the greatest landholders in all of Britain or Ireland, he would die, in the withering assessment of Norman MacDougall, 'as a pathetic pensioner of the Crown'.[28] How did it go so terribly wrong?

'The best laid schemes o' mice an' men / Gang aft-agley,' wrote Robert Burns in his poem *To A Mouse*, and John of Islay II's schemes were audacious in the extreme. Since the days of Somerled, the Islesmen coveted the mainland, in no small part – like the ironborn of Westeros – to have access to the rich, fertile lands denied to them by the scant soils of their island homes. Determined to make them his own, John took one of the most controversial and, to many modern observers, outrageous steps imaginable. He made a deal with the English. At the same time as the Scottish crown was battering the heartlands of the Earls of Douglas in the wake of the second Black Dinner (see Part V for more on this), John decided to take advantage of the royals' divided focus by making a bid for the north. On 18 October 1461, John authorized his kinsmen, Ranald of the Isles and Duncan, the Archdeacon of Ross, to conspire with the beleaguered Douglases against King James III of Scotland. Travelling to London, Ranald and Duncan arranged an alliance with the English king, Edward IV, ratified by the Treaty of Westminster-Ardtornish on 13 February 1462.[29] Their scandalous arrangement was almost precisely the same as that struck by Euron Greyjoy and Cersei Lannister – to defeat a mutual foe and split the North between them. An English invasion was proposed but never materialized, and in the event of victory John was to seize control of all of Scotland north of the Forth-Clyde line,[30] the same frontier established by the Romans nearly 1,500 years prior. Islesmen seized Inverness and demanded that the residents of the north recognize John as their rightful lord.

The plot was discovered, however, and the rightfully enraged King of Scots, James IV, decided that the days of quasi-autonomous lordship in the Isles were long overdue to end. John was summoned to present himself before Parliament in Edinburgh, and when he failed to do so his vast lands were immediately declared forfeit to the crown. A year later, John limped to Edinburgh at last, and could do nothing but cast his gaze to the ground as his lordship was dismembered with the stroke of a pen.[31] He retained the Hebrides, Morvern, Garmoran and Lochaber, but lost all the rest, including the coveted Earldom of Ross.[32] The following twilight years of the Lordship of the Isles are remembered as a time of humiliation and indignity. Internal divisions tore the Lordship apart, with a spate of risings against the mainland being put down with increasing decisiveness. The MacDonalds, so long the anchor of power in the Isles, were set adrift as their title of Lords of the Isles was formally forfeited in 1493. There would be flare-ups in the following decades, such as the Islesmen's raid on the Great Glen in 1545, but the overall trajectory is clear in hindsight.

The final blow came in 1608 with the Statutes of Iona, named after that shining light of sophistication and faith in the Isles despite being created to dim it. James VI, having acceded to the throne of England as well as Scotland following the death of Queen Elizabeth I, demanded that the chieftains of the Highlands and Isles present themselves before him annually in London, a place that was utterly alien to the sensibilities and worldview of the men of the west. The chieftains' eldest sons were to be educated in the Anglicized Lowlands far away from their Gaelic homes, a tried and true method employed by colonial regimes the world over for erasing what were regarded as more 'primitive' identities. In an early echo of the later Highland Clearances, Gaelic was banned by the 1616 Education Act and the bards, so long the bearers of tradition and knowledge in the Isles, were put in stocks wherever they were found. In a little over a century, the Isles had gone from the 'age of joy' under MacDonald Lordship to what must have felt like an age of calamity and silence. There was, as the famous lament goes, no joy without Clan Donald.

Are the Iron Islands fated to suffer a similarly inglorious end? As of the time of writing, Balon Greyjoy is dead and, in the television show at least, two distinct paths forward for the ironborn have emerged. One, led by Euron Greyjoy, is a grasp for greater power of just the sort that doomed John of Islay. Euron has aligned himself with Queen Cersei, and is uncompromising in his stated aspiration – which forms the basis for his leadership amongst many of the ironborn – to carve out a mainland empire from the ashes of war. It is an incredibly bold venture, by no means guaranteed to fail. The other, led by Asha (Yara) Greyjoy, is an altogether new approach: to secure the Iron Islands' independence from the Iron Throne from Daenerys in exchange for permanently abandoning the last surviving vestiges of the Old Way. If Yara's plan succeeds, it will be a peaceful settlement of a kind unknown in the annals of the Isles. If Euron's way prevails, however, the stakes are even higher – either the Iron Islands will dominate the North of Westeros to an extent that the Lords of the Isles could only dream of matching, or, if Euron and Cersei lose, they may be punished to such an extent that no ironborn will ever dream of setting sail in anger again. What is dead may well rise again harder and stronger, or it could sink into the darkness of the Drowned God's halls – history shows that neither Islesmen nor ironborn are like to settle for anything in between.

Warrior Bards

Clearly, the meek will not inherit the Iron Islands. Above wit, wisdom, a fine face or a noble name – traits held dear by soft mainlanders – sheer force of will is the prized asset of the ironborn. Even Vikings, the most famous ravagers in history, ultimately sought land to settle and farm; any ironborn worth the salt in their veins will tell you that they Do Not Sow. 'We take what is ours,' boasted Balon Greyjoy,[33] before falling victim to his brother, Euron, who tired of Euron's pontificating and took the crown he saw as his by pushing him off a rope bridge at Pyke. Balon's subjects did not mourn him long, if at all, and threw their wholehearted support behind the man of action that had murdered him. Ironborn cannot spill the blood of other ironborn, and technically Euron had not shed a drop. He had paid the iron price, fair and square.

The Norse-Gaels of the Isles, though not nearly as radically individualistic as the ironborn of Westeros, were also ready to pay the iron price for their conquests. They called it *còir a' chlaidhimh*, the 'sword-right'.[34] Winning lands by the sword was just as legitimate to the Islesmen as doing so through marriage was to the mainland Scottish nobles. The most common way of asserting power and reducing the enemy throughout the Highlands and Isles was through the *creach*, or cattle raid. Outright conquest was not the objective of the *creach*, but rather to reduce an enemy's capacity to maintain a war footing and, significantly, to engage in an sort of ritualistic exercise in enhancing honour, renown and individual prowess.[35]

In times when opportunities for raiding and warring were scarce at home, the Islesmen would export their excess of skilful troublemakers to chieftains in Ireland as *gallóglaichs*, known in English as gallowglasses, from the 1290s well into the sixteenth century.[36] Many a Hebridean fought and died in the endless tribal wars of medieval Ireland, wielding their much-feared axes which could allegedly decapitate a horse at a single blow. This served the dual purpose of allowing glory-hungry men from the Isles to distinguish themselves and win a little fortune through sword-right, and to reduce the number of otherwise idle warriors milling about the Hebrides. For if there is one constant in the history of war, it is that having a lot of capable and ambitious young men whose identities have become inextricable from the battles they fight hanging around with nothing else to do does not bode well for domestic stability.

If it came down to a battle between the Islesmen of Scotland and the ironborn of Westeros, my money would be on the Islesmen. In terms of raw martial talent, they are on approximately equal footing. Both cultures excelled in producing warriors who were more than a match for their mainland counterparts on an individual basis. A chieftain in the Scottish Isles was supported by an extremely close-knit group of household warriors, typically numbering around twelve, called the *lèine-chneis*, men who most visibly cultivated the warrior persona that the bards were so fond of immortalizing.[37] A similar system seems to be in play in the Iron Islands, seemingly embodied by the force led by Asha Greyjoy (named Yara in the television series) to free Theon from the sadistic grip of Ramsay which is comprised of fiercely loyal men whom Asha has known and fought alongside for many years.

A fight between a Norse-Gaelic *lèine-chneis* and Asha's picked group would be a brutal and close-fought melee, but in a larger pitched battle the Islesmen would almost certainly triumph over the ironborn. Stannis Baratheon, regarded as one of Westeros' finest military minds (a reputation, it must be said, that is very much at odds with the blunt and blundering instrument he turns out to be in *Game of Thrones*), made a prudent observation about the ironborn at war: 'As sailors and warriors the ironborn are unparalleled, but they are not soldiers.

They have no discipline, no strategy, no unity. In battle each man fights only for his own glory.'[38] The ironborn's accomplishments when fighting on the mainland pale in comparison to those of the historical Norse and Islesmen, their strength seeming to quite literally drain away the further they get from the coasts.[39]

Compare that with the conquests of the Islesmen, who at their height dominated more than a third of what we now consider to be Scotland, including huge swathes of the mainland in Argyll, Lochaber, the Northwest Highlands, the Great Glen and Ross. Far from being easily swept aside by mainland armies, large forces from the Isles could wreak havoc. A great raid on Urquhart Castle on the banks of Loch Ness, the largest and strongest castle in the Highlands, in 1545 saw the Islesmen carry away over 8,500 head of livestock.[40] In the summer of 1411, Donald of Islay gathered a force of more than 10,000 Islesmen and marched them as far east as Inverurie in Aberdeenshire, where he fought the bloody Battle of Harlaw against the Earl of Mar. The Islesmen were able to inflict major casualties against Mar's mounted knights, so much so that the battle is remembered amongst many bloody engagements between Islesmen and mainlanders as 'Red Harlaw'. The ironborn, for all their fury, are known to melt away in the face of similar heavy cavalry charges, and could not have hoped to fight the Earl of Mar's small but professional army to a stalemate so far from home.

In the Isles, an army alone counts for nothing. The true measure of power was in ships,[41] without which there could be no Lordship. The MacDonalds knew it well. The sigil they went to battle beneath was completely different from anything used by mainland lords. Rather than depicting the usual Scottish armorial motifs of lions, castle towers, swords or unicorns, the MacDonald arms consist of the solitary and daunting image of a great black galley flying blood-red flags. *Birlinns*, the traditional Hebridean longships, varied greatly in size, with crews ranging from a minimum of about twelve to upwards of 100 men.[42] Smaller vessels called nyvaigs were also used, though more usually for personal transport than for war-making. While the Lords of the Isles would likely get the better of the ironborn when fighting on land, the Iron Fleet would undoubtedly shatter the Lordship's *birlinns* into as much flotsam. Euron's flagship, the *Silence*, would make even the mightiest warship of Scotland's western isles appear as insignificant as a salmon alongside a whale. What we see of the Iron Fleet in battle is truly terrifying. Their multi-tiered warships with masts as high as castle towers are a combination of ancient Greek galleys and Renaissance-era caravels, and they employ a devastating array of weapons. When Euron's fleet ambushes Asha, Theon and the Sand Snakes in season seven of the show, we see them using on-board catapults and nifty underwater rams at their prows that can pierce the hulls of their victims' ships. This is a recent development, however, with *The World of Ice and Fire* noting that Balon Greyjoy built the first true galleys for the Iron Fleet within a generation of the events we are witnessing.[43] All earlier ships in the Iron Fleet were much closer to the kind of classic Viking longship that was also the basis for the *birlinns* of the Isles.

When King James VI sought to smash the power of the Isles, he knew precisely where to strike. One of the more devastating blows dealt by the aforementioned Act of 1616 was that it forbade any individual to possess more than one galley of sixteen or eighteen oars, so that 'in their voyage through the isles they should not oppress the Country people'.[44] Without their *birlinns*, the last stubborn sinews that allowed the Isles to retain their semi-autonomous way of life were cut.

Both Islesmen and ironborn are fierce, of that there is no doubt. Yet there is one light, away from the battlefield, under which the Iron Islands seem barbarous by comparison. The ironborn produce no art to speak of, and bards – so essential to the identity of the Isles – are tolerated rather than glorified. Their royal regalia is a crown of simple driftwood, and the Seastone Chair from which the Lord (and formerly King) of the Iron Islands rules was not carved by any local artisan. There is no evidence of a patronage system for craftsmen or poets, and what glimpses we have of their storytelling traditions seem to amount to little more than a few people huddled around a dampened fire waxing nostalgic about faded glories. There is the odd, eccentric exception – for instance, Asha Greyjoy reminisces fondly on time spent reading her uncle Rodrik Harlaw's many books[45] – but by and large the ironborn are far more interested in destruction than creation. No wonder they take to reiving and raiding so readily – there doesn't seem to be anything else to do.

The average Hebridean of the Middle Ages would not know what to make of such barbarism. Knowledge, creativity, deep memory, artisanal skill and a fine voice were the greatest gifts of all, even more so than a good sword-arm; after all, what good is a great warrior if there is no one to tell and spread their legend? The name for artists in the Isles says it all – they are *aos-dana*, 'the folk of gifts'. Even those who looked down upon the Isles as being a remote backwater had to acknowledge their cultural assertiveness. During his visit to the Isle of Skye with James Boswell, the diarist Samuel Johnson noted with surprise and delight that he was 'never in any [noble] house of the Islands, where I did not find books in more languages than one'.[46] Like wealth, poverty manifests in many forms. What was undoubtedly a materially impoverished land from the perspective of urbanites like Boswell and Johnson was nonetheless a culturally rich one that remembered and cherished its history like few others. Rather than allowing outside observers to have the last word in the matter, however, let us turn to the lamentation of the bard Giolla Coluim Mac an Ollàimh, composer of the era-defining lament *Nì h-éibhneas gan Chlainn Domhnaill*, '*It is no joy without Clan Donald*':

> *I dtosach Clainne Domhnaill*
> *do bhí foghlaim 'gá fáithneadh,*
> *agus do bhí 'na ndeireadh*
> *feidhm is eineach is náire.*

> 'In the van of Clan Donald
> learning was commanded,
> and in their rear were
> service and honour and self-respect.'[47]

Far from being one-note pillagers and plunderers of more sophisticated civilizations like the ironborn, the Norse earldom of Orkney and the *reguli*, or kinglets, of the Hebrides were enterprising and outward-looking in the extreme. They benefited from international contacts that allowed them to import European masons and craftsmen to build their castles and churches in the latest styles,[48] while Iona off the south-west tip of the Isle of Mull continued to be one of the most revered and respected ecclesiastical centres in Europe, despite depredations by the Vikings centuries before. Recall, for instance, that many of Scotland's earliest stone castles were not the work of mainland nobles but of Norse-Gaelic sea lords, including the castles of Sween, Skipness, Dunollie, Dunstaffnage, Tioram, Kisimul and Cubbie Roo's. Bards and sennachies were not merely entertainers in the Isles but were members of the highly respected and professional *Ollamh* class, which included physicians, judges and master craftsmen who often stood at the side of chieftains and the Lord of the Isles himself.[49]

Perhaps most indicatively of all, the relative stability of the Lordship of the Isles was the envy of most European kings and barons. Between 1336 and 1493, when the Lordship of the Isles at last collapsed, it had been ruled by just four leaders, each of which was the son of the last. It was a time remembered in Gaelic tradition as *Linn an Àigh*, the 'age of joy'.[50] By way of comparison, during that same period the Kingdom of Scotland had seen near-total occupation by England and the last gasp of the Balliol claim to the throne and the rule of six kings, Robert II through to James IV, four of which were killed in battle or assassinated by their own nobles. Perhaps the greatest example of this relative harmony, to which we'll now turn, is the Isles' choice of a capital.

Heart Of The Isles: Finlaggan & Old Wyk

For a society so fundamentally reliant on waterways, Finlaggan at first appears to be a completely counterintuitive place for a capital. Loch Finlaggan on the Isle of Islay, itself the spiritual heart of the Lordship of the Isles, takes the form of a shallow tub surrounded by low hills. It is completely landlocked, and from within the surviving ruins on the main island in the loch, Eilean Mòr, the sea is not even visible. Eilean Mòr, meaning 'Big Island', and its smaller companion Eilean na Comhairle, 'Council Island', are islands in a loch on an island in the sea. No ship can sail there, and the smell of salt and seaweed is only occasionally carried in by the winds that are a near-relentless feature of life in the Hebrides. Yet far from being a world apart from the forces that govern the life of the Islesmen, Finlaggan is the Lordship of the Isles in a microcosm.

The cauldron in which Finlaggan rests is like a great lens, the soft slopes on all sides gently bringing the loch in the centre into focus. On the bumpy path that approaches Finlaggan from the east is a standing stone, a reminder that this landscape has been inhabited for thousands of years. The Finlaggan Trust, which also runs an on-site interpretive centre, constructed a timber walkway which carries you over the reed-strewn waters of the loch onto Eilean Mòr. The Lords of the Isles had small ferries and a stone causeway to bring them to the twin islands in the loch, but now this is the only way to reach Eilean Mòr while staying dry.

Eilean na Comhairle is tantalizingly just out of reach, separated by waters that no islesman would be the slightest bit deterred by.

Under the MacDonald Lords of the Isles, who at their height ruled over more than a third of Scotland,[51] Finlaggan was the administrative centre of the Lordship. Their domain extended from the Butt of Lewis in the Outer Hebrides to the tip of Kintyre in south-western Argyll, including much of the mainland's western seaboard, not to mention the deep roots on the Isle of Man and in Antrim. While it may not look like what we expect a capital to be – what structures remain are largely ruinous, though there are treasures such as several masterfully carved Hebridean-style grave slabs to be found amongst them – during the fourteenth and fifteenth centuries it was a thriving Gaelic settlement. When the Council of the Isles gathered on Eilean na Comhairle in the manner of a parliament to affirm the next Lord of the Isles, the number of elite warriors, artisans, singers and dignitaries assembled allowed Finlaggan to take its place alongside the great courts of contemporary Europe. Leave the sky-scraping tenements and the choked warren of alleys to Edinburgh; this capital was everything its kingdom was, built upon the water under the vast open skies and with boats in the place of steeds and carriages. There is another striking difference between Finlaggan and the other capitals of Scotland. While Edinburgh, Perth, Stirling and other royal centres were defended by town walls or mighty castles, Finlaggan had no equivalent, aside from a modest fortified hall house. It is a strange thing to countenance that the fearsome sea kings did not think it was necessary to have strong walls or towers to guard the nucleus of their realm. Yet, is there anything that could more boldly declare their power? Like Sparta, Finlaggan needed no walls – only instead of a phalanx of pikes and shields to defend it, the Lords of the Isles had their fleet of *birlinns*.

The ironborn of Westeros could be similarly confident in the power of their ships to guard their capital. The most revered of the Iron Islands is Old Wyk, where the ribs of the wrathful sea dragon Nagga form a cathedral of bones upon Nagga's Hill. It is here that the ironborn held their kingsmoots in the days of the Old Way before taking to their longships to wreak havoc on the coasts of Westeros and beyond. There is no castle on Old Wyk, and the taboo against ironborn shedding the blood of other ironborn goes some way towards making any fortification redundant. Unlike Finlaggan, however, which can boast of no equivalent tales of bloodshed or butchery, Nagga's Ribs had drowned in blood before. In the *History of the Ironborn*, an in-universe chronicle of the Iron Islands, Haereg records how the great reiver Urron of Orkmont unleashed his axemen during a kingsmoot and gave the Greyirons uncontested power for 1,000 years.[52] The Isles of Scotland witnessed many gory encounters over the centuries, including the aptly named Battle of Bloody Bay off the coast of Mull, yet astonishingly – and despite large groups of armed men regularly gathering here – none seem to have soiled the waters of Finlaggan. There is no greater testament to the power of Scotland's sea kings than their paradoxical capital, a beacon of Gaeldom amidst a sea of troubles.

Chapter 9

Barbarians at the Gates?
Caledonians & Wildlings

'At the end of the known world staring at these distant hills and wondering what lives there and what might come out of it. You were looking off the end of the world. Protecting the civilized world against whatever might emerge from those trees. Of course, what tended to emerge from those trees was Scots, and we couldn't use that.'

- George R.R. Martin[1]

An army of honourless savages had brought death south of the Wall. Babes were cruelly speared with spears in their cradles, the sick, old and injured shown no mercy. Nothing – not homes, sacred places nor livestock – was left unburnt or unsullied. The victims were gruesomely displayed, and by the unspeakable manner of their deaths it seemed that the more pitiable an end they were given, the more their killers rejoiced in the act. While this wild army raided and wrought their depredations, no man, woman or child could sleep sound in the north.

While Bran Stark would no doubt delight in such grisly telling, this is not one of Old Nan's stories. It is an account by Ailred of Rievaulx of marauding Scots.[2] Ailred's words were hardly alone, with a chorus of medieval English sources such as the *Luttrell Psalter* condemning the savagery of the people of the north. Nearly a millennium after Hadrian's Wall had been built, people south of it still seemed to genuinely believe that the land beyond it was, like Procopius described, filled with serpents and a thousand ways to die badly. It probably started with Caesar, who famously remarked in his *Gallic Wars* that the Britons decorated their bodies with permanent, vivid blue dye called woad which made them 'a sky-blue colour and thereby more terrible to their enemies'.[3] This was indeed common practice amongst the locals, but in the eyes of Rome this made them more beastly even than Germans. All kinds of mad tales sprung up as a result, including this description from the third-century Roman encyclopaedist Gaius Julius Solinus that would make a wildling father flush with pride:

> 'The Gaelic people were always rough and warlike with barbaric customs. For when boy babies were born to them, their fathers followed the practice of offering their first food to them on the point of a spear, so that they would wish for no other death than to die in battle fighting for freedom.'[4]

Just as Roman fathers told their children tales of the unimaginable debauchery of the barbarians of Britain, so too do parents in the North of Westeros go a little overboard at story time. Compare Solinus' observations (glimpsed not in person, of course) with Old Nan's description of the wildlings to Bran:

> 'They consorted with giants and ghouls, stole girl children in the dead of night, and drank blood from polished horns. And their women lay with Others in the Long Night to sire terrible half-human children.'[5]

The Skagosi are an especially brutish example. Even other wildlings try to keep their distance from them, and northmen curse them derisively as 'Skaggs'. The Skagosi live on an isolated island east of the Bay of Seals – here again being on an island equates to barbarism – where they practice human sacrifice, feast on human flesh during the winter and ride unicorns (which, incidentally and amazingly, happens to be Scotland's official national animal).[6] There's something of a chain of derision forming here. Folks from King's Landing think that the northmen are retrograde brutes, northmen think wildlings eat babies for fun and wildlings believe Skagosi are little better than hairy grumkins. And, of course, everyone hates the Thenns.

The conclusion we can draw from this is not only that barbarism is a relative concept, but that the people in the far north of Westeros do not actually represent the real people who lived beyond the Roman frontier in Scotland. Rather, they are manifestations of what the Romans imagined the people beyond their frontier to be like. It's as though in creating the wildlings and their various factions, George R.R. Martin packed together all the stereotypes and horror stories recounted in classical sources and turned them into flesh, blood and fur. That is the lens through which we must view them. It is not the reality of Iron Age and early historic Scotland that is being depicted, but the outside, imperial perception of it. As Jon Snow quite rightly points out to the less-accepting members of the Nights Watch, 'They were born on the wrong side of the Wall. Doesn't make them monsters.'[7] The Caledonians and later Picts were only strange due to the geographical isolation of their realm, which was reinforced by Roman geopolitics, rather than in any innate sense to do with their character or questionable parental habits.[8]

In that case, who were they? The problem in trying to construct an accurate account of the peoples beyond the Antonine Wall is that they have no voice of their own to speak to us with. There are no Caledonian chronicles, Pictish parchments or Maeatae manuscripts. Everything we think we know about them comes from the people who tried to conquer them, and to say that is problematic is an understatement. Archaeology has gone a long way towards bringing peoples like the famously mysterious Picts out from the mists of history that once shrouded them, but their identities are still fuzzy, as though we're looking at them without our glasses. We don't even know what they were really called. The term 'Pict', a Latin quip meaning 'painted people', does not emerge into history until a mention by the Roman writer Eumenius in 297 CE.[9] The word was thrown around before that, likely with a derogatory slant by Romans stationed along Hadrian's Wall and the Antonine Wall, a bit like the Allies calling Germans 'Huns' during the First World War. It was also a catch-all term, thrown as a wide-cast net to encompass more or less any tribe beyond the Forth-Clyde isthmus. Though the Kingdom of Pictland did emerge in the early historic period, the people who the Romans built the walls as bulwarks against certainly did not call themselves Picts. What they did call themselves is unknown. The Celts of Ireland referred to the land north of the Antonine Wall as Alba, so perhaps something like 'Albans' is the closest we will manage to get. One way to think about it is this. 'Wildlings' don't call themselves that; they call themselves the Free Folk. In the same way, Picts did not call themselves that (at least not at first), the Romans did. 'Wildling' is to 'Pict' as 'Free Folk' is to whatever name the people north of the

Forth-Clyde line gave themselves. There are a small number of Pictish words that survive, but they are primarily to do with places rather than people. Anywhere sporting the prefix pit-, for instance, such as Pitlochry or Pittenweem, are former Pictish settlements. Such names spanned a huge swathe of Scotland, from Fife into Ross and Caithness, though the vast majority survive in the Grampian region and north-east[10].

In one sense, however, they did leave records, or at least depictions of themselves, and quite literally in stone. We just don't know how to interpret them. Pictish stones have been the object of antiquarian fascination for centuries, with their beguiling blend of abstract yet repetitive symbols such as V-rods and crescents alongside beasties like fish, boars, bears and the famously puzzling 'Pictish beast' that resembles a cross between a dolphin and a horse. An excellent representation of the Pictish beast can be found on a carved stone that stands on the ground of Brodie Castle near the Moray Firth, one of the traditional heartlands of the Picts. The Aberlemno Stones in Angus would be the Pictish equivalent of the Rosetta Stone if only we could find the cipher for them. Still, we can marvel at their depictions of spear-wielding warriors, Christian crosses intertwined with pagan iconography and the usual array of geometric symbols. An exceptional collection of Pictish symbol stones can be found in the National Museum of Scotland in Edinburgh, as well as regional museums including the Meigle Sculptured Stone Museum and the Groam House Museum, but nothing beats viewing them out in the open as they were intended at sites like Aberlemno.

In terms of appearance, we are told by Tacitus that the Caledonians had 'red-gold hair and massive limbs', which sounds like the beginnings of a very flattering biography of everyone's favourite wildling, Tormund Giantsbane.[11] The Scots are, of course, well known for their ginger locks and brawn, but for Tacitus' readers in Rome the subtext was loud and clear yet again: here dwell barbarians. Those traits, he wrote, 'proclaim German origin', which was inaccurate but convincing enough for his audience, who thought of everyone north of the Alps as being more or less the same.[12] The peoples of Iron-Age and early historic Scotland were certainly larger than Romans on average, but that was the case across the Celtic world from Iberia to Germania. Back amongst the Free Folk, while red hair is seen amongst them it is actually regarded as being rather rare and is held to be a sign of favour from the Old Gods. Ygritte and Tormund are both major characters with fiery red locks, and a good number of the extras in any given scene, such as the massacre at Hardhome, have that trait too, but it is not as though the average wildling is a shortbread tin-style depiction of a red-headed Scot.

The truth is that the people in the far north were a typical Iron Age society, with most of its members not being woad-covered warriors but farmers, fishermen, artisans and labourers operating under a landowning aristocracy.[13] That said, one of the greatest parallels between them and *Game of Thrones*' wildlings, a connection which has been confirmed on many occasions by Martin himself, does lie in the domain of war, so it is to the battlefield that we now turn.

The Free Folk at War

One of the most dread-inducing sounds in all of Westeros, aside from the beating of a dragon's wings overhead, is the long bellow of a horn. At the Wall, one blast heralds the return of Rangers from beyond the Wall; two blasts warn of wildlings; three blasts mean the White Walkers are coming and you should make peace with your gods. Euron Greyjoy possesses a horn with Valyrian glyphs along its side that can bind dragons to its owner's will – at the price of the life of the person who sounds it. The Free Folk also use horns to bolster their morale before battle, and one horn that Mance Rayder is said to have discovered, the Horn of Joramun, is allegedly able to bring down the Wall with its arcane power.

If only the Caledonians had such a horn! They did not, of course, but as far as their Roman oppressors were concerned they did wield the next most terrible thing: the carnyx. Taking the form of a bestial head, typically a boar, mounted atop a long hollow stem, carnyces were used throughout the Celtic world and beyond. Examples have been found in Dacia (modern Romania) and there is even a depiction of one on a Buddhist statue in India.[14] Their cry was so distinctive that the Romans used it as a catch-all symbol for many of the northern tribes they fought, and many carnyces are found on Roman sculptures and coinage, including on Trajan's triumphal column in Rome itself.

In fact, we may have some idea of the sound that that resounded across the Caledonian battle lines. The remains of an original carnyx from *c.* 80-250 CE was discovered in a bog at Deskford, Banffshire, in the early nineteenth century. Given its location in Scotland's north-east and its date of construction, there is even a chance – a small chance, but a chance nonetheless – that it was used at the definitive clash between Caledonia and Rome to which we'll soon turn, the Battle of Mons Graupius in 83/84 CE.[15] It was deposited there deliberately and ceremonially, with its components ritually deconstructed to emulate the butchering of the boar. Such objects were priceless in their time and were the result of an advanced artisanal class and hundreds of hours of labour. A replica was crafted in 1992 by Scottish musicologist Dr John Purser and metalsmith John Creed, made of bronze and brass with a wiggling wooden tongue and fiery red and yellow enamel eyes.[16] In 2016, a demonstration for the ages was put on by musician John Kenny, who sounded it as part of that year's *Celts* exhibition at the National Museum of Scotland, where the carnyx is still on display. You would expect a barbarian instrument to be coarse and one-note; you would be very wrong. The sound that emanated from that boar's head was astonishingly complex, striking notes both giddily high and hauntingly low. There is a melancholy to it, and each note lingers a little in the snout of the boar, creating a brief but unmistakable echo. Hearing it while marching through the mist-laden hills beyond the Antonine Wall, it would be tempting to stop and admire its beauty if it was not also so utterly terrifying.

The thing about the Free Folk, despite all their bravado and intimidating weapons such as giants and magical horns, is that the Seven Kingdoms don't have to give them much thought unless they unite. Given how much the dozens of disparate tribes north of the Wall hate each other – especially the Thenns – and how wary they are of authority figures, that's a rare threat indeed. The same was true of the tribes of the far north of Brittania, and the Romans knew it; divide and conquer, after all, was the maxim that built their empire. Tacitus summed up the commonly held and not inaccurate Roman view of the Celtic tribes in his *Agricola*, observing:

> 'In former times the Britons owed obedience to kings. Now they are formed into factional groupings by the leading men. Indeed, there is nothing that helps us more against such very powerful peoples than their lack of unanimity. It is seldom that two or three states unite to repel a common threat. Hence each fights on its own, and all are conquered.'[17]

However, as has already been mentioned, the spectre of Rome eventually provided the northern tribes with the impetus to unite, at least for a time. When they did come together in a confederation, they could be formidable indeed. Such an alliance of tribes, from the Trossachs to the coasts of Buchan, was forged in late 83 CE to stand against the advancing legions.[18] So, too, did an army of 100,000 Free Folk, consisting of ninety clans speaking seven languages united under Mance Rayder, march upon the Wall.[19] The battles fought by Caledonians and Free Folk against their oppressors reveal striking parallels, and so now we wade into the twinned battles for the lands beyond the walls – Mons Graupius and Castle Black.

Battle for the True North: Mons Graupius & Castle Black

In 83 CE, the hardened Roman general Gnaeus Julius Agricola did what no other Roman had done before him: he struck beyond the Forth-Clyde frontier and invaded deep into the heart of Caledonia. With him marched a massive and finely tuned war machine of veteran legionaries and auxiliaries, amongst whom stood the renowned legions Second *Augusta*, Ninth *Hispania*, Twentieth *Valeria Victrix* and Second *Adiutrix*.[20] The precise numbers arrayed by Agricola for this great northern campaign are unknown, but most figures put his force at between 20,000 and 25,000, with 4,000-8,000 legionaries, 3,000-5,000 cavalry and several thousand ferocious Tungrian and Batavian auxiliaries, who, as fellow 'barbarians', could match the Caledonians' ferocity man-for-man.[21] Agricola's brief from Emperor Vespasian was nothing less than the total subjugation of the Caledonians – for their own benefit, of course.[22]

Agricola split his army into three columns as they marched in a great arc from the area around modern Stirling north-east via Perth, Angus and Aberdeenshire all the way to the Moray Firth.[23] They were closely shadowed by the Roman fleet along the way, who provided supplies and scouted ahead to ascertain the elusive enemy's location and threat level. The Caledonians, for their part, played the part of the guerrilla resisters, falling back before the legions before battle could be engaged and frustrating Roman sorties by melting away into the hills and woods as soon as they had struck. The Ninth Legion was nearly destroyed in this fashion, but was saved by the last-minute arrival of the rest of

Agricola's army. When they finally caught up with the Caledonians, it was on the steep slopes of a mountain known only as 'Mons Graupius', where, according to Tacitus, the Caledonians were at last arrayed in battle formation and ready to make their stand.[24] Battles almost as fierce as the one that followed have been fought over where the Graupian Mountain actually is. The most popular theory places it on the slopes of Bennachie, an imposing hill near Inverurie that bears a striking if shrunken resemblance to the arrowhead-shaped mountain glimpsed in fiery visions by Sandor Clegane in *Game of Thrones* (the mountain in his vision is in fact Kirkjufell in Iceland). Other theories swing as far south as Moncreiffe Hill, several miles south of Perth, and just about everywhere in between those two extremes.[25] Figuring out the precise location is a battle for another day.

Tacitus estimated the Caledonian force to be around 30,000-strong, though some scholars reckon that to be too high for the fighting-age population of the north at the time and put it closer to 20,000, making them approximately equivalent in numbers to the Romans.[26] They were equipped with swords, spears and shields, with the chieftains and their companions wielding great two-handed swords that were the precursors to the great claymores made famous by their Highland descendants.[27] Their weapons were fierce, but their armour was negligible compared to that of the Romans; many Caledonian warriors fought with no armour at all save whatever protection they believed their woad tattoos afforded them[28].

They would have presented a formidable front arrayed upon the slope of the Graupian Mountain, a great host seething with hostility towards the conquerors who had stolen their land and were now seeking to take their lives and liberty. As men shouted and steeled themselves, the Caledonian war chariots thundered back and forth in front of their lines, making as much noise and stirring up as much ground as possible in a display of psychological warfare.[29] Chariots had been abandoned for several centuries in the rest of the Celtic world, but here in the Old North they had not yet been cast aside. Though the chariots made a mighty din, they were of little practical use against an enemy that had seen it all, from scythed chariots to war elephants, and who could use their iron discipline and organization to open up gaps in their ranks to allow the chariots to pass harmlessly through. The Caledonians, for all their courage, were not nearly so organized and their force effectively functioned as a great mass of individuals rather than as a cohesive army like the Romans.

Caledonian courage, they hoped, would be enough. Their chieftain Calgacus, meaning 'the Swordsman', stepped forward and – if Tacitus can be believed – delivered a stunning rebuke of Roman imperialism and encouraged his men, the 'last of the free', to defy tyranny with the sword and descend upon the Romans in the names of their country and kin.[30] Stirred by Calgacus' defiant words, the Caledonians charged headlong down the slope, sounding their carnyces and giving a final, defiant howl before they crashed into the empire's lines.

The Free Folk at the Battle of Castle Black also did not lack for raw bravery. Anyone who can confidently stand alongside a giant riding a mammoth and charge headlong at a 700ft-tall wall of ice with nothing but a spear of ash in their hand is a bolder sort than most. Bravery alone does not guarantee victory, however. 'A shout, a slash, and a fine brave death', is how Jon heard the wildling's fighting style described, and given their track record of unsuccessfully invading south of the Wall seven times, it's not an entirely unfounded assessment.[31] Any given soldier in a Westerosi army south of the Wall was no stronger, braver or more determined than any tribal warrior beyond it – if anything, the barbarian archetype that the Free Folk embody gives them an edge in individual combat. But individuals do not win wars; armies do. When Mance Rayder's force, said to be 100,000-strong, emerges from the treeline of the Haunted Forest and prepares to attack Castle Black, it is not an army but a very great gathering of individual warriors. There is no semblance of battle formations, and for all their intimidating chanting and horn-blowing they are still 100,000 people milling about at the bottom of the Wall. Jon Snow's prescient warning to Ygritte comes to mind: 'You don't have the discipline, you don't have the training, your army is no army. You don't know how to fight together. If you attack the Wall, you'll die. All of you.'[32]

And attack they did. Yet before coming within bowshot of the Wall, Mance's army made a great show of just the sort performed by the Caledonians at Mons Graupius. The wildling chariots, made of walrus bone and drawn from the shores of the Bay of Seals, rode out before their great host and made as much of a clamour as they could. Against fellow wildlings or even a force of Night's Watchmen in the open field, this tactic would no doubt have stoked fear in their foe's hearts. But given that their enemies stood 700ft above them atop an impenetrable wall of ice, the proud display of the charioteers amounted to nothing more than background noise. Then all at once the wildling force pushed forward, and the chariots took the lead. The chariots got far ahead of the rest of the host, but without anyone to mow down they could only get in the way of the advancing mass of infantry. 'The wildlings had not crossed a third of the half mile yet their battle line was dissolving,' Jon observed contentedly from above.[33] His suspicions were confirmed; Mance may have lit the greatest fire the North had ever seen, but it burned so wild that there was simply no controlling it.

The Caledonians fought Rome furiously. The sheer momentum of their initial charge drove back the auxiliaries, and they wrought terrible carnage with their great two-handed swords. After some time, however, the discipline of the legions began to inexorably grind down the Caledonians, who had spent all their fury at once, whereas the Romans revolved their battle lines so that fresh troops were always at the front. After much bloodshed on both sides, the killing blow came as the Roman cavalry, until now held in reserve, struck the Caledonians from the flanks and caused death and panic amongst them. The Caledonians, so formidable on foot, simply had no answer to a coordinated cavalry charge, melting away before it. Soon the battle turned into a rout, the deadliest stage of any battle. Some Caledonians preferred to die as free men rather than live as vanquished ones. Tacitus recounts with admiration how some tribesmen flung themselves fully exposed onto the Roman ranks, many of them not even carrying weapons, embracing their deaths and terrifying their foes with their fatal resolve.[34] When Agricola reined in his men from the pursuit, the slopes of the Graupian Mountain resembled a vision of hell. The dead were everywhere, crushed under the hoofs of the horses with the contents of their guts spilled by the deadly thrusts of the Roman short swords. Tacitus describes how the 'silence of desolation fell over the field'.[35] Official Roman estimates say 10,000 Caledonians died that day, taking only 360 Romans with them. While these numbers are almost certainly inflated and reduced, respectively, to add to the glory of the victory, the butcher's bill was undoubtedly much higher for the Caledonians. And yet the Romans' victory would not transcend the battlefield. The surviving Caledonians, as many as 20,000, melted back into the mountains and left Rome with no spoils or slaves to show for their triumph. The battle had been won by Rome, but the war would be won by the north.

The Free Folk faced a very different obstacle than the Caledonians, of course, given that they were assaulting the Wall and not fighting the

Night's Watch in the open field. The result, however, was much the same. After taking substantial losses, the wildling army fell back, the vast majority of its numbers having played no part at all in the attack. They established their camp in the forests just beyond the reach of the Wall and settled in to what they were sure would be merely a waiting game. It was not to be. The next morning, their breakfast was interrupted by the trembling of the ground. Stannis Baratheon had come with thousands of heavy horse, and the Free Folk – who had no cavalry to speak of and no time to organize into anything resembling a battle line – were cut down like as much grass. Thousands died under their hooves, and thousands more took flight without grasping a weapon. 'When they break,' Jon Snow observed, 'they break hard.'[36] The survivors, still numbering in the tens of thousands, faded back into the Lands Beyond the Wall like winter mist. In death and in life, the Free Folk and the Caledonians proved their bravery beyond a doubt. They also were defeated at their definitive battles for the same reasons, though their wars were far from over. Eventually the Free Folk would pass through the Wall without a fight, and the Caledonians would gather in their Highland holdfasts and descend upon the Antonine Wall, only to find it, and the imperial ambitions it represented, abandoned. Despite suffering a grave defeat, if the story of the Caledonians is anything to go by then the glory days of the Free Folk are still ahead of them.

Chapter 10

The King Who Knelt

The King in the North and the conquering dragonlord faced off across the Trident. Torrhen Stark had brought 30,000 battle-hardened northmen with him to do what northmen always do: throw back the southern invader. But what Torrhen Stark saw across the water, and what he had heard from the trickle of news that reached Winterfell, melted his northern valour. Aegon Targaryen sat astride Balerion the Black Dread at the head of an army at least 40,000-strong. Northmen think nothing of fighting superior numbers – every northman, after all, is said to be worth ten southron swords.[1] But alongside Balerion were his sisters, Meraxes and Vhagar, all three fresh from the Field of Fire where they had burned 4,000 of the last men to defy them. Before that Balerion had incinerated the castle of Harrenhal, the largest ever built in Westeros, in a single night. Torrhen Stark had a choice. Charge headlong into the Targaryen host, wreak what havoc he and his 30,000 could and perish defiantly in a blaze of dragonflame; or kneel and feed honour to the crows instead of northern dead.

Torrhen Stark bent the knee. When he rose the North was a kingdom no more, and though he saved untold thousands of his men and their families from an agonizing death, he will forever after be remembered as the King Who Knelt.[2] Torrhen gave his men their lives, but had taken their honour – and if there is one thing a northman prizes above his life, it is his honour. There is more than a hint of moral absolutism woven into the culture of the North, exemplified most radically by Ned Stark's honourable but self-sabotaging actions upon learning the truth about King Joffrey's parentage. Staring down the agent of his people's imminent annihilation on the far bank of the Trident, however, Torrhen Stark chose the path of survival and his 30,000 returned to their homes and families. If that is less heroic than mass suicide by dragon, then glory be damned. To paraphrase Balon Greyjoy, who knew a thing or two about bending the knee, no one ever died from doing it, and besides, the kneeling man can rise to take vengeance, but a dead one cannot.[3]

There is no monument to Torrhen's capitulation. The only reminder is the Inn of the Kneeling Man which stands more or less upon the spot where his once-royal knee touched the ground. Since that day, 'kneeler' has become a derogatory slur in Westeros. It is mostly hurled by the Free Folk at anyone to the south of them, for the Free Folk kneel to no one, though there is also a robust disgust at the notion of kneeling amongst the northern houses like the Umbers and Glovers. Torrhen Stark's bannermen were likely more grateful to not melt in a storm of dragonfire than they were ashamed not to fight, yet it seems that their descendants are convinced, with the bravery bestowed by hindsight, that they would not have gone so quietly. When the Night King descends on them to extinguish the fires in their hearths forever, we shall see if their deeds live up to their words.

There may not be an inn to mark the spot where the King of Scots bent the knee to a southern conqueror, but there is a tea room. A few miles south of Perth, the ancient capital of Scotland, is the quiet village of Abernethy. Tucked away just off the edge of the old town square where the mercat (market) cross stands is Abernethy Round Tower, one of the oldest surviving stone structures in the north. It is one of only two Irish-style round towers in Scotland, built by Celtic Culdee monks and harkening back to 1100 CE. There was a church on the site from at least the start of the seventh century, when the Picts dominated the area, and they too left their mark. At the entrance to the kirkyard in which the round tower stands is a Pictish symbol stone incised with a crescent and V-rod, hammer and anvil, and several other motifs. Though the round tower arrived just a little too late, this special little stone was almost certainly standing watch when King Malcolm III 'Canmore' – the Big Head or Great Chief – knelt before William the Conqueror in 1072.

Ironically, the course of events that led to Malcolm bending the knee started with a wedding proposal. An exodus of Anglo-Saxon nobles followed the victory of Guillame le Bâtard – known to us as William the Conqueror – at the Battle of Hastings. As refugees from invasions and political machinations within the Kingdom of England would continue to do for centuries, the Anglo-Saxon prince, Edgar Atheling, along with his mother Agatha and sisters Margaret and Christina, sought refuge in Scotland in the summer of 1067.[4] They were warmly received by

Malcolm III, and the course of Scottish history was changed forever as a result. Not only did Malcolm wed Margaret, who is known to posterity as Saint Margaret and was one of the most consequential reformers of medieval Scotland, it also inevitably drew Scotland into the political maelstrom of the Norman invasion. Looking on from his castellated bases in the south, William the Conqueror had every reason to see the exiled Edgar and this new union as a threat to his nascent kingship. After all, if Edgar died without an heir, then the King of Scots would have a claim to the throne of England through Margaret no less legitimate than William's own claim on the realm.[5]

William struck first. He scourged the northern shires of Danes and Edgar's supporters in a blood-soaked campaign remembered to this day as the Harrying of the North. The scales were weighted heavily in William's favour, not least because of his formidable mounted Norman knights, the first true knights to ride through the valleys of Britain. Although Malcolm could field a significant cavalry force of his own, head-to-head the light hobelar horsemen would be no match against William's barded knights armed with mail and lance. William duly invaded Scotland with a great host by land and sea in 1072, and it became clear to Malcolm that the Kingdom of Scotland could either reach an accommodation with the William or be subjected to his will against their own.[6] So Malcolm rode out to the banks of the River Earn to meet the Conqueror on the other side upon the hallowed ground of Abernethy.

It would be fascinating to be able to see through that Pictish stone and witness the moment that the two kings came face to face. We do not know exactly what happened next. The *Anglo-Saxon Chronicle* tells us only that Malcolm 'came and made peace with King William, and was his man, and gave him hostages, and afterwards he turned home with all his army'.[7] Many battles, both actual and academic, have been fought over the precise nature of the phrase 'and was his man'.

What did bending the knee to William really mean? It was not the first time that something like this had happened, and it would not be the last – Constantine II of Scotland submitted to Athelstan of England outside the walls of Dunnottar Castle in 934 CE, and William the Lion would be forced to sign the humiliating Treaty of Falaise, making him a vassal of England's Henry II from 1174-89.[8] Paying homage, however, is not as clear-cut a term as it sounds. From the perspective of the kings of Scots, the paying of homage to the kings of England was a personal act of fealty, not a national one, no different than the kings of England paying homage to the kings of France for lands that they held across the Channel.[9] The English perspective, understandably, was rather different, treating acts of homage as recognitions of England's feudal overlordship over Scotland.[10] It was certainly possible to pay homage to a king whilst remaining a king yourself, but future kings of England, including most notoriously and effectively Edward I, 'Hammer of the Scots', would use Malcolm's submission to William at Abernethy and terms of the Treaty of Falaise of 1174 to bolster their legal case to rule the whole of Britain.

Content not to conquer Scotland outright, William returned south. Malcolm Canmore barely waited until he was out of sight to rise once more against him. Throughout his reign, Malcolm launched no less than five major assaults on the north of England, hoping to secure Scotland's claim on Cumbria and Northumbria. The fifth expedition was Malcolm's last, for he was struck down at the Battle of Alnwick.[11] Despite this disaster, the Kingdom of Scotland not only survived him but reached new heights in the decades to follow. Part of this success was down to the fact that, while the Normans did not conquer Scotland by force of arms, many Northern European knights were invited to Scotland by twelfth-century kings such as David I to build their newfangled castles and help expand the boundaries of the nascent kingdom. Many of Scotland's most renowned noble families, including the Murrays, Frasers, Comyns and Bruces, were founded by such incomers, who quickly mixed with the locals, self-identified as Scots and even spoke Gaelic. If avoiding mass slaughter and creating the national heroes of the future are the consequences of bending the knee, it's hard to argue against a little flexibility.

Chapter 11

The Lion and His Claws: Edward I & Tywin Lannister

All a King Should Be?

A few rare individuals throughout history have played their parts so well that they have become synonymous with their archetypes. Leonidas of Sparta, the warrior; Attila, the barbarian; Joan of Arc, the saviour; Einstein, the genius; and Edward I of England. Whether you see the latter as a great hero, a tyrant or some combination of both, all seem to agree that Edward I was a king – or, more accurately, he was at least all a king should appear to be.

He certainly looked the part. With the exception of a drooping eyelid, a trait inherited from his father Henry III,[1] Edward was head to toe the ideal image of nobility. Making an authoritative impression is always easier when you literally stand head and shoulders above your contemporaries, and an exhumation of his body at Westminster Abbey in 1774 proved that he did just that at the commanding height of 6ft 2in. His features were handsome and his hair put on an impressive lifelong performance, transforming from a silvery yellow in his youth to a black that matched his temper in manhood and ultimately, in old age, to an almost saintly pure white.[2] Though he could not have planned it, unlike so many of the other details of his life, Edward's visage could not have been more perfectly constructed to convey the lion within.

Tywin Lannister, Lord of Casterly Rock and Warden of the West, benefited from the same natural gifts, and *Game of Thrones'* Charles Dance perfectly captures the regal menace of the Lion of Lannister. Though Tywin never sat upon the Iron Throne, few in the realm were in any doubt as to who built the foundation the throne rested on. If not for Tywin's guiding hand during the rueful reign of the Mad

King, the realm would almost certainly have fallen to pieces far sooner than it did. Whispers in the streets of King's Landing of the real power behind the throne soon became a cacophony, and when Ser Ilyn Payne was caught touting Tywin as the uncrowned king of Westeros, the Mad King, in his jealousy, ensured it was the last thing Ser Ilyn would ever say. That could hardly silence the truth, however, and Tywin's authority only grew in the minds of the people. He was uncompromising in war, diligent in administration, ever playing the short and long games simultaneously, and above all unwavering in his commitment to building a dynasty to last 1,000 years. 'The gods made and shaped this man to rule,' wrote one of Tywin's most fawning contemporaries, Grand Maester Pycelle,[3] echoing the eulogy given to Edward I by the author of the *Chronicle of Lanercost*: 'Throughout his time he had been fearless and warlike, in all things strenuous and illustrious; he left not his like among Christian princes for sagacity and courage.'[4]

Aside from their superficial regality, the most obvious parallel between Edward I and Tywin Lannister is the symbol that above all represents their respective houses: the lion. The Plantagenet dynasty of which Edward I is arguably the most distinguished member took the lion as their standard by the mid-twelfth century, and it remains the iconic image that most people around the world immediately associate with England. The Plantagenet arms were eventually amended so many times to the point of becoming absurdly crammed, but it started simply enough with three lions *passant guardant*, meaning laid out horizontally walking on all fours with their faces turned towards the 'audience'. There is a fierce debate afoot among students of heraldry as to whether that in fact makes them leopards rather than lions, but that is a hill we can die on another day. Tywin Lannister's arms are a nod to the English lion, yet its disposition is actually closest to the royal arms of Scotland. Adopted by the heirs of David I, including the aptly named King William 'the Lion' (r. 1165-1214), the Scottish lion is rampant, meaning it is standing upright on its hind legs with its forepaws extended before it as if to maul some unseen foe. It can still be seen flying from castle walls across Scotland, and at the main gate of Edinburgh Castle it stands astride the combative motto of the Stewart dynasty of Scotland, *Nemo me impune lacessit* – 'No one provokes me with impunity'. The lion rampant, known officially as the Royal Standard of Scotland, was borne into battle against England on countless occasions and would have stood in stark contrast, as it did upon the field of Bannockburn, to the Plantagenet and later English lions. The Scottish lion rampant is red upon a golden field, the inverse of English heraldry whose lions are golden upon a red field. In creating the sigil of House Lannister, Martin seems to have fused the two beasts together into a golden lion rampant upon a red field. I wonder how Edward I and Robert the Bruce, avowed enemies whose identities were inextricably linked to their respective lions, would feel about this fusion.

Bastards in Their Fathers' Eyes

Of all the troubling familial relationships in *Game of Thrones*, the neglect and scorn poured on Tyrion Lannister by his father, Tywin, is one of the most consistently heartbreaking. There are several wellsprings from which Tywin draws his hatred of his son. The first, and most unfair, is that the one person in the world who could make Tywin Lannister smile was Joanna Lannister, and she perished in the act of bringing Tyrion into it. 'Lord Tywin's bane', the small folk called Tyrion upon his birth, and Tywin seems convinced of the truth of it. Further vexing Tywin was how Tyrion proceeded to live his life, the sum of which Tywin – with characteristic ego – saw as little more than a calculated insult to him. As we learned the very first time we meet Tyrion in *Game of Thrones*, if you need to find him it is best to check his bedroom, the local brothel or wherever a strong Dornish red is served first. While Tyrion's debauchery gives us some of the best moments of levity in the series, it could not be in starker contrast to Tywin's fixation on legacy and, most of all, keeping up at least the appearance of nobility and competency. Tywin eventually grows so weary of Tyrion's hedonistic antics that he disowns him and even condemns him to death at trial for the regicide and kin-slaying of the heinous King Joffrey. 'You are an ill-made, spiteful little creature, full of envy, lust and low cunning,' Tywin berates him. "To teach me humility the gods have condemned me to watch you waddle about wearing that proud lion.'[5]

It was a charge that Edward I could relate to in sorry detail. His son, Edward II, has gone down as one of the most wayward kings in English history, and though the extent of the depredations ascribed to him are somewhat exaggerated in the chronicles, it is resoundingly clear that

Edward II was all his father was not. Unfortunately, much of the scorn poured upon Edward II relates to his homosexual relationship with a Gascon nobleman and confidant, Piers Gaveston, a reflection of the prejudices of the time. Of actual concern was the fact that Piers was an objectively awful influence, diverting Edward's attention from matters of state to frivolity and leisure and becoming hated by every lord in the land for the way he openly basked in the king's favour to the detriment of others.[6] On this Tywin Lannister and Edward I would agree: a king is only as wise as his counsellors, whose accumulated experience go well beyond that of any single man, so it is paramount that a king chooses his advisers with care and consideration. Tywin tells the newly crowned King Tommen as much whilst standing over the barely cold corpse of Joffrey in one of *Game of Thrones'* finest articulations of his cunning.[7]

Unlike Tyrion, Edward II was not held back by his physicality. Far from it; he was tall, handsome and strong. The *Vita Edwardi Secundi* laments that if only Edward II had trained more diligently in the use of arms, studied more astutely the stratagems of war and dedicated himself more wholly to the business of governance, then instead of presiding over a period of ruin he could have 'raised England on high'.[8] Where Tyrion's vices are, to Tywin, a product of his physical form, Edward II was undone by his choice of company and pursuits. Edward was, at any given moment, more likely to be found rowing on a lake with Piers Gaveston, thatching roofs or shoeing horses – respectable enough endeavours in their own right, but hardly the concerns of the king of one of the most powerful nations in Europe. The historical verdict on Edward II is that far from fulfilling or continuing his father's legacy, he was consumed by his passions rather than his nation's imperatives.[9] Though we cannot delve into detail here, there is also much to be said for the follies and disruptive ambitions of the English nobles during Edward's reign – for instance the bickering which plagued the English side at Bannockburn – so before coming to too damning a verdict we should recall Tacitus' observation of failure, that 'all claim for themselves the credit for success, failure is blamed on a single man.'[10]

Tyrion Lannister knows the weight of those words more than perhaps any other individual in Westeros, having been turned into a lightning rod for every grievance and suspicion in the viper's pit of King's Landing. But, unlike Edward II, will he rise above them? Tyrion may have begun his days doing cartwheels for guests at court and sleeping his way through the brothels and wine sinks of Westeros, but at the time of writing he finds himself as Hand of the Queen to Daenerys Targaryen, mostly sober and wholeheartedly engaged with tremendous responsibilities. Despite some miscalculations, there is no doubt that Tyrion has the capacity to be a truly great man, greater even than Tywin, for Tyrion pairs wit and strength of spirit with justice and compassion. These are kingly virtues of which, despite the praises of the chroniclers, Tywin – and as we shall now see, Edward I of England – were found wanting.

A Legacy of Woe

The long shadows of past evils cast a pall over almost every major character in *Game of Thrones*. Just as we can all remember one or two major events in our own lives that shook our worlds and sense of safety to the core, so too can the inhabitants of Westeros. The day that the Mad King roasted Rickard Stark alive in his armour was one. So too was the day that Joffrey ordered Ser Ilyn Payne to bring him Ned Stark's head on the hallowed steps of the Sept of Baelor. Yet no day was as woeful as the day that Tywin Lannister marched into King's Landing and, instead of saving the city like the hero he presented himself to be, proceeded to butcher it.

Tywin's uninhibited wrath consumed King's Landing. When Eddard Stark arrived in his wake and waded through the blood-soaked streets to the Red Keep, he witnessed horrors he would never forget or forgive: countless innocents raped and slaughtered, children cut down at play and whole neighbourhoods reduced to simmering ruins.[11] Even by the brutal standards of Westerosi warfare this was excessive, yet one act above all cemented Tywin's reputation in the minds of many as not just a man capable of evils, but an evil man – a critical distinction. Ser Gregor Clegane forced his way into the royal chamber where Elia Martell, Prince Rhaegar's widow, and her children were hiding. Gregor seized the infant Aegon and dashed his head on the cold stone wall before brutalizing and murdering Elia herself. Whether or not Tywin gave Gregor the order to do this is immaterial; in the minds of much of the realm, the blood of Elia, her children and the thousands of dead in the streets was on Tywin's hands as much as Ser Gregor's.

Edward I also had many sins to answer for. One of the most vile was his expulsion of the Jews from England in 1290, which systematically and cruelly rooted out a community that had been well-established since at least the Norman Conquest and would not return for nearly four centuries.[12] While crusading in the Holy Land, Edward presided over the slaughter of nearly the entire population of Nazareth.[13] Yet to contemporary chroniclers, even this act was overshadowed by what befell the innocent residents of Berwick, then a part of Scotland but now known as Berwick-upon-Tweed astride the border of Scotland and England. Arriving there nowadays by train, it is all too easy to glimpse the unremarkable and heavily deteriorated stone wall across the tracks, surrounded by crates and an unsightly car park, and not give it a second thought. Yet these are the fragmentary ruins of Berwick Castle, a reminder of Edward's shocking opening gambit in the Wars of Independence. Berwick was once Scotland's wealthiest trading town by a considerable margin, and in Edward's day its population likely rivalled or even exceeded that of Edinburgh. On 30 March 1296, having assembled an army of some 20,000 outside the town, Edward, the image of nobility, gave the most dreaded order that a medieval commander could issue. A black flag with a red dragon fluttered in the breeze, and Edward's men charged forth to 'burn, kill and raise the dragon'.[14]

Under that ominous banner none would be spared. 'Raising the dragon' meant that all the restraints of chivalry would be thrown off and anyone – soldiers, peasants, even livestock – that got in the way would be killed without question. The town's makeshift ditch and palisade were quickly overrun by Edward's army, and Berwick was reduced from the jewel of the south to an ashen wreck. One of the flashpoints of the slaughter was at the Red Hall, a mercantile institution where Flemish merchants attempted to make a stand. The English army set the Red Hall ablaze, and all inside perished. Edward's rage was stoked when he learned that his kinsman, Richard of Cornwall, had fallen in the act.[15] It is impossible to know how many died at Berwick, but estimates range from as high as 15,000, which would have been nearly the entire population, to a more probable 7,000-8,000 as recorded in the *Lanercost Chronicle*[16] and *Scotichronicon*.[17] Scotland's total population at the time was a little under 400,000,[18] so even if the most conservative estimate for the number killed on Edward's command is taken as true, that amounts to just under 2 per cent of the national population. For context, the United Kingdom and its colonies suffered roughly the same proportion of fatalities relative to its total population during the First World War.

Like the Westerosi chroniclers who lay the victims of King's Landing directly at the feet of Tywin Lannister, historians are unequivocal about who bears the historical burden of the massacre at Berwick, 'for which the king alone must be held responsible'.[19]

If you must commit evils, argued Machiavelli, the best way to do it is all at once.[20] The theory holds that people will more easily move past merciless yet selective use of evils than they will a steady stream of moderate ones. While the fundamental assumption of this premise is very much up for debate, given how tragically inured individuals and populations can become to systemic injustices, Tywin Lannister seems, at least at first, to follow Machiavelli's advice to a T. His first major act of cruelty was the extermination of the Tarbecks and Reynes, the same act that gave us the incomparably ominous *Rains of Castamere*. By destroying his competitors root and stem in one swift wave of violence, Tywin abided by the Machiavellian principle that 'men are either to be flattered and indulged or utterly destroyed – because for small offences they do usually revenge themselves, but for great ones they cannot'.[21] Unless you're north of the Wall or find yourself in the grip of Lady Stoneheart, the dead cannot seek revenge. It is a cruel fate for the Tarbecks and Reynes that their names will forever be synonymous with the singular act that brought their houses crashing down.

Indulging in a somewhat fanciful comparison for a moment, we can almost think of the Machiavellian premise of accumulation of evils like a point counter in a video game. With each reprehensible act the bar rises another notch towards a limit at which point one's reputation for evil is irreversible. It is the crucial threshold between being feared and being hated, the latter of which is the worst of all outcomes for someone wishing to keep hold of the reins of power.[22] It seems that by the end of his life, Tywin had indeed crossed that threshold. A popular observation about Tywin is that while he was widely viewed as the power behind the throne, he was little loved for it. In fact, his less noble yet most memorable characteristics were pride, cruelty and humourlessness, traits not likely to leave behind a flattering legacy.[23] He did not go quite so far as Ramsay Bolton, a relentlessly and, worst of all, arbitrarily cruel figure who embodied the very worst type of ruler according to Machiavelli. Tywin was respected by all and hated by some, while Ramsay was hated by all and only obeyed as far as his sadistic hand could reach. Ultimately, however, Tywin had more in common with Ramsay Bolton than saintly figures like Baelor the Blessed. Whether such criticism would have bothered Tywin is unlikely. In an almost verbatim recitation of the Melian Dialogue that international relations scholars point to as the birth of the theory of political realism – 'the strong do what they can and the weak suffer what they must' – Tywin remarked in life that 'A lion doesn't concern himself with the opinions of a sheep'.[24]

The reality is that despite the superficially convincing illusion that the medieval world operated on chivalry and codes of honour, the most effective military commanders and governors of the age largely ignored chivalry whenever it limited their ability to achieve their desired ends.[25] It was an approach that rings close to the Machiavellian concept of *virtù*, being the means to direct one's will towards the realization of great accomplishments, with the absolute morality of said means being of secondary concern. The trick is not taking that principle too far. Edward I did just that when blood flowed through the streets of Nazareth and Berwick, as well as when he cruelly ordered Robert the Bruce's wife and sister to suffer the indignity of swinging in outdoor cages from English walls. He wanted the same fate for Bruce's young daughter, Marjorie, and was only deterred by pleas of clemency from members of the clergy.

Tywin, too, seems to have accumulated scuffs on his lion banner to permanently colour his legacy. The annihilation of the Tarbecks and Reynes had largely been forgiven when he ordered the massacre of King's Landing, an act which has not been forgotten by the city and those who waded through the aftermath.[26] With that evil still festering, he orchestrated the Red Wedding, perhaps the most reviled act in all of *Game of Thrones*, and though the bulk of the blame for it stuck to the Frey puppets rather than the Lannister puppet-master, many in Westeros knew where the orders came from. Tywin's funeral attempted to maintain the façade of chivalry. The silent sisters bedecked him in his most magnificent armour, and with hands folded as though in prayer and noble features upon his face even in death, it almost worked.[27] Yet the highly symbolic smell of rot nevertheless became overpowering. No matter how regal Edward I and Tywin Lannister may appear, their legacies will forever be stained by several bloody spots that soaked in too deep to wash out.

And what of that legacy? For all their talk of building dynasties and creating order, neither Edward nor Tywin's glories and aspirations survived them. Immediately upon Edward's death, Robert the Bruce's cause was greatly bolstered, and Edward II would go on to be humiliated by Bruce at Bannockburn and murdered by a conspiracy involving his own wife and her lover, Roger Mortimer. Bruce, whom Edward I spent his final days dying at Burgh-on-Sands cursing, restored Scotland's independent status and pushed the frontier of the war deeper and deeper into the northern English shires than would ever have been possible while Edward lived. Edward I may not have died on the privy like Tywin (though he did once famously remark, in regard to Scotland, that 'A man does good business when he rids himself of a turd'), but the fate of his son and heir was just as undignified.

If a standard of Machiavellian *virtù* is that a king can commit evils so long as his subjects remain obedient and loyal,[28] then Tywin also fails the test. Even while he lived, the Tyrells successfully murdered his grandson, the North rebelled under their restored king and, most damning of all to him personally, his son and daughter's incestuous relationship and children that came of it made mockery of Tywin's obsession with family and reputation. The pedestal of cruelty that Cersei Lannister now stands upon is unstable indeed, and it is very likely that within a single generation of Tywin Lannister's death there will be no trace of his family left in Westeros – except, perhaps, for Tyrion, the son who embodies the best of him yet never knew his love. There could be no more fitting a legacy for a man whose stature made him king in all but name, but whose deeds left much of the realm smiling at the death of a man who never did.

Chapter 12

The Banner with the Bloody Heart

Of all the sigils one could carry into battle, a bright red cartoon-style heart does not seem like a choice to instil fear in your foe. The residents of Westeros had certainly never seen anything like the arms of Stannis Baratheon, which placed a crowned Baratheon stag inside the flaming heart of the Lord of Light. To them it was every bit as alien and bewildering as rumours of Dothraki savagery or tales of depraved decadence in Slaver's Bay. To us in the twenty-first century, the classic heart shape is inseparable from the notion of romantic love and seems farcical as a symbol to march to war under. There is good precedent to fear it, however. To those living in the northern shires of England in the early fourteenth century, few sights were as dreaded as that of the 'bluidy heart' of James Douglas.

If Edward I was the Hammer of the Scots, then James Douglas was the unrelenting 'hammerer of the English'.[1] Douglas, Robert the Bruce's indomitable captain, is overshadowed only by Bruce himself as the most intriguing wartime personality of fourteenth-century Scotland. He is something of a Janus figure. While many Scots came to know him as 'the Good' Sir James for his championing of Bruce's cause, it was his mastery of fear as a tool of war, his personal ferocity in battle and his brutally effective raiding style that caused his victims to bestow on him his most enduring moniker, 'the blak Dowglas'.[2] His bogeyman reputation amongst the English was such that, while he was still very much alive and active, mothers in the north of England sang to their children:

> 'Hush ye, hush ye, little pet ye,
> Hush ye, hush ye, dinnae fret ye
> The Black Douglas shall not get ye.'

A chilling folk story has this refrain followed by a calloused hand grasping the mother's shoulder, and a growling voice uttering, 'Don't be too sure of that'.[3]

Even his name is ominous. Douglas, a common first and last name in Scotland and, as a result, across much of the world, is derived from the Gaelic *dubh-glas*, meaning dark or black water.[4] There is technically a 'Blackwater' – and many variations thereof – in Scotland. The Douglas Water, a tributary of the River Clyde which courses through Lanarkshire and past James' home, Douglas Castle, lives up to its name. It is a plodding serpent that often takes on a deep silvery-blue and black hue, its surface seeming to stop all light in its tracks. James' shoulder-length hair shared this characteristic with the river and contributed to his grim visage in battle. That's not to say that James was constantly brooding. If Barbour can be at all relied on to impart anecdotes, James even had a pretty good sense of humour. In response to an English knight who doubted that Douglas could possibly live up to his reputation since he did not have any visible scars to show for all his war-making, James shot back, 'Praise God! Always had I / Strong hands with which to guard my face.'[5] In other words, no one had ever got close enough. Apparently nobody laughed.

Douglas led and partook in many dramatic episodes in the period between joining Bruce in 1306 and his death in 1330. He became infamous for the 'Douglas Larder' in 1307, in which he recaptured his family home, butchered the English garrison, stuffed their bodies into a cellar along with the castle's stores and set it all ablaze. In the wake of the Battle of Bannockburn, Douglas pursued the defeated Edward II to Dunbar, nearly seventy miles to the east, with a cavalry force outnumbered as much as ten to one by the king's. Barbour gave the memorable detail that Douglas allowed Edward 'not so much leisure / As to make water'.[6] These and other actions gave James the reputation among friends and foes alike of being 'mair fell [fierce] than was ony devill in hell'.[7] His battle record speaks for itself: according to Walter Bower's *Scotichronicon*, Douglas gained fifty-seven victories to thirteen losses, a remarkable and not unrealistic ratio, especially considering that Douglas was not exactly in the habit of holding himself back from the thick of a good fight.[8]

The final and most enduring episode of all came with the death of Robert the Bruce on 7 June 1329. In his final days, Bruce assembled his captains by his bed and tasked Douglas to bear his heart on crusade to the Church of the Holy Sepulchre in Jerusalem. This could be read as a kind of posthumous repentance for Bruce's sins, including the murder of his rival for the crown, John Comyn, at the High Kirk in Dumfries in 1306.[9] Jerusalem, however, was firmly in the hands of the Mamluk Sultanate, but an alternative cause was readily available in the form of King Alfonso XI of Castile's campaign against the Moors in Andalusia. A hand-picked group of Scottish knights, including Sir William Sinclair of Rosslyn and Sir William Keith, bade their homeland farewell, with Douglas bearing his king's heart in a metal cask worn round his neck.

A battle ensued in the shadow of the Castillo de la Estrella, the 'Castle of the Stars', near the village of Teba between Seville and the Moorish power base in Granada. True to form, Douglas and the Scots were the first to throw themselves into the fray and even threatened the personal division of the Berber general Uthman bin Abi-l-Ula.[10] Without support from the rest of the Christian army, however, they were soon overwhelmed by sheer numbers. With his end clearly upon him, the story as recounted by Sir Walter Scott goes that Douglas removed the cask from around his neck, declared aloud, 'Pass first in fight ... as thou wert wont to do, and Douglas will follow thee, or die', then charged forward one final time.[11]

When the few surviving Scots searched the field following the crusader's indecisive victory, they found Douglas dead, hewn with 'five deep wounds'.[12] Despairing, they lifted his body up to carry from the battlefield, only to rejoice when they found the heart protected to the very last underneath. Bruce's heart now rests at Melrose Abbey, while Douglas was interred in St Bride's Church in the small village that gave him his family name.

The specifics of this tale vary depending on who you ask. A passage in Barbour's *The Bruce*, for instance, contains the first recorded use of a now iconic and much misunderstood moniker. Barbour wrote that Douglas began his final proclamation with the words, 'Brave heart, that ever foremost led'.[13] The oft-sought 'real' braveheart, it turns out, is not William Wallace but the bond between Robert the Bruce and James Douglas. Neither Barbour nor Walter Scott, however, could possibly have known Douglas' true last words. The minutiae, as in all great stories, are perhaps best left to the imagination. Whatever the case, in honour of James' noble cause, whoever assumed the title of Earl of Douglas from 1356 onwards was known as the 'Black Douglas'. Their banners and even armour were adorned with the bloody heart of Bruce, which together with the cry of 'A Douglas, A Douglas!' became the most menacing presence on any battlefield it entered.

Chapter 13

A Tale of Two Roberts:
Bruce & Baratheon

The Warrior Kings

The moment that Robert Baratheon won the Battle of the Trident was the moment that he became the ruler of the Seven Kingdoms. King's Landing had yet to fall and the Mad King still lived, yet that battle is what Westeros' maesters will recall in a thousand years.

Winning a kingdom through force of arms was a legitimate route to power in the Middle Ages. While a blood claim certainly helped, skill in war and the guile to outwit an otherwise superior enemy was a sort of wisdom and, therefore, a kingly virtue alongside justice, piety and the gentler aspects of rule.[1] Strange as it may seem at first to view the carnage of medieval battle through a legalistic lens, the 'verdict of battle' carried a strong moralistic component in which battle was seen as a wager between two or more parties and victory corresponded to the rightness of a cause.[2] The link between martial success and leadership is one that emerged at least as far back as the Iron Age, as we saw with Calgacus at the Battle of Mons Graupius, and it strengthened during the Early Historic period of approximately 400-1000 CE.[3] If a king could defend his people and land in person and not just by proxy, that went a long way towards building legitimacy. A king who could not, such as the neglectful Edward II of England, could quickly become thought of as no king at all.

Robert the Bruce, King of Scots from 1306-29, and Robert Baratheon, first of his name and King of the Andals, the Rhoynar and First Men, both held claims to their respective thrones through ancestry. Bruce was a descendant of David I, whose pivotal rule lasted from 1124-53, and the Bruce family was able to put forward a strong but unsuccessful claim

116

1. Stirling Castle
Stirling Castle, Scotland's most strategically important castle situated at a pinch point in the land. Old Stirling Bridge, the Abbey Crag with the Wallace Monument, and the Ochil Hills can all be seen to the right beyond the castle. ©Neil Robertson.

2. Stirling Bridge
Old Stirling Bridge crossing the River Forth. A stone bridge replaced a timber one in the 15th century. For nearly 2,000 years this crossing was the key to controlling Scotland. Author's Image.

3. Map of Britain by Matthew Paris
Matthew Paris' 13th century map of Britain. Notice the emphasis on Stirling Bridge near the top and how the whole island appears to be severed by the 'Scottish Sea'. Wikimedia Commons.

4. Dumbarton Rock
The volcanic plug of Dumbarton Rock, Britain's oldest continually occupied fortification, astride the River Clyde. Author's image.

5. Castle Sinclair-Girnigoe
The impossibly precipitous castle of Sinclair-Girnigoe in Caithness. Built upon the sheer cliff face alongside several sea stacks, the castle made the Sinclairs a major power on both land and sea. ©Chris Sinclair.

6. Kisimul Castle
Kisimul Castle in Castlebay, Barra, seat of the Clan MacNeil and one of the most distant strongholds of the Lords of the Isles. Author's image.

7. Duart Castle
Duart Castle on the Isle of Mull, a major power centre of the Lords of the Isles, viewed from the ferry at the start of the 'castle corridor'. Author's image.

8. Dunnottar Castle
The ancient and precipitous fortress of Dunnottar on the coast near Stonehaven, Aberdeenshire. Author's image.

9. Goatfell
The mountain of Goatfell rises sharply at the north end of the Isle of Arran, known as 'Scotland in Miniature' for being cut in two by the Highland Boundary Fault. Adobe Stock #242044957 ©Matthew.

10. Ring of Brodgar
Several of the standing stones that comprise the 4,500 year-old Ring of Brodgar in Orkney, with blossoming heather on a late summer's eve. Author's image.

11. Achnabreck cup and ring markings
Cup and ring markings at Achnabreck, Argyll. The meaning of these abundant 5,000 year-old symbols remains enigmatic. Author's image.

12. Aberlemno Stone
One of five Class I and II Pictish sculptured stones at Aberlemno, Angus dating from 500 to 800 CE. Like the cup and ring marks, their meaning remains a mystery.
Adobe Stock #135484310
©Richard.

13. The Scottish Crannog Centre
A reconstructed crannog on Loch Tay. Crannogs are exclusive to Scotland, Ireland, and Wales.
©The Scottish Crannog Centre.

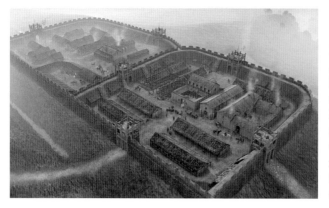

14. Rough Castle at Antonine Wall
Digital reconstruction of Rough Castle in Falkirk, a Roman fort along the Antonine Wall where some of the best remains of Rome's final frontier can still be found.
©Bob Marshall.

15. Roman cavalry tombstone
A Briton being trampled by the might of Rome on a Roman cavalry tombstone. The mismatched scale between the cavalryman and Briton reinforces the supposed inferiority of the natives in the eyes of the Empire. ©Trimontium Trust and Ribchester Roman Museum

16. Duffus Castle
Duffus Castle near Elgin, Moray, is Scotland's largest surviving motte and bailey castle. Author's image.

17. Craigmillar Castle
Craigmillar Castle in the south of Edinburgh is Scotland's closest approximation to Winterfell. Author's image.

22. (*Above left*) The Bloody Heart
The heart sigil of the Douglases emblazoned on plate armour worn by Andrew Spratt, medieval re-enactor and castle reconstruction artist, at Dirleton Castle. Author's image.

23. (*Above right*) King Edward I
A depiction of King Edward I of England conveying his effortlessly regal air, backed up by the menace of the sword. Wikimedia Commons.

24. Bruce's shield and axe
The lion rampant of King Robert Bruce emblazoned upon a shield and crossed by Bruce's favourite weapon, the axe, lying upon the grass at the battlefield of Bannockburn. Author's image.

25. Robert Bruce v Henry de Bohun
King Robert Bruce slays the English knight Sir Henry de Bohun with a single swing of his axe in the opening moments of the Battle of Bannockburn. Wikimedia Commons.

26. Bothwell Castle
Bothwell Castle, with its great donjon nearest the bend in the River Clyde, was one of Scotland's premiere baronial castles. ©Neil Robertson.

32. Old Man of Storr
The iconic Old Man of Storr north of Portree on the Isle of Skye, said to be the fingers of a buried giant. Adobe Stock #211471192 ©Fulcanelli.

33. (*Left*) Ballachulish Figure
A sketch from the 1880 edition of the Proceedings of the Society of Antiquaries of Scotland depicts The Ballachulish Figure, some 2,500 years old, a possible representation of the Cailleach or 'Queen of Winter' in Gaelic lore. ©The Society of Antiquaries of Scotland.

34. (*Below*) Face in Dunino Den
The face of the old gods? A modern carving on the rock of Dunino Den, an ancient Pictish ritual ground near St Andrews. Author's image.

35. Declaration of Arbroath
The Declaration of Arbroath, composed in 1320 under King Robert Bruce, is one of European political history's most important documents. ©National Records of Scotland SP13/7.

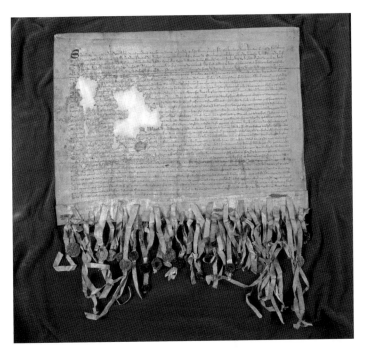

36. Edinburgh Castle
Edinburgh Castle upon its crag in the heart of the modern capital of Scotland. It is the most besieged castle in Britain and played host to the Black Dinner which inspired *Game of Thrones'* Red Wedding. Author's image.

37. Black Dinner
Illustration of the Black Dinner at Edinburgh Castle in 1440. The young King James II can be seen pleading with Sir Alexander Livingston, architect of the Black Dinner, while 18 year-old William Douglas is seized by armed guards.

38. Glencoe
Glencoe, scene of the infamous massacre of 1692. A place heavy with the weight of history. ©Ana Soldatenko.

to inherit the throne following the sudden death of King Alexander III in 1286. Baratheon's grandmother, Rhaelle Targaryen, was a daughter of King Aegon V, who wed into House Baratheon. Yet it was a different kind of blood that made them both into kings – the kind spilled on the battlefield. Bruce had, after all, broken his oath to Edward I and murdered his main rival for the throne, John Comyn, in cold blood at the altar of a kirk. In the eyes of many he was no less than a usurper,[4] a condemnation also applied by Daenerys and Viserys Targaryen to Robert Baratheon, and no one casting this accusation in either Scotland or Westeros was entirely wrong.

Trial and victory through battle combined with the support of the people could help an aspiring king to overcome such technicalities,[5] and following the Battle of Bannockburn, Bruce could decisively lay claim to both. In addition to the countless raids, hit-and-run attacks and assaults on castles conducted prior to Bannockburn, Bruce could boast of three victories at Glen Trool (April 1307), Loudoun Hill (10 May 1307) and the Pass of Brander (late summer 1308). This was a significant reversal from the situation in 1306, which saw near-total defeats at the battles of Methven and Dalrigh. Success in feats of arms was crucial to Bruce's transformation from 'King Hob', the disparaging name meaning something like 'King Nothing' given to him by English propagandists and Scottish rivals, to being widely acknowledged by the people and nobility alike as the rightful King of Scots.[6]

One key difference between the two warrior-kings seems to be that while Baratheon yearned for combat and felt most alive in the brute chaos of war, Bruce frequently pulled out every trick in the guerrilla playbook to avoid open battle and unnecessary loss of life. 'I swear to you,' Baratheon complains to Ned Stark when he finds out no one will ride against him in a tournament, 'I was never so alive as when I was winning this throne, or so dead as now that I've won it.'[7] Contrast this with Bruce, who during the desperate early years of his reign often went hungry, slept with not even canvas between him and the elements, and was bed-ridden with a mysterious illness on several occasions. Though there is no doubt that Bruce believed in his right to the throne, there is little evidence that he enjoyed winning it. After the first day's fighting at Bannockburn, for instance, Bruce was strongly considering withdrawing his men into the hills, thinking it was enough to have bloodied the nose and pride of the English army. After the next day's battle, upon learning that his cousin the Earl of Gloucester had fallen while leading the English vanguard against the Scots, Bruce put aside the jubilation of victory to mourn him. In this regard he is perhaps more reminiscent of Rhaegar Targaryen than Robert Baratheon, an extremely capable warrior who nonetheless knew that war, while sometimes necessary, is always hell.

That is not to say he wasn't very good at it. Robert the Bruce was not just a capable commander but a force to be reckoned with in individual combat. Similar to modern sports stars, there was a widely recognized ranking system for the best warriors in the land. At the time of his death in 1329, Bruce was rated as one of the top three fighters in all Christendom, alongside the Holy Roman Emperor Henry VII and the French knight Giles D'Argentan.[8] A duel between Bruce and Baratheon – the axe and the hammer – would truly be a clash of titans! Bruce's preferred weapon was the axe, a brutally effective tool. A well-made handaxe can crunch bones, even under mail and partial plate armour. Bruce's axe came with a nasty spike which could be driven through the visor of a knight's helm or, when swung with enough force, punch a hole clean through armour like a hungry raven's beak.

Both men's ferocity in battle was driven in part by tremendous personal loss. Robert Baratheon was consumed by the death of Lyanna Stark, and his obsession with exacting revenge on any and all surviving Targaryens was all-consuming. It was a sort of madness in him,[9] and Baratheon often fantasized about the violence he wished he could inflict on Rhaegar, lamenting that he was only able to kill him once.[10] Bruce must have entertained similar fantasies about Edward I and II. In addition to the destruction of much of his lands and the general suffering of the population of Scotland under English military occupation, Bruce had endured loss after loss. Three of his four brothers – Neil, Thomas and Alexander – were given traitor's deaths of the same brutal kind met by Wallace. His steadfast queen Elizabeth de Burgh, as well as his 12-year-old daughter Marjorie and sisters Christina and Mary, were captured at Tain and subjected to brutal imprisonment. Elizabeth and Mary's fates were especially wretched, being held in cages swinging from the walls of Roxburgh and Berwick in all weathers for four miserable years.[11] How they endured, and how Robert must have been tormented by the knowledge of his loved ones' suffering, is beyond reckoning.

Definitive Duels

History is a great diminisher, often reducing entire lives to one or two definitive acts. To the storytellers of Westeros, Robert Baratheon will always be the man who slew Rhaegar Targaryen with one rage-fuelled blow with his hammer. Robert the Bruce, for all his faults, nuances and triumphs, will forever be known to schoolchildren as the king who split Henry de Bohun's head in two with his axe at Bannockburn.

Precisely what occurred between the two warriors will never be known, yet a number of near-contemporary sources such as the *Vita Edwardi Secundi* and Barbour's *The Bruce* allow us to piece together something of what unfolded. Sir Henry, a young and bold knight in his prime, was at the head of the English army, a lumbering beast that stretched out for many miles. The first whiff of action came when the Scots were sighted pulling back from the Tor Wood, where they had been training, to the New Park, where the modern Bannockburn Visitor Centre stands. Sir Henry must have thought himself blessed by the heavens above, for amongst what he saw as rabble was a man mounted on a grey pony and armed with only a handaxe, the golden circlet upon his head unmistakeable in the late morning light: Robert the Bruce, so-called King of Scots.

Heroic moments like these would have been drilled into Sir Henry's head since childhood, and had things gone differently he would have been celebrated – by English chroniclers at least – as a paragon. Sir Henry took his shot at immortality and achieved it, though not in the way he had hoped. His destrier, bred for battle, thundered towards the king with the stab of a spur. A missile made of horseflesh, it shot towards its target with furious momentum. Bruce was expecting no such thing, and when he saw de Bohun's lance levelled towards him, the king had a choice to make that would echo across the centuries. Should he do the prudent thing, withdraw behind his lines and let his men take care of this upstart knight? Or should he ride and meet his enemy head on? With the eyes of his army upon him, this was no true dilemma at all. Bruce charged back.

Barbour relates the moment it all went wrong for de Bohun:

> 'Together charged they galloping.
> Sir Henry missed the noble king!
> And he, that in his stirrups stood,

Lifted his axe, so sharp and good,
And such a mighty stroke he aimed
That neither hat nor helmet stemmed
The force of that tremendous blow.
Down did the bold Sir Henry go.
The hand-axe shaft was broke in two.
His skull was almost cleft right through,
And there he lay, bereft of might.
So fell the first stroke of the fight.'[12]

The reaction of the Scots army must have been like that of a stadium of football fans when their team scores a winning goal in injury time. Nails were surely bit ten to the quick while watching Bruce and de Bohun charge inexorably towards each other, only for the tension to be released in a wave of jubilance at the result. Imagine, too, the emotion that went into that murderous stroke. The rage and despair that Bruce felt at the killing of his brothers, the capture of his wife, sisters and daughter, as well as other compatriots like the Bishop of Glasgow Robert Wishart, was channelled into that axe. No wonder it split de Bohun's head in two.

There are variations on this narrative, though they all end the same way. The *Vita* proposes that upon seeing the king, de Bohun attempted to return to his fellows, only to be cruelly pursued and struck down by Bruce.[13] This seems incredibly reckless on Bruce's part, far more so than the already risky gambit of turning to meet an oncoming knight in full armour. Bruce was never shy about getting stuck in at the front lines, but this version seems more like an attempt to paint de Bohun as the victim of a bloodthirsty king than an accurate record.

The encounter between Bruce and de Bohun was a microcosm of the battle to come, an experienced but materially outmatched Scot against the very picture of English military might in the form of de Bohun. This would not have been lost on Bruce's men. The prospect of victory against Edward's army, which only moments ago seemed impossible to many, was now tangible. Nonetheless, Bruce's captains scolded him for putting himself at risk so brazenly. After all, if Bruce fell, then so too did the Scottish cause. In a laconic response worthy of Bronn the sellsword, Bruce replied that the only thing he regretted was that he had broken his favourite axe in the process.[14]

Rule, Reconciliation and Repentance

It is almost never a good sign to find yourself agreeing with Grandmaester Pycelle, one of the most persistently loathsome characters in *Game of Thrones*. However, he did get it right when he said that 'winning a kingdom and ruling a kingdom are rather different things'.[15] It's a rare individual indeed who can do both capably. Peace was the bane of Robert Baratheon, whose kingdom only held together due to the competency of his small council while he himself became so torpid that he could joke of needing breastplate stretchers to get into his old armour.

If Robert Baratheon failed to understand or care about this principle, then Robert the Bruce certainly did not, proving as capable a statesman as a warrior and being heralded by later generations at the 'Good King Robert'.[16] There are several major accomplishments we can attribute to his reign that make him worthy of the moniker. One of Bruce's proudest moments was the consecration of St Andrews Cathedral on 5 July 1318, four years after his great victory at Bannockburn. Such a sign of prosperity, not to mention holy favour, must have seemed like a just reward for the great suffering and poverty that Scotland had experienced for the past two decades. Bruce, ever stalked by the whims of outrageous fortune, suffered even through this – for it was at the time of the consecration that he learned of the death of his last surviving brother in Ireland. As ever, he persisted. The Declaration of Arbroath, one of the most significant documents in Western political history, was issued in Bruce's name to the pope at Avignon in 1320. Amongst other things, including the blood-stirring line about resisting English rule until but 100 Scots remain alive, it challenged the notion of divine right to rule and laid out an early form of social contract between king and kingdom. The culmination of Bruce's efforts and sacrifices finally came in 1328, just one year before his death, with the ratification of the Treaty of Edinburgh-Northampton. The treaty recognized Scotland as a fully independent kingdom, and Robert the Bruce and his heirs as its lawful rulers, though Edward III of England would not long keep his word after Bruce's passing.

While Bruce was a grievous enemy to make, as the Comyns and MacDougalls learned, he could also be magnanimous to those who fought against him. The most successful example of this is undoubtedly his nephew Thomas Randolph, who initially fought for the English but was captured and brought, spitting defiance, before Bruce by James Douglas in 1308. Randolph would go on to be one of Bruce's most ardent and effective captains, engaging in a game of one-upmanship with Douglas that spanned twenty years and shifted the balance of war in Scotland's favour. In other cases the blood was not yet dry before Bruce sought reconciliation. Philip Mowbray, the commander of Stirling Castle at the time of the Battle of Bannockburn, surrendered the castle to Bruce after denying the defeated Edward II shelter inside. Bruce, recognizing that Mowbray had acted with honour, gave him the option of returning home or joining his ranks. Mowbray chose the latter and 'loyally maintained his faith until his very day of death',[17] which he met while fighting at the side of Bruce's brother Edward in Ireland at the Battle of Faughart in 1318.

Robert Baratheon, too, recognized the value of bringing enemies from old wars onside as allies for new ones. Ser Barristan Selmy, a member of the Mad King's Kingsguard and one of the greatest swordsmen to ever live, was gravely wounded fighting on the Targaryen side at the Battle of the Trident. Though Robert was also injured from his duel with Rhaegar, he insisted that his own maester tend to Ser Barristan, a man who would have cut him down on sight mere hours before.[18] Admittedly this was mostly motivated by Robert's admiration for anyone who could make battle into an art, as only legends like Ser Barristan the Bold and Ser Arthur Dayne, the Sword of the Morning, could. The restraint with which Robert Baratheon treated Balon Greyjoy after his failed rebellion, however, hints at a deeper commitment to reconciliation.

On that note, both kings ended their lives in a way that seems at odds with how they lived them. They did so not with calls for revenge on their enemies or for wars to see through, but with attempts at spiritual redemption. Having spent so much of his life with little else in his heart but hate for the Targaryens, Robert Baratheon ended it with a plea to spare the life of Daenerys. This about-face seems motivated at least in part by a concern for legacy. Robert is concerned that he will be remembered as being as bad as the Mad King, and asks for mercy from the gods.[19] Robert the Bruce also feared for his legacy and soul, which is why the final task he set for his companions was to bring his heart to Jerusalem as a posthumous act of penance.[20] Perhaps there was more than a hint of Bruce's conciliatory and devout spirit in Baratheon after all.

Both kings also left behind a legacy that is more complex than the simplified personas often ascribed to them, and which had profound implications for their realms following their deaths. For all their might, neither could secure the safety of their kingdoms or heirs beyond their own lifetimes, and the seeds they sowed during their reigns often resulted in what international relations theorists term blowback – the unforeseen yet logical negative consequences of past actions. The Seven Kingdoms plunged into the War of the Five Kings within days of Robert Baratheon's undoing by a boar, in no small part due to concerns about the legitimacy of King Joffrey's parentage and the dynastic rivalries that festered under the king's administrative negligence. Within three years of Robert the Bruce's death in 1329, all but five Scottish castles would fall to an invasion force led by Edward Balliol, the vengeance-seeking son of the man whom Bruce murdered in 1306, sponsored by Edward III of England. Scotland recovered faster from this fallout than the Seven Kingdoms seem set to, perhaps thanks to Bruce's emphasis on nation-building in his latter years; in contrast, can the chaos that engulfed Westeros be blamed, in part, on Robert Baratheon's total lack of interest in governance? We are faced with deciding the legacy of two kings, both of whom showed heroism of the highest order while also committing acts of extreme violence whose repercussions would haunt those who survived them. Robert the Bruce, nearly 700 years after his death, is almost universally regarded as a hero-king. What will the maesters say of Robert Baratheon, the warrior-king whose kingdom crumbled? Only Martin knows.

PART IV

THE WHEELS
OF WAR

Chapter 14

Under Siege

Heroes are born on the battlements, at least if the legends can be believed. Nothing distils the perils of medieval war, or the journey of the protagonist in a historical or fantasy epic, like getting stuck into a siege. A forlorn few separated from the ravenous multitude by only a few feet of stone is so engrained in our collective consciousness as the most dramatic way to convey impossible odds that it is often the only note that films and books in the genre can satisfactorily end on. From the Battle of the Hornburg in *The Lord of the Rings: The Two Towers* to *Game of Thrones'* own Battle of Castle Black or Battle of the Blackwater, the siege is here to stay as the storytelling spectacle *par excellence*.

If the truth got out, there would be far less enthusiasm. The sorry reality – which Martin goes out of his way to repeatedly call attention to – is that sieges, the most common form of medieval warfare aside from raids, were often inglorious at best and downright miserable at worst. Getting involved in one was far more likely to end with death from dysentery or starvation than with anything worth putting in a song. Bronn the sellsword hit closest to the mark, as he tends to, when he told Tyrion before the Battle of the Blackwater that during a siege it isn't the fighting that kills most people, but the starving and the desperation that precedes it.[1] Also the boredom. Everyone knows that war is hell; what the stories and songs don't tell you is how mind-numbingly tedious sieges and campaigning can be. A bored guard is a negligent – or at worst a bribable – guard, and over the course of most sieges there were plenty of opportunities to exploit the inclination towards both negligence and self-preservation. The siege of Stirling Castle that led to the Battle of Bannockburn, for instance, endured from the autumn of 1313 to Midsummer's Day 1314, while the aptly named Lang (long) Siege of Edinburgh Castle dragged on for two years, during which either side could do little except take occasional pot-shots at each other.

Recall that Dumbarton Rock, one of the mightiest forts in Scotland, fell to the infamous Ivar the Boneless and his Norsemen not due to a direct assault but because after many weeks the fort's well ran dry and the defenders surrendered out of thirst. In *Game of Thrones*, the suffering of Stannis' famished garrison at Storm's End, relieved only by Davos Seaworth smuggling onions and other supplies in with his skilful sailing, is far more representative of the reality of siege warfare than the grand spectacle of battles like the Blackwater or Castle Black. It wasn't pretty, noble or honourable; it was tedious, miserable and desperate. You can see why producers tend to prefer more climactic alternatives.

How to Crack a Castle

Thankfully, for us as observers at least, there are plenty of examples from history to break the monotony. One of the earliest recorded attacks on a Scottish castle was the Norse assault on Rothesay Castle on the Isle of Bute in 1230. The Stewart defenders, whose arms still adorn signs and lampposts on the island today, were besieged by a ravenous army of Norsemen led by Gillespec, grandson of the mighty Somerled, King of the Isles.[2] For three days the circular curtain wall of the castle held out as the Norse landed their longships nearby and assailed it furiously from all sides. Eventually, so the story goes, the Norse used their great bearded axes to hew right through the relatively soft stone of the wall. Imagine thinking yourself safe behind a wall only for your enemy to start simply hacking through it – if it did indeed happen, the effect on the defenders' morale must have been devastating. The castle still bears a gaping wound on its south-west side that possibly attests to it. Rothesay Castle was stormed and its garrison likely received all the mercy you would expect from men who had just cut through walls with nothing but axes. There is no direct equivalent of this happening in *Game of Thrones*, though it sounds like the kind of thing a Thenn would try.

Aside from that admirably unorthodox approach, there are plenty of excellent demonstrations of the principles of a siege in both the show and books, covering most of the strategies that were actually employed. Ladders were perhaps the most straightforward means – after all, for every wall there is a ladder at least as tall. We see siege ladders employed during the Battle of the Blackwater by Stannis' army. Scaling a stretch of wall with ladders in a direct assault was deadly work, as Stannis' men learned as they were cut down by arrows and had their heads bashed in by rocks thrown from the battlements above. While a commander could choose to accept these losses, the best way to use ladders was with stealth. Thomas Randolph was able to retake mighty Edinburgh Castle this way on 14 March 1314 by climbing the perilous Castle Rock and using rope ladders to get over the walls. Nowadays there are nets which prevent climbers from scaling the rock, but within living memory of the time of writing it was something of a rite of passage for Edinburgh schoolchildren to make the climb. Barbour's *Bruce* tells of a local man, William Francis, who showed the way to Randolph, having lived in the castle in his youth and climbed the Rock many times to visit his sweetheart in the town below:

> 'And I was a little licentious,
> And loved a wench here in the town.
> So that I might, all unbeknown,
> Repair to her lodgings privily,
> I made a rope-ladder secretly,
> And over the wall I slid thereby.
> A narrow crevice followed I,
> That I had noticed from above.
> Thus, often, went I to my love.'[3]

Edinburgh Castle Rock may look insurmountable, but since time immemorial all it took was the right motivation.

Rather than going over a castle's walls, with the right experts to hand you could also try going under. Siege mines were amongst the most feared methods of assault, for once one was begun there was often little a defender could do but watch as the tunnel progressed excruciatingly slowly and inexorably towards the wall. Engineers would dig a passage into the earth or stone upon which a castle wall rested, ideally starting from far enough away so as to be beyond bowshot. Timber frames were constructed within the tunnel to keep it from collapsing until the tunnel was under the wall itself, at which point the timbers would be set ablaze and the collapsing tunnel would bring down the masonry above. In *Game of Thrones*, mines were used at the siege of Storm's End by the Lannister-Tyrell alliance, though Ser Loras Tyrell, the 'Knight of Flowers', lacked the patience to wait for them to work and instead led a conventional assault.[4] He seized the castle but was also gravely injured. Had he been a little more patient, it's likely that the garrison would have surrendered once their wall was undermined.

While not for the faint of heart, one of the most unique experiences you can have at any Scottish castle is to delve down into the siege mines used in the assault on St Andrews Castle in 1546-47. They are the only accessible siege mines in Europe, and few places convey the sweat and blood that went into medieval warfare like they do. The mine, whose entrance is directly underneath the street that now passes by the castle, has stone-cut steps and is large enough for pack animals to have been brought in to help clear the rubble more quickly.[5] It's surprisingly spacious. Compared to the countermine, it is as an open field to a prison cell. The defenders, who included a young John Knox, decided not to stand helplessly by as the mine, and therefore defeat, crept nearer, but to intercept it with a tunnel of their own. The desperation of those who toiled away in it is hard to fathom. To enter you must crouch and crawl your way through its confines, and at no point in the countermine is it possible for even a child to fully stand. Two false starts were made before the defenders managed to get it right, which must have been infuriating given the time-sensitive nature of their ordeal. The look on both sides' faces in the moment when an exhausted defender burst through into the attacking mine with a swing of his pick must have been one for the ages.

Time and again we see that the best way to take a castle was not through brute force, but with a little creativity and a lot of luck. Crawling through the sewers and latrine chutes of Casterly Rock may not have been the most dignified way for Daenerys' Unsullied to capture the Lannisters' supposedly impregnable home base, but Tyrion was more than willing to trade a little dignity for efficacy. Scotland's own James 'the Black' Douglas would have heartily approved. On 19 February 1314, he seized Roxburgh Castle, one of the strongest castles in all the land, by pretending to be a cow. Douglas and several dozen companions wore black cloaks over their armour and, with the aid of the low February light, crawled on hands and knees in meandering zigzags, doing their best impressions of the local black cows (which were far smaller than modern cattle, so it's not quite as absurd as it sounds).[6] They were then able to overcome the unready watchmen and remove one of the greatest thorns in the side of Robert the Bruce's hold on the south. Oh, to hear the tales that Douglas and Tyrion could share over some Dornish red!

If none of those other options appealed or proved fruitful, you could almost always pay the gold price rather than the iron or steel one to make a castle yours. While gold leads to many betrayals great and small in *Game of Thrones* – Dany is betrayed for gold by Hizdahr zo Loraq in Meereen, and Littlefinger pays off the Gold Cloaks to capture Ned Stark, for instance – nobody in the series outright buys their way into a castle. In reality it was such a common tactic that it's surprising that no one, especially the Lannisters, have tried it. One true story of betrayal did, however, end with the traitor receiving a golden reward à la Viserys Targaryen at the hands of Khal Drogo. In 1306, the Prince of Wales Edward Caernarvon, the future Edward II, laid siege to Kildrummy Castle, one of the premier castles of the north. Barbour boasted that it was 'impossible to take' by conventional assault, and as the siege dragged on it seemed that those words may have rung true. It was undone from within when the castle's blacksmith, Osborne, was successfully bribed by the prince. Osborne set fire to Kildrummy's grain stores, which were in the hall, and the blaze intensified to such a degree that even the English soldiers outside the walls were forced to pull back by the searing heat. Sir Neil Bruce, Robert the Bruce's brother, held the castle and was given a traitor's death by the English. Sure that he had earned the reward he was promised, Osborne sought payment from Prince Edward, only to have molten gold poured down his throat.[7]

Another tactic, employed with trademark ineptitude by the Freys at the siege of Riverrun, was to threaten to execute noble prisoners unless the garrison surrendered. A pathetic spectacle plays itself day in and day out as Edmure Tully, the groom of the Red Wedding, is brought up to the gallows and threatened with hanging unless his uncle, Brynden 'the Blackfish', opens the gates to the Tullys' otherwise unassailable ancestral seat. Knowing full well that the Freys lack the spine to follow through, Brynden ignores them and takes solace in the simple arithmetic of the siege: the defenders in Riverrun have nearly inexhaustible supplies – enough, he says, for two years – while the attackers' resources diminish with every passing day. Besides, he later scoffs, 'Sieges are dull', and at least it was something to break the monotony.[8]

One of the more memorable acts of defiance in Scotland's long tradition of them was every bit a match for Brynden's wry rebuff. With all but five of the castles in Scotland having fallen to the English and Edward Balliol in the 1330s, Lady Agnes' situation appeared dire indeed. Popularly known as 'Black Agnes' for her olive skin, dark hair and formidable character, she was besieged in Dunbar Castle by the Earl of Salisbury in 1338. Dunbar was once one of the most powerful redoubts in southern Scotland; for that very reason it was systematically destroyed and now stands as little more than a few stony spires clinging to the rocks of Dunbar Harbour. But not on Agnes' watch.

When Salisbury had siege equipment including mangonels and battering rams known as sows shipped in from England, most commanders would have despaired. Instead, after Salisbury's war machines did their worst, Agnes would calmly walk the battlements with her handmaids in their linens to delicately dust off the spots where projectiles had hit their mark. She taunted her besiegers with curses, songs and even prophecies, foretelling that 'the Thistle would out-thorn the Rose', portending the ascension of the Stuart King of Scotland, James VI, to the throne of England with the death of the last Tudor monarch, Elizabeth I, in 1603.[13] Salisbury sent a sow forward to batter down the gates, but Agnes simply dropped a large chunk of masonry from the wall which shattered the ram and killed the men operating it.[14] In a direct echo of Edmure Tully's ordeal at Riverrun, Salisbury even brought Agnes' brother, John Randolph, within sight of the walls and threatened to hang him if she did not surrender. Agnes called his bluff in astonishing fashion, telling Salisbury that she would be most thankful if he did for she would then inherit the powerful Earldom of Moray. John was probably a little nonplussed to say the least, but Salisbury backed down and John survived the siege. For five months it went on, with Agnes little worse for wear, until at last the doom of almost every aggressor in history arrived – winter. The English were forced to withdraw and Black Agnes became not only the pride of Dunbar, but one of the most tenacious champions of Scotland's Wars of Independence. If ever a Scottish hero was indeed born on the battlements, it was Black Agnes.

Anatomy of a Donjon

Shifting into the realm of defence – the function of castles that usually springs to mind first – let's explore one of the most ingeniously designed towers in Scotland, Bothwell Castle. Built of red sandstone on a rocky outcrop above the River Clyde near Uddingston, Bothwell would have been Scotland's largest castle if war had not broken out and disrupted its founder's best-laid plans. Even as a ruin it is exceptionally impressive, heralded by the antiquarian W.D. Simpson as 'the grandest piece of secular architecture that the Middle Ages have bequeathed to us in Scotland'.[9] In terms of defence, Bothwell's donjon – a great round tower corrupted in English into dungeon – is nothing shy of genius. The *donjon* was separated from the courtyard by a moat cut from the sandstone bedrock which was crossed by a drawbridge. This drawbridge would retract into the 'beak', a stone projection at the side of the *donjon* which housed the entrance, thereby adding yet another layer to the already 5-metre-thick walls. The beak itself is angled away from the courtyard, from which enemies would approach, in such a way that it would have been nearly impossible to bring a battering ram or other siege engine to bear against the awkwardly angled gate.[10] Anyone trying to force their way in would have to deal with a barrage of missiles and boiling liquids hurled from an overhanging stone or wooden projection called a hoarding, positioned directly above the entrance. Similar hoardings are seen at *Game of Thrones'* Castle Black and are used to deadly effect when the wildlings attack the Wall; more real-world examples of this type of defence can be found at Threave Castle, Hermitage Castle and even smaller castles like Preston Tower. Two crosslet arrow slits in the *donjon's* walls covered the courtyard and drawbridge, providing archers with additional opportunities to make the task of assaulting Bothwell a miserable one.

Once inside, the travails of the attacker were far from over. They would have had to pass at most two abreast through a zigzag corridor, severely restricting movement. This feature, somewhat surprisingly given its obvious defensive merit, is thought to be unique amongst the castles of Scotland and England.[11] If they could then fight their way single-file up the tight turnpike stairway then the castle's holders would likely consider fleeing, and this too was all planned for. A secret passage led from the lord's bedchamber on the top floor of the *donjon* to a sheltered wall-walk, where they could make their way to the adjoining prison tower and escape via an external stair at the postern gate. The triangular grooves for this wall-walk can still be seen near the top of the *donjon*, though the wall-walk itself is no more.

To further impress just how thoroughly both defence and comfort were thought through, the donjon's *garderobes* (toilet chambers) had chutes leading down the wall's exterior in such a way that water from the moat could be channelled to cleanse them. These chutes could theoretically be used to access the castle, but a barrier pillar guarded them against the small but not unprecedented chance – like the one that Tyrion exploited when taking Casterly Rock for Daenerys – that some poor soul would attempt the pungent climb![12]

A Siege Worthy of a Song

Every now and then sieges did live up to our modern, climactic expectations of them. Bothwell was besieged in 1301 in an operation that included thousands of soldiers, siege towers and all the panoply of war we have come to expect at sieges. One of the best documented sieges in Scottish history was Edward I's assault on the shield of the south, Caerlaverock Castle, in 1300. Caerlaverock, which means 'fort of the lark' and uses the common Welsh prefix for fortified sites, *Caer*, is the quintessential picture of the medieval castle. It is entirely surrounded by a broad moat, traversable only across a drawbridge, and bristles with arrow slits, a murder hole and machicolations. The Solway Firth, with its treacherous sinking sands, and the River Nith lay nearby, making the surrounding ground so soft that the first castle built by the Maxwells in the early thirteenth century sank into the clay. The walls they raised 200 yards away are unique, for Caerlaverock is Britain's only triangular castle. Approaching them head-on or, better yet, from a bird's eye view, it appears as a great shield planted in the ground.

Caerlaverock is a near-perfect shrunken version of *Game of Thrones'* Riverrun, the great Tully Castle in the Riverlands. According to Brynden 'the Blackfish', Riverrun was the product of the same sort of cunning logic that compelled the Freys to build their bridge and castles at the Twins – soldiers can't swim.[15] Accordingly, Brynden's ancestors built a castle at the junction of two rivers, the Red Fork of the Trident and the Tumblestone. The rivers provided protection on three sides, but to cut off the western approach to the castle the Tullys built a moat that could be flooded at will. This innovation turned Riverrun into an island stronghold that could hold out indefinitely so long as the garrison's bellies were full, attested to by the fact that it has never been taken by force in its 1,000-year history.[16] While Caerlaverock Castle does not stand at the confluence of two rivers like Riverrun (though nearby Threave Castle, another very good fit for Riverrun, does), the moat dug around it effectively made it an island, too. The gatehouses of both Riverrun and Caerlaverock are protected by two massive drum towers, and the entire length of both castles' walls have battlements. If any castle in the south of Scotland could prove Ned Stark's adage true – that fifty men inside a castle are worth 500 outside one[17] – it was Caerlaverock.

Its defenders in 1300 would have preferred those odds. Edward I of England was not only the 'Hammer of the Scots', but an undisputed master of siege warfare.[18] The old lion brought a fearsome arsenal to the walls of Caerlaverock, numbering at least 3,000 footsoldiers and eighty-seven knights. Each of the nobles involved are described in the remarkable *Roll of Caerlaverock*, a document composed by a herald in Edward's camp that is one of the best first-hand accounts of a medieval siege in existence. Edward brought not just soldiers but specialized engineers, carpenters and miners under the direction of a fighting friar, Brother Robert.[19] So long as Caerlaverock's walls held there was little that could truly threaten the defenders, but their anxiety must have grown as Brother Robert built a ram, a siege tower, a small stone-hurling device called the robinet and, most daunting of all, three huge trebuchets.[20] The robinet incessantly harassed the garrison, hurling so many stones that they were collected and dropped back down on any attackers who reached the gate. As the trebuchets took on their menacing form, several direct assaults were launched against the walls, but to little avail. Knights scrambled for glory while 'huge stones and bolts and arrows rained down upon them till they reeled'.[21] Many were wounded and slain in the attempt, and the raw valour of Edward's knights alone proved no match against the castle's red walls.

Then, with a loud roar like a waking giant, the trebuchets flung into action. It is possible that one of them was none other than Edward's pride and joy, the dreaded *Loup-de-guerre* or 'War Wolf', then the largest trebuchet in all of Europe. So large that it filled thirty wagons when unpacked, the War Wolf could hurl 200lb projectiles with unparalleled force at a rate of about ten per day.[22] It and its smaller counterparts threw no fewer than ninety such missiles at Caerlaverock on the first day of the siege, shaking loose the stones of the castle's towers and sweeping the defenders from the ramparts. After two days of constant bombardment and regular attempts to storm the walls with sheer numbers alone, one of the trebuchet shots caved in the roof of the gatehouse. The garrison, bloodied and beleaguered, had no choice but to submit themselves to the mercy of the notoriously unmerciful King Edward.

The king had borne witness to many wonders during his well-travelled life, but what he saw next was one of the most remarkable spectacles in his long career. As the defenders marched with heads held high out from the ruins of Caerlaverock's gatehouse, the English could not believe their eyes – there were only sixty of them. For two days a group that would be annihilated with a single hail of arrows in the open field managed to fend off the might and genius of one of the greatest commanders and fighting forces in all of Europe. Accounts are conflicted as to their fate. The herald behind the *Roll of Caerlaverock* insisted that, marvelling at the bravery of these noble few, Edward spared them and even dressed them in fresh garments before allowing them to leave.[23] Given Edward's history, which as we have seen included the massacre of over 7,000 civilians at Berwick as recently as 1296, this seems unlikely. The account in the *Lanercost Chronicle* is probably closer to the truth, which is that most were hanged while some were spared to spread tales of terror throughout Scotland of Edward's castle-smashing war machines.[24] Still, despite their ultimate defeat, the defenders of Caerlaverock had taught a bloody lesson in the ability of a good castle to defy, if even for a time, impossible odds. Never mind Ned Stark's boast that a castle could allow fifty to stand against 500; at Caerlaverock, sixty stood against 3,000.

Chapter 15

Raiders in the Riverlands

Most people in Westeros don't seem to be particularly enjoying themselves. It's little wonder, what with the countless miseries inflicted on them. The true scourge of the common people in *Game of Thrones* is not the big set-piece battles that tend to close out each season, but the much more pernicious rhythm of violence carried out through raids and banditry in the absence of justice. Calling it 'low-intensity' or 'low-level' warfare is a disservice to its victims. The countless common folk in the Riverlands terrorized by Gregor Clegane and the Bloody Mummers, or the women hanged by Stark bannermen encountered by Brienne and Jaime, are no less dead than the soldiers who fought at the Blackwater or Battle of the Bastards. That is the unglamorous, and certainly unchivalrous, reality of medieval warfare.

Aside from the oft-heralded but exceptionally rare pitched battles, warfare from prehistory through to the early modern period mostly consisted of raids, skirmishes and lightning strikes into enemy territory. These enterprises were largely carried out by groups numbering in the tens or hundreds rather than the thousands, and the theatre of war was predominantly on a local rather than national or international scale.[1] The object of this type of warfare was not to capture a key stronghold or defeat an opponent in one fell swoop like in a field battle, but rather to chip away at an enemy's resources by destroying productive lands, put pressure on population centres through the displacement of people from the countryside and undermine a foe's authority by targeting those who they are supposed to protect.

In the vast majority of cases, as with the Scots' raids into the north of England during the reign of Robert the Bruce, conquest was not the objective of these expeditions. Instead, raids could be used to bring an enemy – even a materially superior enemy – to the negotiating table, where you could achieve favourable terms that your opponent would never otherwise consider. This was the case with the Treaty of Edinburgh-Northampton in 1328, which recognized Scotland's independent sovereignty, something that English kings had stubbornly refused to concede for centuries and which was brought about in large part by the Scots' seasonal devastation of the northern shires. The suffering brought about by this type of warfare should never be underestimated. Northumberland in particular suffered considerable depopulation and, in the words of G.W.S. Barrow, one of Scotland's greatest historians, was 'reduced to a miserable anarchy'.[2]

An excellent example from *Game of Thrones* is the harrying of the Riverlands by Ser Gregor 'the Mountain' Clegane on the orders of Tywin Lannister. After Jaime Lannister's defeat and capture by Robb Stark at the Wolfswood, Tywin commanded Ser Gregor to 'head out with 500 riders and set the Riverlands on fire from the God's Eye to the Red Fork'.[3] Tywin knew that such a force would never be able to capture a power centre like Riverrun, but he hoped that the sustained pressure on some of the northern alliance's most productive lands would erode Robb's ability to continue the war. Westeros has no paucity of other examples of professional marauders: the Bloody Mummers, dispatched by Clegane from Harrenhal, and the Brotherhood Without Banners, who were originally appointed by Ned Stark to end Clegane's raids, are two of the most notable groups from either side of the war. That's an important point: all sides, whether Stark and Lannister or Scottish and English, participated in this kind of sustained terrorization. No one can claim to have clean hands, no matter how much we may want to divide antagonists up along the simple yet false dichotomy of heroes and villains.

Nowhere else in Scotland or England blurred the lines between the two quite like the Borders. The lands where two hostile nations meet will always be places of suffering for the common people, and this was true of those living on both sides of the border, where the constant threat of violence and impoverishment was a fact of life.[4] It wasn't always this way. The Borders were a place of relative peace until the outbreak of the Wars of Independence in the late thirteenth century. The Lowlands – particularly the Borders and Lothians – were scourged time and again in the years to come, and this repeated abrasion allowed only the toughest grit to survive.

Much is made of the hardiness of Highlanders, yet the high moors of the Cheviot Hills and the dark recesses of the Ettrick Forest are every bit as inhospitable as the most rugged northern glen. Many a modern adventurer, myself included, have made the mistake of underestimating the Borders, expecting to find a landscape of tranquil hills and sunlit valleys. It is indeed a beautiful area, yet its beauty is not timid. It is, instead, a landscape of windswept moors, treacherous mosses, high roads relentlessly exposed to the elements and deep-cut rivers that tax the endurance of the fittest walkers and cyclists.[5] This was the perfect landscape for the bandit, who could find innumerable hideouts and hidden passes, and could descend on an unsuspecting farm or village with the speed of the winds upon the hillsides. Though many now call them home and remember them fondly, historically the Borders were no country for old men.

Wherever the border between Scotland and England was fixed, be it where it has stood since the fifteenth century or 100 miles further south, that land would have become a battleground. The residents of towns like Hawick, Peebles, Langholm and Lockerbie were the victims not of geography but more specifically of political geography. There is nothing inherent about these places, or the people in them, that fated them to become centres of banditry, though it is admittedly easier going for outlaws here than in the more placid lands of the Lothians to the north. The simple fact that they stood on the frontier between two nations more often at war with each other than not meant that what we call the Borders became one of Europe's most persistently violent regions. In the event of war, they were the first to be struck. One can pity the twelfth-century builders of the magnificent Borders abbeys, such as Melrose, Jedburgh, Kelso and Dryburgh, for little could they know that they were building on the most tumultuous man-made fault line in Britain.

The extent of the devastation is difficult to come to terms with. During the Earl of Hertford's campaign into Scotland in 1544 as part of the 'Rough Wooing', the butcher's bill counted 192 towns, towers, churches and farmsteads burnt, over 400 Scots slain and more than 12,000 sheep killed or taken.[6] It would take years for the Borders to recover from such a ravaging, and by then the next round would likely have already begun. To many there would seem to be little point in trying to live a peaceful life in these circumstances. John Leslie, the sixteenth-century Bishop of Ross, wrote: '[O]n the restoration of peace, they entirely neglect to cultivate their lands, though fertile, from the fear of the fruits of their labour being immediately destroyed by the new war.'[7] Violence begat violence, as the victims of raids and campaigns soon took up arms in hopelessness and themselves became the perpetrators.

Life Outside the King's Laws

The Borders were so estranged from the authority of either the Scots or English crown that a whole specialized system of regional governance had to be established to try – mostly in vain – to bring the region to heel.[8] In 1286, six Scottish knights and six English knights met and set down the terms of the *Leges Marchiarum*, or Law of the Marches, which was confirmed the following year and went beyond the remit of the national laws of both countries. Under the terms of the *Leges Marchiarum*, both sides of the Border were split into three areas, or Marches, with each March – the East, West and Middle – governed by a warden. On the Scottish side of the border it was necessary to go one step further and appoint a Keeper of Liddesdale,[9] an area centred around the menacing Hermitage Castle that more than earned its moniker of being the 'bloodiest valley in Britain'. There was also an area extending from the Solway Firth to Langholm known as the Debateable Lands which were so porous and fought over that they became a sort of no-man's land.

We have to remember that until as recently as the middle of the seventeenth century at the earliest, the concept of national allegiance was far less absolute than it is today. Scottish and English nobility commonly held lands in Scotland, England and France, with homage being paid to the kings of each realm without any stigma of treachery or duplicity. The loyalties that these nobles held had far more to do with personal obligations and allegiances than national identity.[10] Most Borderers thought nothing of raiding what we now think of as 'their own side' – after all, the boundary lines on maps are for more absolute than the rolling hills of the Cheviots, where large swathes of Scotland and England, not to mention the people living there, were, and to an extent remain, indistinguishable from one another. By the end of the fifteenth century, it was common for expeditions to carry multiple sets of banners and even wear both the cross of St Andrew and that of St George, allowing them to 'be Scottishe when they will, and English at their pleasure'.[11]

The Law of the Marches tried to account for this, with many acts being treasonable in the Borders including the selling of weapons, arms and horses across the Border, intermarrying without the express permission of your warden or assisting raiders from 'the other side'.[12] The reality, however, was that the vast majority of transgressions went ignored or unpunished. Sometimes the need to appear to appear loyal and law-abiding led to almost farcical scenes. Alistair Moffat records how one sixteenth-century Borderer on the English side, Sandie Armstrong, was so fed up with the lack of protection afforded by local authorities that he threatened to become a Scot if things didn't improve.[13] Reaching levels of absurdity that would make Monty Python blush, an account of the Battle of Pinkie in 1547 reported that Scots and English Borderers were seen openly and amicably conversing with each other in the middle of the battlefield. When they realized that they had been spotted, they put on a good show by pretending to attack each other, though 'they strike few strokes but by assent and appointment'.[14]

In practice, enforcing laws in such a society proved futile more often than not. Communities would organize into graynes, a sort of extended kin group broadly comparable to modern organized crime families. Allegiance to your grayne came before allegiance to the king and warden, and blood feuds developed between graynes that could endure for generations. If one grayne was harmed by another, the aggrieved party would rally their companions and seek revenge by burning homesteads, pillaging villages and stealing livestock, mostly at night by the light of the moon to conceal their plots and movements.[15] Historians have made much of the incessant feuds between Highland clans, using it as an example of their supposed barbarism, yet the Borderers were, if anything, even more deeply drawn into this spiral of cyclical violence. Many young men with little to do and less to lose had no other option but to join in and add their blood to this toxic brew. If your surname is Armstrong, Bell, Bourne, Elliot, Graham, Irvine, Johnstone, Kerr, Maxwell, Nixon, Robson or Scott (amongst many others), you can likely count them amongst your less than noble ancestors.[16]

This cycle of raiding became so institutionalized by the sixteenth century that the English language acquired several words from it that are widely used today, over 400 years after the Borders were pacified. The men who engaged in this life of coordinated banditry were known as Reivers. To be a victim of their violence – for instance, to have your cattle stolen or one of your kinsmen hurt or killed by them – was to be 'bereaved'. Perhaps George R.R. Martin was aware of this when he titled a chapter from the point of view of the dreaded ironborn captain Victarion Greyjoy 'The Reaver' in *A Feast for Crows*.[17] The other term we inherited from the Reivers is no more friendly. The Reivers were experts at extracting wealth from the terrified population. Tenant farmers could pay off bands of Reivers in exchange for being kept off the list of targets. Some agreements even offered protection from other groups of Reivers. This was not some nickel and dime operation but a massive enterprise that could extend for many miles beyond a Reiver's homelands, with one group of Scottish Reivers extracting protection monies as far south as Morpeth, just a few miles north of Newcastle.[18] This probably sounds familiar to anyone who has watched gangster films where thugs threaten small business owners along the lines of 'it would be a shame if something were to happen to this place'. The word, you will no doubt have already guessed, is 'blackmail', which translates literally as 'black rent'. Blackmail was practised openly and unapologetically, and a tenant farmer or small landholder could be paying blackmail to several groups of Reivers at once. If making a living was already difficult enough in medieval and early modern Scotland, it was doubly so in the Borders.

Ride of the Reivers

The raiding season was autumn to spring, when the Reivers were not busy tending to what lands they held. To begin a raid, men would assemble at a meeting place known as a tryst and hammer out the details. The average reiving party numbered a few dozen, though far greater numbers could be raised in exceptional circumstances with extraordinary speed that could put formal armies to shame. Johnnie Armstrong, one of the most successful and therefore infamous of the sixteenth-century Reivers, was apparently able to muster 3,000 cavalrymen in a matter of hours,[19] which, if true, would equal the number of mounted men that followed Edward II to Bannockburn – and it took Edward many weeks and much coercing to make it so. Johnnie's Reivers, however, were no knights on heavy destriers but lightly equipped men on exceptionally hardy mounts. Some of the best light cavalry in the world come from the Scottish Borders, with their small but sturdy mounts, known as Galloway nags, being nearly indefatigable and capable of traversing terrain that would prove challenging even for men on foot. Their riders wore a padded vest known as a jack, which is where we get the word jacket, as well as an open-faced helm. They wielded a wide array of arms, combining more traditional melee weapons such as 8-10ft-long steel-tipped lances, basket-hilted swords, dirks, polearms such as the popular Jedburgh stave and gunpowder weapons like wheel-lock pistols for the wealthiest of them.[20] This made them a very flexible fighting force, and Borderers were often employed in formal warfare to harass enemy lines, raid supply trains and generally cause as much inconvenience as they could. The reiving culture of the Borders was a nightmare for administrators, yet it also produced what were arguably the finest guerrilla fighters of their time.[21]

Once assembled, the Reivers would set out, all on horseback, towards their target, which could be upwards of 50 miles away from their tryst point. Though comparisons to *Game of Thrones*' Dothraki are probably too much of a stretch, the Borderers were renowned for their skill on horseback and the extent to which they lived their lives in the saddle. Given that their livelihood was the long-distance lightning raid, the horse was by far the Reiver's most treasured possession, being the terrestrial equivalent of the *birlinn* war galleys for Scotland's Islesmen. Jean Froissart, a fourteenth-century chronicler, reported that a determined group of Scottish raiders could cover 60-70 miles one-way in a single outing by day or night.[22] This was hungry work, and the Reivers came prepared. Any modern Scot will instantly recognize the Reiver's preferred snack for the road, as described by Froissart:

> 'each of them carries a flat stone under his saddle flaps, and a little bag of oatmeal behind the saddle: when they have eaten so much meat that their stomachs feel weak and ill, they put the stone on a fire and mix a little oatmeal with water. When the stone is hot, they lay this thin paste on it and make a little cake, like a biscuit.'[23]

The Scottish love affair with oatcakes, it seems, is long-established and battle-tested.

Their hunger sated, the Reivers would descend on their target and seek to steal pretty much anything that was of worth and portable. Livestock, the primary currency of much of the rural medieval world, was the main but by no means exclusive quarry. Metal tools and wares, cloth and victuals were also prized. Unlike with the military campaigns of England in the Scottish Borders or the Scots campaigns on the English side, the human cost of reiving expeditions was usually rather low. Buildings would be set alight, flocks of animals driven off and the land itself greatly despoiled, but relatively few people were killed.[24] There were, however, episodes of extreme violence. Following an assault on Lockerbie by the Johnstones against their hated rivals the Maxwells, the downward slashes inflicted on the heads and faces of reiving victims by mounted assailants became known throughout the Borders as 'Lockerbie Licks'.[25] After the battle, known as the Battle of Dryfe Sands, Lord Johnstone recovered Lord Maxwell's body and 'did cut af baith his hands, and careit the same with thayme on speir points, as a memorial of his perfidie'.[26] Consider, too, the very real human costs of material devastation. Sir Robert Bowes tallied the total cost of Scots' reiving in the English Marches for just one year, 1597, at £93,000 – equal to between fifteen and twenty million pounds today.[27] That's a lot of livestock and essentials that the residents of the Marches would have to go without, leading inevitably to malnourishment, starvation and more and more men abandoning the plough for the sword to add to the cycle of violence.

The Price of Peace

The tumult that 'shook loose the Border' for over 300 years began with the death of a king and ended with the ascension of another. Though Scotland and Britain would see many wars yet to come, including the devastating War of the Three Kingdoms and the Jacobite Risings, when James VI of Scotland also became James I of England with the Union of Crowns in 1603 it turned the Borders from a frontier region between two warring nations into the 'Middle Shires' of James' kingdom.[28] One of King James' first orders of business was to rein in the rogues of the Border, and this he did with brutal efficiency. 'Jeddart Justice' – execution without trial for those accused of reiving – became commonplace, and in 1603 alone thirty-two Johnstones, Elliots, Armstrongs and Batys were executed and another 140 were formally made outlaws.[29] The tried and true method of simply exporting the troublemakers was also adopted, with many Borderers being resettled in Ulster, having lost little of their appetite for warring.[30]

The king did not content himself with these superficial methods, for where one Reiver fell or was shipped off, several more could be counted on to take his place and redouble the authorities' headaches. The next step was to make owning a horse worth more than £30 (Scots) illegal in the Borders, which is tantamount to tackling modern urban street racing by banning cars worth more than around £4,000. Carrying weapons was also strictly prohibited, meaning that the crown, after centuries of almost total impotency in the Borders, now held a monopoly on militarism.[31] No one was going reiving 60 miles into England on a pack horse, no matter how much their blood boiled. The reiving way of life came to an end when the Borders, for so long the flashpoint between two warring nations, came under the authority of the same king in 1603. Just as castles became redundant when the conditions that gave rise to them – decentralized power and feudalism – waned away, so too did the Reivers when the structural conditions upholding their *raison d'être* were no more.

That is not to say that all trace of the Reivers has disappeared. 'Common Ridings', originally conceived as ways for local authorities to police and inspect their territories, still proceed through, at the time of writing, twenty-nine towns in the south of Scotland. They are majestic affairs, with resplendent riders coursing over river fords, through market squares and, in the grandest display of them all which dates to at least the early sixteenth century, down Edinburgh's Royal Mile. In the Borders one can walk or ride the Reiver's Trail, which takes you through the lands most hotly contested by them and stops at the towerhouses, tryst points and towns that defined their lives. Perhaps one day, too, the Riverlands of Westeros will greet the arrival of bands of riders as a spectacle rather than a terror. It seems a naïve hope for a land so chronically beset by violence, yet to a sixteenth-century resident of the Scottish and English Borders, a peaceful life was just as distant a dream until rather suddenly it became a reality. Perhaps, with the endgame now in sight, the Riverlands are not doomed to run red forever after all.

Chapter 16

A Steamroller of Spears: Schiltrons & Battle Of The Bastards

The moment during the Battle of the Bastards when Ramsay Bolton's infantry encircles the remnants of Jon's army and thrusts forth their spears is the moment the latter's doom seems certain. Outmanoeuvred and pressed in so tightly that many Free Folk cannot even swing their swords, the battle descends into butchery. Men are crushed under the heels of their desperate companions as they seek somewhere, anywhere, to escape the onslaught. The forlorn helplessness of Jon's men is tangible. There is simply nothing they can do but pray that death comes quickly.

This same excruciating fate befell as many as 10,000 men as they floundered against the banks of the Bannock Burn on the morning of 24 June 1314. Only hours before, this seemed unthinkable. The Scots, led by Robert the Bruce, had a mere 7,000 against Edward II of England's 20,000. Some contemporaries observed that 'never in our time has such an army marched out from England'.[1] The English had brought more than 2,000 men-at-arms mounted on hulking destrier warhorses, the tanks of their day, while the Scots fielded only around 500 light horse under the Marischal, Robert Keith.[2] Edward's archers also vastly outnumbered and outclassed their Scottish counterparts, numbering around 4,000, with many of them drawn from South Wales,[3] where the best longbowmen came from. In a traditional engagement on open ground, the result of the Battle of Bannockburn would have been a foregone conclusion. Many factors made a Scottish victory possible, but the most significant were the masterful reading of the land by Robert the Bruce and his lieutenants, and the schiltron.

The schiltron, alternatively spelled schiltrom, is a formation of massed infantry equipped with iron-tipped 10-15ft-long spears. It has often been compared to a huge, bristly porcupine or a thick-set hedge[4] with spear

145

points projecting out in many ranks, though perhaps a steamroller is a better comparison. When assuming a defensive stance, the men in the very front would kneel and plant their spears in the ground or against their feet angled up at roughly forty-five degrees. Immediately behind them, with barely an inch to spare, the second rank thrust their spears straight forward. The third rank, requiring extraordinary strength, would hold the spears above their heads. The spears of the fourth, fifth, sixth and even seventh ranks would project in front of the first rank, such that even lacking shields, the men in the front line were protected by a forest of spear points. To go on the offensive, the front ranks simply rose up, added their spears to those pointed straight ahead and pushed with the weight of an army behind them. There is debate about whether schiltrons took a roughly rectangular or circular shape, with the latter being much more difficult to coordinate; whatever the case, it was almost invincible against unsupported cavalry and lighter infantry.

The schiltron drew its strength from the discipline in its ranks. The men were trained to hold firm even in the face of a head-on heavy cavalry charge, and to move together as one cohesive fighting unit. Much like its ancient predecessor the Greek and Macedonian phalanx, used by Alexander the Great to smash the Persian Empire, if even one man wavered the whole formation could be compromised. Robert the Bruce knew this well, and at Bannockburn he turned away many well-known warriors from his front lines because they had arrived too soon before battle to drill convincingly in schiltron formation. One soldier on a battlefield wielding a 12ft spear is a sitting duck; several thousand working as one are nearly unstoppable.

A fascinating bird's eye shot during the Battle of the Bastards shows how the Bolton formation works in comparison.[5] The front ranks are bearing large rectangular shields not unlike the Roman legionary *scutum* or the late Medieval and Renaissance-era pavise. They are able to establish a line using their interlocked shields as a mobile barrier capable of withstanding most assaults by light infantry. The second rank are the spear-wielders, using both hands to maximize the power behind each thrust and allow for better control in the press. Their spears appear to be roughly the same length as those used in schiltrons, though the Bolton spears have iron counterweights to help with balance while schiltron spears typically did not. The Bolton spear formation resembles Renaissance-era pike and shot arrangements, where crossbowmen and harquebusiers peppered the enemy from within the protection of pikemen. This is a more flexible formation than a standard schiltron and has the added advantage of being able to pepper an enemy from a distance. Still, the principle is the same – to turn your infantry into a wall against which the enemy can only crash and recede.

The one bane of the schiltron is a well-placed volley of arrows. Wearing little by way of armour and with no shields to protect them, the densely packed spearmen could hardly make for better targets. This was the decisive factor at the Battle of Halidon Hill in 1333 where, seemingly forgetting less than five years after his death all that Robert the Bruce had taught them about warfare, the Scots engaged a dismounted English army head-on in open ground. The English infantry hardly had to assert themselves at all, so devastating were the hails of arrows loosed by the skilled longbowmen in their ranks. The Scots in the front lines were so wounded and harassed by arrows that they had no choice but to turn away and shield themselves with whatever was to hand,[6] causing the integrity of the schiltrons to crack and opening up gaps which could be exploited decisively by the rest of the English forces.

A better-known example was the Battle of Falkirk on 22 July 1298, a clash still recalled with bitterness as the place where William Wallace, who has since become the epitome of Scottish defiance, was defeated. His schiltrons held up well against Edward I's cavalry, who repeatedly probed the Scottish lines for weakness but found precious few to exploit. Then came forth the longbowmen. Skilled longbowmen could loose upwards of ten arrows per minute with extraordinary accuracy – capable, for instance, of sending an arrow clean through the narrow eye slit of a great helm from over 100 yards away – the equivalent of a medieval machine gunner. Wallace's men fell, as one English chronicler put it, 'like blossoms in an orchard when the fruit has ripened', many of them having not struck a single blow in anger. At Bannockburn, the English archers were unable to spread out and fire effectively into the Scottish ranks, and when some of them managed to do so amidst the chaos, a reserve of Scottish cavalry under Sir Robert Keith, held back by Robert the Bruce for just such an eventuality, swept them from the field. Had Edward II's great multitude of archers been able to meaningfully partake in the battle, Bruce could well have suffered the same fate as Wallace at Falkirk.

As an aside, one example of where *Game of Thrones* falls foul of history is when, during the Battle of the Bastards, Ramsay Bolton orders his archers to loose repeated volleys of arrows into the thick of the fighting, killing as many of his own men as Jon Snow's. The show seems to have taken a page from *Braveheart* here, for in that film's extremely inaccurate depiction of the Battle of Falkirk, Edward I, in a memorably vicious moment, orders his archers to do the same. While this may seem to be in character for both Edward and Ramsay, there is not a single known example of a medieval commander issuing such an order. To do so would break the fundamental agreement underlying the feudal system, being the reciprocal obligations upon lord and subject to defend one another. While neither Edward nor Ramsay seem to mind shedding their own men's blood, their lords would be livid. Recall that in the medieval period, soldiers were not full-time fighters but were also the farmers who grew your food and the foundation of baronial wealth. To pepper them with arrows deliberately was to directly impoverish your own side. If Ramsay had not been defeated by Jon Snow and the Knights of the Vale, I would not have been at all surprised if the lords whose subjects he filled with arrows, like Harald Karstark or Smalljon Umber, didn't stick him with a few of their own in return.

The Schiltron's Finest Hour

The seminal use of the schiltron was undoubtedly at the Battle of Bannockburn. The first major test of Bruce's schiltrons, albeit bolstered with confidence by previous smaller-scale victories at Glen Trool and Loudoun Hill, must have been an agonizing one to watch. In the late morning or early afternoon of 23 June 1314, Robert Bruce watched from his slightly raised position at the New Park south of Stirling as the schiltron commanded by his nephew, Thomas Randolph, was seemingly swallowed up by an English cavalry charge near the kirk of St Ninian's. For infantry, and lightly armoured infantry at that, to stand against a massed heavy cavalry in 1314 seemed as unlikely as a dog besting a direwolf. Amidst the flurry of arms, it was at first hard to tell if Randolph and his men had held firm or been trampled down, but as the dust settled an extraordinary sight sent a righteous clamour up amongst the Scots. Though bloodied, Randolph's men endured – not only that, the bodies of many of the English knights lay skewered at their feet, and a great many more were thrown from their mounts. Robert de Clifford and Gilbert de

Clare, knights of considerable experience who led the cavalry charge, must have thought themselves to be in a waking nightmare. Every moment of their training had taught them that they should have ridden down the Scots like grass, yet here they were, impotent against the schiltron. Many amongst their ranks grew so frustrated at their inability to get anywhere close to the enemy due to the length of the Scots' spears that they hurled their secondary weapons, including maces, knives and axes, into the schiltron from a distance.[7] While some found their mark, many more would have deflected harmlessly off the densely packed Scottish spears. The day, against all odds, belonged to the Scots, a David versus Goliath match if ever there was one. The *Vita Edwardi Secundi*, written from the English perspective, lamented this dishonour: 'Oh! Famous race unconquered through the ages, why do you, who used to conquer knights, flee from foot soldiers?'[8] Yet this was merely a prelude, the first major test in what became a two-day battle whose result, despite this initial success, still seemed grim.

The second day was essentially a repeat of the first on a far larger scale. Having constricted the English army between the Bannock Burn and Pelstream Burn, Bruce had turned his foe's superior numbers into a liability with their men packed so close together that they could not properly deploy for battle. The Scots advanced on Edward's ensnared lines, and in a noble attempt to reverse a suddenly desperate situation, Gilbert de Clare once again led a cavalry charge headlong into the Scots' spears. The crunch of snapping spears and cries of injured horses would have been sickening. The *Chronicle of Lanercost* records how the English knights rode 'as it were into a dense forest', and a 'terrible crash' arose at the impact.[9] Once again the flower of Edward's chivalry was impotent against the schiltron, which then began to steamroll over the compressed English infantry, who struggled, like the Free Folk against the Bolton spears, even to draw their weapons for lack of space.

Caught in the Crush

One of the most harrowing parts of *Game of Thrones*' Battle of the Bastards is the sense of utter helplessness and inevitability as Jon Snow and the Free Folk are trampled and suffocated under a pile of their own dead and panicking men. Jon's claustrophobia and powerlessness in the crush as all the oxygen is battered out of him was one of the most realistic depictions of melee warfare ever put to film. The deadliest moment for an army is not, paradoxically, while they are in the thick of the fighting; it is when one side's morale collapses and a once-cohesive body of armed men abandon all hope and scramble to save themselves at any cost. An army in flight is no army at all, but something closer to a human stampede of the sort that occasionally and tragically claims lives at sports matches or pop concerts when panic takes root.

In the final hours of Bannockburn, many of the English were killed not by Scottish spears but in the chaos and panic of the rout, being crushed by their own men, knocked down by errant and flailing horses and drowned in a mere few inches of mud. Barrow details how the English were hemmed so tightly between the schiltrons and the Bannock Burn that if any man fell he would have no room to rise again, and so would be trampled underfoot.[10] While the veritable and suspiciously tidy mountain of corpses that suddenly appeared on the field during the Battle of the Bastard was strikingly unrealistic, that is not to say that nothing like was ever seen in reality. Barbour wrote that at the Battle of Loudoun Hill in 1308, a similar situation of English cavalry charging the schiltron unfolded, and that 'those that had been first to charge / Were clustered here and there at large'.[11] Of Bannockburn, it was observed grimly how the waters of the Bannock Burn itself were so filled with the dead that it could be crossed dry of foot by using the backs of the drowned as stepping stones.[12] If you think the Battle of the Bastards was hard to watch in its darkest moments, spare a thought for the thousands who died forsaken, afraid and breathless in the Bannock Burn.

Chapter 17

Firepower: Guns & Dragons

A million men could march on Harrenhal, claims Tywin Lannister, and a million men would be vanquished.[1] Within the walls of the largest castle in Westeros, Black Harren, an ironborn lord who ruled the Riverlands through a reign of abject terror, was effectively invincible. Harren had played the game of thrones and seemed poised if not to win, then at least to be impossible to vanquish. Then along came Aegon Targaryen on the back of his dragon, Balerion the Black Dread, and suddenly the size and strength of Harren's walls counted for nothing. Aegon had changed the rules, and House Hoare was roasted alive the same as if they had rode out to the Field of Fire.

Dragons did not just change the balance of power in Westeros, they obliterated the foundations upon which that balance rested. Castles, which for thousands of years had been the ultimate redoubt of the powerful, were rendered impotent. Why bother spending forty years building the most gargantuan fortification in history, as Black Harren did, when a single dragon could wipe it and your family name off the map in a night? This was the very same dilemma faced by the noble houses of Scotland in the middle of the fifteenth century. Just as Balerion the Black Dread had been the bane of Harrenhal, the king of Scots fell upon rebellious nobles such as the Lennox Stewarts and the Black Douglases with something almost as monstrous: *Mons Meg*.

The Black Dread

Weighing in at over 15,000lb and measuring just over 15ft in length, *Mons Meg* is one of the largest calibre cannons in world history.[2] With a sound that must have shaken the earth, it could fire a stone cannonball up to 150kg in weight at an effective range of over 3km. Its barrel diameter is 51cm, large enough that stewards at Edinburgh Castle, where *Mons Meg* now resides, have to stand watch to ensure that no one climbs inside. Like Daenerys' dragon eggs, *Mons Meg* was a wedding gift. Phillip the Good, Duke of Burgundy, presented it to James II of Scotland, his nephew through James' marriage to Mary of Gueldres, in 1454. We can only imagine Mary's reaction to this, but James was ecstatic. This was by far the biggest toy in his arsenal, and he could not wait to play with it. Meg's mere presence at a siege could force a surrender and some of Scotland's greatest castles, including Dumbarton, Roxburgh and Threave, fell to its wrath. Staring down the mouth of *Mons Meg* was no less lethal than the jaws of a Targaryen dragon. Weapons like *Mons Meg*, or more accurately the broader developments that possession of them represented, changed the rules.

In the early days of gunpowder weapons, this advantage was far from obvious. The first use of ordnance in Scotland was likely during Edward III's invasion of 1327, when Hainault mercenaries on the English side used them during an unspecified siege.[3] They cannot have been terribly convenient or decisive. Early bombards were slow, unwieldy and required draft animals such as oxen to lug around. The lack of good roads in Scotland, along with the famously soggy weather, meant that ordnance regularly got stuck in the mud and brought whole armies to a halt.[4] Despite their expense they were often the first pieces of kit to be abandoned in a pinch, and many commanders must have wondered why they bothered with them. Compare, for instance, the longbow with the early harquebus. A skilled longbowman could loose around twelve arrows per minute, and a crossbowman two or three bolts. Against that, a harquebusier as late as the early sixteenth century would be lucky to manage eight shots per hour.[5] Hardly dragons among sheep, then.

Backfire

There was another problem. While the Targaryens made devastating use of dragons as weapons of shock and awe, they did not own the dragons they rode. Dragons' primal, elemental power is too great and wild to be wholly controlled by any man or woman, and the history of the Targaryens is replete with examples of dragon riders being consumed, crushed, abandoned and thrown mid-flight by their own mounts. Think of Daenerys' frustration with Drogon, who refuses to hunt or return to Meereen in the aftermath of the attack by the Sons of the Harpy in the Great Pit of Daznak; or of the tragic fate of the Targaryen Princess Aerea, carried unwillingly and helplessly by the dragon Balerion to the cursed lands of Old Valyria to suffer an unspeakably agonizing death.[6]

Early cannons were hardly more predictable than dragons. As a case in point, if ever curiosity killed a cat then that cat was James II of Scotland. The king had a penchant for personally inspecting his artillery, and enjoyed few things more than to be nearby when a volley was unleashed. We all know the sort. During the siege of Roxburgh Castle in 1460, James was indulging in his love of these fire-breathers when one of his cannons, named *The Lion*, burst its barrel and sent shrapnel flying through the air. The *Auchinleck Chronicle* records how James 'unhappely was slain with ane gun the quhilk [which] brak in the fyring, for the quhilk was great dolour throu all Scotland'.[7] James' thigh bone was split in two and he bled to death in moments,[8] a victim of the volatile nature of his favourite pets.

Given all of these complications, it is hardly surprising that there is no Scottish equivalent of the Field of Fire, the battle in which Aegon the Conqueror's dragons incinerated thousands of foes in mere moments in the parched fields of the Reach. While artillery would not become capable of anything like that level of destruction until the late eighteenth century, it could force an army's hand in a way that precipitated mass slaughter. Few things are as demoralizing as getting picked off by enemy cannons from afar while being unable to retaliate, and under such a deadly and impersonal barrage most soldiers would take one of two actions: flee the field or charge into the proverbial dragon's jaws and try to deal some damage up close. At the Battle of Flodden on 9 September 1513, the Scots chose the latter and charged to their doom. Fought just over the border on the English side, the Scots were led by none other than their king, James IV, and for once they outnumbered their English adversaries, who were led by the Earl of Surrey. Despite this, their artillery was not on a par with the English army's and the Scots had to endure a bombardment made all the more devastating by their position on an exposed hillside. Their charge was brave but fatal, and the Scots' spears were hacked apart by the English billhooks. It was the first battle on British soil to begin with an artillery barrage, and it ended with over 10,000 Scots, including the king, massacred on the field.[9]

How Dragons & Cannons Changed the Rules

By the middle of the sixteenth century, the rules of engagement had irrevocably changed.[10] Improvements in gunpowder technology meant that holing up inside a defensive position did not confer nearly the advantage it did a century or two before. Instead, the initiative was usually with the attacker.[11] This change did not come overnight like Aegon's assault, but it was no less revolutionary.

There were a few stubborn holdouts. Tantallon Castle in East Lothian, which is effectively one massive wall cutting off an enclosed seaside promontory, defied two major artillery bombardments in 1491 and 1528 by James IV and James V respectively. In the 1528 siege, the royal cannons fired at Tantallon for twenty days and the castle emerged 'never ane hair the worse'.[12] The king won the castle through bribery, paying the gold price when iron proved insufficient for the task, and Tantallon would not fall to a direct assault until Cromwell's cannons bent against it in 1651. By that time even Dunnottar Castle, perhaps Scotland's most dramatically and defensibly situated castle, could not withstand the trend – though it put up an admirable final stand in 1651-52, holding out for eight months against relentless bombardment. Looking at Harrenhal, Westeros' mightiest castle, you can't help but wonder how long even it could hold out against a well-supplied battery of mortars and culverins.

The castle age was effectively over by the mid-seventeenth century, its end brought about as a direct result of the dominance of artillery and the resultant emphasis on offence rather than defence. However, these were proximate, rather than an ultimate, causes. To understand how artillery was able to end the 700-year dominance of the castle, we need to look not just at individual pieces of ordnance like *Mons Meg*, but the broader social and political changes that they represent.

Aegon the Conqueror didn't sweep aside centuries of Westerosi power structures simply because he had dragons; he was able to do that because he had the only dragons. When the last dragons died a century-and-a-half before the events of *Game of Thrones*, the balance of power began to shift. The greatest symbol of Targaryen authority became a memory, and the Lord of the Seven Kingdoms' main advantage amounted to nothing but a name and title. Had dragons still been in the skies when Rhaegar and Lyanna stole away from Robert Baratheon, would he still have risen and triumphed against the Mad King? The significance of dragons is that they are the ultimate weapon in the arms race for the Iron Throne. When one side holds them all, there is the danger of tyranny. When all sides hold them, the ladder of chaos is unfurled. Dragons are flying, fire-breathing stand-ins for the monopolization of power.

Back in Scotland and indeed across Europe, the late sixteenth to the eighteenth centuries were pivotal in the development of the first centralized nation states. War in this time became less and less about factionalism between regional and baronial competitors, of the sort that drove so many Scots to build castles and towerhouses, and more about national and religious ideologies that involved a much higher percentage of the population and could brook little compromise. From this revolutionary tumult emerged a more highly militarized state apparatus than had ever yet been seen in Europe. The Wars of the Three Kingdoms of 1639-51, as well as the five Jacobite Risings between 1689 and 1745-46, were especially significant as they saw castles systematically targeted and demolished to deny their advantages to the enemies of the crown.[13]

A sort of positive feedback loop was formed. The power once exercised by regional magnates was shifting towards the crown, and that meant more tax revenues, which could in turn be invested in maintaining a permanent armed force equipped with the latest technologies.[14] This, along with legislation designed to demilitarize the countryside, eventually gave the governments of emerging nation states a near-monopoly on armed force. For instance, the 'Act Anent Removing and Extinguishing of Deidlie Feuds', which became law in Scotland in 1598, demanded that feuding nobles present their case before the king rather than act as judge, jury and executioner in their own lands as they had done for centuries.[15]

With this momentum behind them, the kings of Scots were able, eventually and with several significant stumbles, to isolate and grind down their domestic rivals. Over-mighty nobles could no longer simply take refuge inside their 'closed-up shells',[16] but had to either face royal armies in the field or join what it was increasingly clear they could not beat. The real equivalent of Balerion the Black Dread, then, was not *Mons Meg*, awe-inspiring as it was and still is, but the emergence of the centralized nation state and the crown's near-monopoly on violence.[17] That's admittedly much less dramatic than being obliterated by a dragon breathing fiery death from on high, but the effect on Scotland was no less profound.

PART V

THE LAWS OF GODS & MEN

Chapter 18

Gods & Monsters

Every year on the last night of April, Calton Hill in central Edinburgh pulses with the light of a dozen bonfires. Thousands assemble upon the volcanic crag to witness the May Queen, resplendent in flower-trimmed white robes and a cornucopia upon her head, undertake her ceremonial procession to reclaim the land from the King of Winter. As she makes her way from fire to fire, a frenzied group of nearly naked demons, named the Reds for their head-to-toe body paint, whip revellers into a hedonistic frenzy with bestial grunts, provocative gestures and unbridled displays of euphoria. Drums pulse for hours into the long night, the rhythm helping to defy the bitter cold and rains that have beset the ceremony every year in recent memory in an apparent final act of wintery defiance. This is the Beltane Fire Festival, and for one ecstatic night Scotland's enlightened capital goes pagan.

The irony of the festival's location could not be greater. The May Queen descends from steps built onto the National Monument, a failed nineteenth-century attempt to build a full-scale replica of the Parthenon atop Calton Hill and manifest Edinburgh's reputation as the 'Athens of the North'. A stone's throw from that folly is the Nelson Monument, shaped like an upturned looking glass, and across from it is the city observatory, where astronomers unfurled the secular mysteries of the cosmos on the rare occasions when clouds did not obscure the view. The New Town of Edinburgh, which Calton Hill punctuates, has been described as the 'Enlightenment in stone', and its fertile intellectual soils gave rise to innumerable brilliant and determined minds including David Hume, Adam Smith, James Clerk Maxwell, Robert Louis Stevenson and countless more. The very layout of the New Town, built upon a then-revolutionary gridiron pattern proposed by the 26-year-old architect James Craig in 1767, is designed to facilitate rational thinking and discerning character.

At first glance, there seems to be no place in Scotland more ill-suited to celebrating Beltane. Scratch but a little under the surface, however, and the enlightened veneer quickly gives way. Long before Calton Hill was a beacon of the Enlightenment, it was apparently home to much older and more mysterious powers. The old ways endure in the north, often right under the nose of civilization. Scarcely a mile from where John Napier discovered logarithms or where James Young Simpson experimented with early anaesthesia, Calton Hill was said to be the home of faerie folk who dwelled in a cavern beneath the crag concealed by invisible gates. They could whisk people away at extraordinary speeds across Europe, and in a popular local tale a young drummer boy from Leith, who could tap out an almost supernaturally perfect beat, served as an intermediary between their realm and ours.[1]

Silly as all that may sound to us, one of the greatest disservices we can do when discussing traditional beliefs in entities like giants, faeries or tree gods is to dismiss them as mere stories told for wont of other entertainment. As evidenced by the tale of the Faerie Boy of Leith, many people saw no conflict between the advancing Scottish Enlightenment and the idea that otherworldly creatures inhabited the hills and neuks at the fringes of modern society. The distinction between magic and religion, with the former seen as a children's fancy and the latter taken more seriously, is a strikingly recent and non-linear one.[2] When many late eighteenth-century Edinburgh citizens looked from the Old Town across the valley that became Princes Street Gardens as the lights of the New Town began to multiply, they were in no doubt that the darkness of Calton Hill concealed mystical forces. Learned men and women may have looked down upon such superstitions, just as Tyrion Lannister once dismissed any notion of snarks and grumkins, but we cannot deign to put ourselves in the shoes of past peoples without treating such beliefs as an integral part of their lived experience. To be absolutely clear, that is not to say that beasts like giants actually existed – they definitively did not. Just for this chapter, however, let us explore the realm of the fantastical like a Ranger of the Night's Watch, who knows better than to dismiss the shadows in the forests and the faces in the trees.

When Giants Walked the Land

Where giants walk, lamentations follow. The lingering suspicion that, despite the marvels achieved by civilization, we have lost something essential in ourselves through our taming of the uncorrupted wilds is impossible to fully escape. We have reckoned with this unease for millennia – the earliest known work of epic literature, the Sumerian Epic of Gilgamesh from 2100 BCE, grapples with the relationship between Gilgamesh, the king of what was then the world's greatest city, and the wild man Enkidu, formed from clay and water by the gods. Nearer our own time, the minds that coalesced into what we call the Scottish Enlightenment of the eighteenth and nineteenth centuries paradoxically looked back to ancient Athens and Rome as a means to move their own society forward; yet, if you had asked the historian Tacitus in the first century what he thought of the same Rome that Enlightenment scholars would later exalt, he would tell you that it was already well past its best. What better representation of this eternal ennui than giants, grander yet more primal versions of ourselves?

In Westeros, when giants are not spoken of in terror by the people they are about to pull apart they are treated with a remorse usually reserved for beloved long-lost family members. Leaf, the child of the forest whom Bran meets at the Three Eyed Raven's den beyond the Wall, delivers a sort of eulogy saying that giants were 'our bane and our brothers ... In the world that men have made, there is no room for them, or us.'[3] The Free Folk, too, sing a dirge called 'The Last of the Giants', with lines like 'Oh, the smallfolk have stolen my forests / They've stolen my rivers and hills ... For these men who are small can never stand tall / while giants still walk in the light.'[4] There is hardly a great monument in the North that does not involve giants in their legendary founding during the Age of Heroes, the walls of Winterfell and the Wall itself being the two greatest examples. How tragic that the Wall ultimately cut the giants off from the world, severing them from their ancient domains and relegating them to children's stories. At the conclusion of the Battle of the Bastards, when Ramsay Bolton puts an arrow through the eye of Wun Weg Wun Dar Wun, the last living giant, we as an audience are left in no doubt that the world of Westeros is left profoundly diminished.

Flocking to ascend what has become one of Scotland's most photographed locations, I wonder how many visitors feel the same existential pangs upon catching up with the Old Man of Storr on the Isle of Skye. The iconic pillar of rock is said to be the finger of a giant buried high upon the ridge overlooking his ancestral domain. Medieval chroniclers like Geoffrey of Monmouth – who brought Arthurian lore into literary vogue with his *Vita Merlini* in the twelfth century – were entirely serious when they wrote that Britain was a land of giants long before its settlement by people. Writing as late as the fifteenth century, the Scottish chronicler Walter Bower still felt obliged to mention the long-since passed 'time of the giants'.[5] Recounting the traditional tale of Brutus, a survivor of the Trojan War and the first mythical settler of Britain, in his *Historia Regum Britannie*, Monmouth claimed that the land was uninhabited save for a scattered population of giants.[6] Conflict kicked off immediately, with Brutus' follower Corineus providing some entertainment by wrestling them. One giant in particular, the 12ft-tall and especially brutish Gogmagog, could 'tear up an oak-tree as though it were a hazel wand'.[7] Eventually the giants were driven, like the one whose finger breaches the earth at the Old Man of Storr, into the caverns, mountains and desolate places of the land, their bellowing songs sung in the hills no longer.

How do the giants of Scottish myth stack up against those of Westerosi reality? Intimidating as the giants north of the Wall are, at a paltry 10-14ft in height they are dwarfed by the giants of Scottish and Irish lore, whose strides could span whole seas. Westerosi giants like Wun Weg Wun Dar Wun, known affectionately as Wun Wun, reach a maximum height of around 14ft. Poor Wun Wun would not even be able to reach the ankle of Fionn mac Cumhaill, a giant of Irish and Scottish lore (known as Fingal in the latter since the late eighteenth century) who supposedly created the Giant's Causeway in Antrim and sat upon a titanic stone throne in his cave on the Isle of Staffa. In some iterations of the legends of Fingal and his accompanying heroes, known as the Fianna, he stood as tall as 500 men.[8] Such a giant could step over Westeros' Wall as easily as we step over a sandcastle. Even Fingal's hound, Bran, would stand head and shoulders above Wun Wun. Just off the road leading north from Oban in Argyll is a pillar of stone over 40ft high that was once a sea-stack in the days when the water lapped further inland. Erosion has carved a remarkable ring around it, like a caricature of a man tightening his belt in a poor attempt to conceal a beer belly. Known as the *Clach-nan-con*, the 'Dog Stone', Argyll legend holds that it got its distinctive shape when Fingal tied Bran to the rock and the great hound restlessly circled it, his strength and speed wearing a great groove into the pillar. Judging by the size of the stone, Bran would make a light snack of even the greatest Westerosi giant.

Scottish giants clearly win out with pure physicality, but the question of culture and cognition is more complex. Both sets of giants are intelligent enough to domesticate animals, for instance, no small feat considering the vast majority of humanity's time on earth was spent without canine companions or beasts of burden. Fingal has his hound, loyal to the end, and Wun Wun's folk have mammoths that they ride as we do horses. Maesters have also put forward evidence that Westerosi giants bury their dead, hinting at a well-developed sense of community, individuality and even something approaching a religious belief system.[9] As Tormund Giantsbane, who should know, observes, 'they are not the monsters you southerners think'.[10] They do not, however, craft tools, forge their own weapons or build permanent dwellings. In contrast, the only thing that would give away the fact that you had stumbled into a Scottish or Irish giant's home rather than that of a regular medieval family is that everything would be bigger. Giants like Fingal build sturdy and cosy homes for their families, craft furniture, adore ornamentation, hunt with spears and bows and all devise all kinds of schemes and stratagems. Westerosi giants, like those fighting alongside the wildlings at the Battle of Castle Black, can be taught to use tools – one wields a monstrous bow that can fire to the top of the Wall, and others use hooks and chains to tear open Castle Black's outer gate – but cannot produce them independently. It seems that Scottish giants win this round as well, though we shouldn't be too hard on Westerosi giants like Wun Wun – they are clearly much smarter than the average ogre.

The Queen of Winter

In the mountain passes and shivering shores of the Highlands dwells the Queen of Winter. She rides from sea to sea in a chariot drawn by otherworldly black hounds until, on the hallowed eve of Samhain (31 October), she reaches the fearsome Corryvreckan Whirlpool.[11] While washing her plaid in the maelstrom, a thunderous noise can be heard across the land, and when she hangs the plaid up to dry icy crystals are carried by the winds to usher in winter.[12] White Walkers may be exclusive to *Game of Thrones*, but for thousands of years the Celts of Scotland, Ireland and the Isle of Man have lived in fear of a strikingly similar force of nature - the *Cailleach*.

The Cailleach, meaning 'Veiled One', is a potent mix of goddess, guardian and tyrant. On the one hand, she is a great creator. Celtic lore says that the mountains of Scotland were her handiwork, as were the Isles which formed as she strode across the ocean and dropped several pebbles into the water. Ailsa Craig, the volcanic plug off the Ayrshire coast which is best known for being the source of the majority of the world's curling stones, was apparently an accident – it slipped through a hole in her apron.[13] She is also a guardian of wild animals and has, on rare occasions, struck mutually beneficial agreements with humans. On the other hand, she has a temper. The Cailleach seems to be a queen of both ice and fire, for one of her powers is the ability to hurl flames from her chariot that char her path.[14] Her reign, lasting from Samhain to Beltane on 1 May, is only ended through rebellion. To break her icy grasp, her subjects must ritually rise up and overthrow her to make way for Angus and Bride, King and Queen of Summer and Plenty. She then retreats to her Highland fastnesses, with traditional connections to Ben Cruachan in Argyll, Glen Nevis in Lochaber, Beinn na Caillich on Skye and, perhaps most of all, the tiny shrine of Tigh nam Bodach in Glen Cailleach.

It is here that the Cailleach bears more than a superficial resemblance to the White Walkers of Westeros or, more specifically, the nightmarish Night's Queen. Long ago during the Age of Heroes, the thirteenth Lord Commander of the Night's Watch returned from the depths of the Haunted Forest with a woman as cold as ice with bright blue eyes.[15] He assumed the mantle of the Night's King, and for thirteen years he and his 'corpse queen' ruled the Wall from the Nightfort through cruelty and dark sorcery.[16] Their tyrannical reign was only ended when the Stark King of Winter, Brandon the Breaker, forged an unprecedented alliance with the wildlings led by Joramun, the King-Beyond-the-Wall, and with much bloodshed cast off their icy grip.[17] While the Night's Queen was wholly malevolent, unlike the Cailleach, the terror instilled by her reign and its undoing through collaborative force by her oppressed subjects rings familiar to anyone who has watched the ceremonial broadsword duel between the Kings of Summer and Winter that unfolds each year on Edinburgh's Royal Mile at Samhain.

Still, not all the Cailleach's subjects seek to overthrow her. Some have learned to live in harmony. An unassuming and ancient ritual takes place at Tigh nam Bodach, one of the oldest uninterrupted pagan observances in all of Britain. Standing all together as a family at the doorway of a tiny shieling are a set of stones, tapered in a vague and uncanny take on the human form. They are the Cailleach, the Bodach (her husband), the Nighean (their daughter) and the rest of their children. Upon Beltane, the family is brought out into the light to look across the glen, and at Samhain they are returned into their home. So long as this is done, it is said, the glen will prosper from the goodwill of the Cailleach. The precise intention of the ritual is unknown, though perhaps the Cailleach's power as a protector of animals is harnessed to safeguard the local herds while they are out to pasture. The old tale that the Cailleach and her family once sought shelter in the glen and offered their protection as thanks also brings to mind that other timeless Highland tradition of guest right, which we'll soon turn to. The last named custodian of Tigh nam Bodach, as reported by folklorist Anne Ross in 1975, was the shepherd Bob Bissett,[18] and though he passed away some years ago the Cailleach and her family still make their miniscule migration with the coming and going of each winter.

Faces of the Old Gods

The deep, dark corners of the world, both our own and Westeros, have ever been the redoubt of the old gods.[19] Places where transience and timelessness can be felt at once – like a forest grove, its colours dying and being reborn with the seasons while remaining fixed in place year after year – have been revered for thousands of years.[20] Some continue to be. Go a little south of St Andrews and such a place awaits at Dunino. The only facilities are those you bring in your mind or your car boot, and at first glance the quiet churchyard appears indistinguishable from hundreds of others like it throughout Scotland. Wander, and look closer.

Alongside a shallow slope at the edge of the churchyard is a weathered stone shaped like an altar, and at any given time its basin is likely to be overflowing with coins, many of them minted within the past year or two - offerings by modern adherents of an ancient ritual. The stone has stood since at least the ninth century, and it is possible that the Christian church was built on the site of a much earlier stone circle.[21] Clearly there are secrets here, and to uncover them you must enter the woods. A short path leads to one of the most remarkable sites of pagan worship anywhere in Scotland.

You may well be in the footsteps of kings. The first thing to greet you upon entering Dunino Den is a rocky promontory with a footprint carved into it. Similar footprints track across the Gaelic world, like the one at Dunadd in Kilmartin Glen into which the early rulers of Dál Riata stepped to assume their mantle. Next to the footprint, a black pool as still as the night sky plunges straight through the stone to unknown depths, perhaps fed by the Dunino Burn, whose trickling is one of few sounds to break the silence. Such pools and wells were venerated by the Picts, as they were throughout the Celtic world, in the belief that they plunged into the deep Otherworld and realm of the gods.[22] Descending stone-cut steps into the bowels of the den, you pass by several Celtic-style knots and crosses, fusions of the old ways with the new faith that swept over Pictland by the eighth century. Some may well have been carved by the Picts themselves, while others have appeared as recently as the last few decades.

At the bottom of the stairs the den opens up, the trees all around forming a partial canopy, and something much older is revealed. Hanging on the branches are strips of cloth, glass baubles, shoelaces, medallions and other personal effects left for the faerie folk in the timeless tradition of clootie wells. Such offerings may be for fortune or a blessing, but they can also simply be signs of respect and neighbourliness towards the forces that dwell amidst the elements. However archaic or quaint it may seem to us to leave trinkets for faeries and water spirits, Dunino Den is a remarkable example of elements of Celtic polytheism surviving the upheavals and revolutions that swept around it, including the arrival of Christianity, the Protestant Reformation and the Enlightenment.[23] Neither the medieval nor the reformed Christian Church held as much sway over the day-to-day beliefs of the inhabitants of Northern and Western Europe as they liked to believe; while Christian ceremony and doctrine were certainly dominant, they existed alongside a host of earlier pagan and animist beliefs that adapted to new ways more often than they vanished beneath them.[24]

If at this point while exploring Dunino Den you get the feeling that you are being watched, it's because you are. Rarely are Celtic gods given anything as tangible as a face, yet if you examine the cliffs opposite the burn that is exactly what you will find staring back at you. Its flowing beard fades into the smooth surface of the stone, and a heavy, concerned brow accentuates deep-set eyes that are as dark as the waters of the den's mysterious well. I am aware of nothing else quite like it in all of Scotland, and the impact of it – especially when coupled with the atmospheric weight of its setting – is unparalleled. Who is this Old God keeping watch over Dunino Den? It turns out that the person responsible for the carving may well still be alive to ask. As tempting as it is to think that the Picts carved this visage as part of some arcane ceremony or to channel the will of their divine entities, locals swear that the face only appeared within the last thirty years or so. Some may be disappointed by this, but it can also be seen as a continuation of a tradition, enacted countless times in this very place, that has withstood the fall of Rome, the coming of Christianity, the scourge of the Norse, the depredations of the Reformation and the inexorable encroachment of modernity. The face at Dunino may only be thirty years old, but in spirit it harkens back to prehistory.

Celtic belief systems, diverse and highly localized as they were, put great emphasis on natural havens resembling Winterfell's godswood, and on oak trees in particular.[25] The people who worshipped – if that is indeed what they did – at Dunino Den 2,000 years ago would have been baffled and outraged by the restrictiveness of churches and cathedrals. The amphitheatre of their gods was the great outdoors: the forests, caves, hidden valleys, deep pools and running waters were the abode of the gods, not any book or building. There is a good chance that the image of the pagan god, if that is indeed what it is, carved into Dunino Den either goes by no name at all or one that would be unrecognizable to someone even 50 miles away. Classical sources – and accounts written by outsiders are unfortunately all that we have from so many vital episodes in Scotland's story – mention over 400 Celtic gods inhabiting the island of mainland Britain, with 300 of those being mentioned only once and so likely inhabiting a very restricted geographical territory.[26] They were not, furthermore, anthropomorphized like the Dunino face or Greco-Roman gods, and some possessed no physical form at all.

It is impossible for anyone who has read *A Song of Ice and Fire* or watched *Game of Thrones* to see the face and not be instantly transported to the godswood at Winterfell. Next to a small pool so black and cold it resembles a void stands an ancient weirwood tree, the most sacred survivors of a time before the First Men, Andals, Targaryens and Starks.[27] Is there anything more powerful in all Westeros than whatever eldritch powers pulse through their roots? Through them the Three-Eyed Raven can traverse time and space; the Children of the Forest seem to prosper or suffer in tandem with their well-being; and Andals in all their iron armour so feared them that they sought to fell each and every one in Westeros.

When marked with a face, a weirwood tree is called a heart tree,[28] and it is beneath such a heart tree that Ned Stark would retreat to solemnly contemplate his choices while sharpening his Valyrian steel greatsword, *Ice*. Every castle worth the name in the North has a heart tree within its godswood, though none are so magnificent as Winterfell's. They are places were one can go to seek answers, though none are promised. While the Old Gods of Westeros are not nearly so fickle and demanding as those of the Faith of the Seven – one of the most insightful lines into the religious mentality of the North versus the South comes from Ned, who tells Catelyn that 'It's your god with all the rules'[29] – the precise nature of their influence and will is perhaps even more unknowable. At least the Seven have well-defined rules and personalities; the Old Gods are inherently beyond categorization. All that a good Northerner can be sure of is that if they step within a godswood and present themselves to a heart tree, something is watching.

The face at Dunino is not alone in helping the old gods to see. In 1880, a strange artefact was recovered from under a thick layer of peat moss along the north shore of Loch Leven, not far from Glencoe. She is known as the Ballachulish figure, an almost life-sized goddess carved of a single piece of dark alder. For the first time in over 2,500 years, someone was able to gaze into her white quartz eyes.[30] Would she have recognized her domain? In recent years, historians and archaeologists have paid increasing attention to the historic environment in which such discoveries are made, considering not just the object itself but its placement within a broader ritual landscape, and the Ballachulish figure's environment was, and remains, rich indeed. A stone burial cist was found near her former post, and since she stood vigil the water levels of the loch have receded, allowing someone to carve cup marks into the small islet of An Dunnan, which lies directly in her line of sight.[31] She once stood freely upright overlooking the strait that connects Loch Leven to the sea, perhaps ensuring the safety of those who made the voyage and standing guard against any uninvited guests.[32]

Who is she? It has been the better part of two millennia since anyone could say for sure. Her location near the water, like the carvings and Dunino Den, is surely significant – was she a local deity of the straits? Her arms are folded just above her abdomen, conveying a sense of motherly protectiveness, and as she is depicted nude one of the most immediately visible features is a crudely etched vulva – was she a fertility goddess meant to bring health and plenty to the denizens of the lochside? Perhaps her true identity lay in the surrounding hilltops. The twin peaks of Beinn a' Bheithir, a precipitous horseshoe-shaped mountain, are easily visible from the banks of Loch Leven and loom like a giant sentinels over the narrow strait leading into Loch Linnhe and the sea. Beinn a' Bheithir translates as 'hill of the thunderbolt' and is named after the Cailleach Bheithir, a local iteration of the Queen of Winter. As the crow flies, it is not a great distance away to Ben Cruachan, that other storied haunt of the Cailleach. Perhaps here on the banks of Loch Leven, one of the watery arteries leading in to the heart of the Highlands and out towards the vast realm of the waves, the Queen of Winter struck a bargain with her subjects. An interpretive illustration in Ian Armit's *Celtic Scotland* depicts the Ballachulish figure placed inside near a hearth fire alongside two other wooden watchers.[33] Perhaps, like the stones at Tigh nam Bodach, she was brought inside at certain times of the year and then placed back on the banks in a cycle of vigilance.

Her home is now the National Museum of Scotland, though her visage has been badly warped due to drying out for the first time in 2,500 years. Her new realm is a shadowy corner of the museum, tucked away as though in secret, though the room contains awe-inspiring treasures like Pictish carved stones depicting boars and mysterious beasts – relics from over 1,000 years after the Ballachulish figure's watch had ended. She greets visitors at the end of a corridor of which she is the focal point, a level of attention that, judging by the somewhat aghast and nervous expression she has taken on as a result of warping, she has yet to warm to. Her expression evokes the morbid serenity of the bog bodies recovered in the liminal parts of the lands between earth and water throughout Northern Europe. There is a sadness to the Ballachulish figure that strikes at the heart immediately. She is the only one of her kind found in Scotland, the last of the old gods.

However, there is hope. A recreation of the Ballachulish figure was erected on the banks of Loch Leven in 2017, reviving her original dignity and inspiring much interest from locals, few of whom grew up without hearing at least a tale or two of her presence. The mysterious face carved within living memory at Dunino Den, the revelry of Beltane upon Calton Hill and the telling of tales that have been heard since before there was a Scotland, ensure that she is once again in good company.

Chapter 19

The Last of the Free

'Ah! Freedom is a noble thing!
Great Happiness does freedom bring.
All solace to a man it gives;
He lives at ease that freely lives.
…
If bondage he has ever known,
Then freedom's blessings he will own,
And reckon freedom worth in gold
More than the world will ever hold!'

- John Barbour, *The Bruce*[1]

Putting the 'Free' in Free Folk

Searching for historical source material in the pages and episodes of *Game of Thrones* sometimes means making some loose extrapolations. Other times, the myriad inspirations that were combined, scrambled and inflated in Martin's work seem to stare right back at you and wink. I half-expected a wildling chieftain in the season six episode *The Broken Man* to do just that. Protesting to Jon, the recently resurrected Lord Commander of the Night's Watch, that they did not risk coming south of the Wall just to fight the Boltons, the chieftain implores him, 'If we lose this, we're gone. Dozens of tribes, hundreds of generations … We'll be the last of the Free Folk.'[2] Though he could not have known it, that wildling chieftain precisely quoted another leader of a seemingly doomed yet defiant people facing off against the might of expansionist southerners. He was Calgacus, the Caledonian warrior-chieftain who dared to stand against the legions of Rome.

Calgacus speaks to us not with his own voice but through Tacitus, the Roman author of the *Agricola* and our best – though far from unbiased – source for the campaign that culminated with the Battle of Mons Graupius. There are a number of issues that prevent us from taking Tacitus' reporting at face value. Firstly, he was not present on the campaign, though his personal relationship with the Roman commander Agricola surely provided vivid and broadly accurate details. Tacitus was also disaffected with Rome, seeing it as past its best and having entered an age of political self-interest, aggrandizement and excess. There is every likelihood, therefore, that Tacitus invented Calgacus not only as a worthy opponent in battle for his father-in-law, but also as a manifestation of what we would now call the 'noble savage', standing in defiance of the insatiable imperial appetite of a corrupt Roman Empire. Still, the speech ascribed by Tacitus to Calgacus stands as one of the greatest anti-imperial treatises ever written, repurposed time and again throughout history and applied to wars as recent as the invasion of Iraq in 2003. Stepping out from the Caledonian ranks as first amongst his fearsome peers, Calgacus valiantly assailed the logic of empire. His alleged words are worth reciting at length:

> '[F]or we, the noblest in all Britain, who dwell in her innermost sanctuary and do not look across at any subject shores, had been keeping our eyes free from the defilement of tyranny. We are the last people on earth, and the last to be free: our very remoteness in a land known only to rumour has protected us up till this day … But now there is no people beyond us, nothing but tides and rocks and, more deadly than these, the Romans. It is no use trying to escape their arrogance by submission or good behaviour. They have pillaged the world: when the land has nothing left for men who ravage everything, they scour the sea. If an enemy is rich, they are greedy, if he is poor, they crave glory. Neither East nor West can sate their appetite. They are the only people on earth to covet wealth and poverty with equal craving. They plunder, they butcher, they ravish, and call it by the lying name of "empire". They make a desert and call it "peace".'[3]

If the King-Beyond-the-Wall Mance Rayder had delivered this speech verbatim before the Battle of Castle Black, only substituting Rome for the

Seven Kingdoms, none of us watching or reading it would have doubted that they were anything other than George R.R. Martin's invention. Just as Martin drew upon Machiavelli's *The Prince* and *Discourses on Livy* to craft much of the moral fabric underpinning *Game of Thrones*, I am in no doubt that at some point, perhaps after standing atop Hadrian's Wall and retiring to reflect on the experience of looking off the edge of the world, he opened a copy of Tacitus' *Agricola* and wondered what being free truly meant in the north.

Right to Rule?

The greatest threat posed by the Free Folk to the Seven Kingdoms is not their sword arms, but their minds. The subjects of the Iron Throne may bicker about its occupant and even occasionally rebel against its authority, but the worldview of the Free Folk goes much further than that to question the fundamental assumptions underpinning that authority. King Joffrey may have been reviled by anyone with a shred of morality, but so long as it was generally agreed that Robert Baratheon's blood flowed through his veins – which it did not – his tyranny was propped up by feudal legitimacy. The Free Folk have other ideas. They don't follow a man or woman just because their parents happened to hold a title or wear a circlet of some shiny metal upon their heads. If the child of such folk was strong, then perhaps they may find people rallying behind them, too. If they were weak, cowardly or inept, then abandonment or a spear of ash to the back in the middle of the night was all they were entitled to.[4]

Operating somewhere on the spectrum between a Hobbesian state of nature – solitary, poor, nasty, brutish and short at the worst of times – and a radically egalitarian meritocracy, the pillars of power beyond the Wall are built of different stuff than in the kingdoms to the south. Whether this makes the Free Folk stronger or weaker as a whole is not our concern; what matters is that they think about power, and indeed the source of power, in a fundamentally different way. No wonder the Starks have engaged in an existential struggle with them for thousands of years; if the Free Folk overran the walls of Winterfell, a Stark by blood would be worth no more than a bastard Snow.

While not exercised as radically as amongst the Free Folk, similar ideas of merit-based rule are found in the ancient, early medieval and even high medieval eras in Scotland. The rulers of Pictland, who clashed against Roman Britain in the late fourth century and endured until the creation of the Kingdom of Alba in the ninth, were elevated not through hereditary right but from amongst a roster of candidates that often included individuals from beyond the traditional boundaries of the realm.[5] A king in this period effectively exercised sole rule in the absence of a bureaucracy, and the extent to which their rule was effective very much depended on the force of their personalities and reputations,[6] though a distinguished lineage on top of all that certainly couldn't hurt. If their mind or body weakened, or the people felt that the ruler no longer truly held their interests at heart, there would be little sentimentality involved in removing them from power and finding someone better suited to the task.

One of the consequences of this was that early kings were viewed as first amongst equals and not divine agents or unimpeachable authorities. Jon Snow got his first taste of this when he was captured beyond the Wall by Rattleshirt and brought before Mance Rayder for the first time. En route, several Free Folk – notably Ygritte, who can always be counted on to voice an opinion – don't hesitate to speak back to Rattleshirt, the warband's leader, and outright disagree with his preferred course of action. 'These are a free folk indeed,' Jon thinks to himself while watching them debate as equals.[7] Reading this passage, I was at once reminded of the exchange between King Alexander III and the humble servants who attempted to see him safely across the stormy waters of the Firth of Forth that fateful night of 18 March 1286. Alexander asked the ferryman if he was afraid of making the crossing in such awful weather, to which the man quipped sardonically that, 'I could not die better than in the company of your father's son.'[8] Upon landing at Inverkeithing on the opposite shore, Alexander, third of his name and King of Scots, was reprimanded by Alexander the cook, master of the sauce kitchen: 'My lord, what are you doing in such weather and darkness? How many times have I tried to persuade you that midnight travelling will bring you no good?'[9] The storm would claim King Alexander's life within a few hours, but that is a tale for another time.

Returning to Jon Snow, the lack of deference shown by the Free Folk is only reinforced during his introduction to Mance, the King-Beyond-the-Wall. Jon gets a laugh out of Tormund Giantsbane when he drops to his knees before him in the belief that Tormund is the king, only for Mance to appear unassumingly from the shadows dressed no differently than any of the others around him. How alien this must have seemed to Jon, who had so internalized the feudal concept that some men are inherently worth kneeling before that he could think of nothing else to do.

By Alexander III's reign in the thirteenth century, hereditary kingship was a long-established institution in Scotland, as in the rest of Europe. The 'Great Cause', the term for the process arbitrated by Edward I of England to determine who would inherit the Scottish throne following Alexander's death, was premised entirely upon blood, with the Bruces, Comyns, Balliols and numerous other noble families all putting forward claims based on lineage. Still, some of the old ways endured. One of the most remarkable interpretations of kingly power in western political history can be found in the Declaration of Arbroath. The Declaration was one of a trio of diplomatic letters sent by Robert the Bruce and the nobility of Scotland to Pope John XXII in 1320, in an ultimately successful attempt to get papal recognition of Scotland's sovereignty in the struggle against England. By far the best-known passage from the Declaration is an unreservedly national, rather than merely governmental, statement of defiance[10] that most modern Scots still know more or less by heart:

> 'As long as but a hundred of us remain alive, never will we on any conditions be brought under English rule. It is in truth not for glory, nor riches, nor honours, that we are fighting, but for freedom – for that alone, which no honest man gives up but with life itself.'

Immortal as these words rightly are, they pale in significance to the almost revolutionary statement that immediately precedes them. It is worth quoting in full:

> 'Yet if he [King Robert the Bruce] should give up what he has begun, and agree to make us or our kingdom subject to the King of England or the English, we should exert ourselves at once to drive him out as our enemy and a subverter of his own rights and ours, and make some other man who was well able to defend us our King.'

The better part of 500 years before the American and French Revolutions threw off the shackles of divine right monarchy, the Declaration of Arbroath had already begun to articulate the idea of a social contract between rulers and the people they ruled. The seeds of this radical notion were planted by the Scottish philosopher-theologian Duns Scotus as a counter to the feckless reign of King John Balliol, a puppet ruler beholden to the increasingly assertive Edward I of England from 1292-96. Scotus was visited at his Paris residence in 1302 by the Bishop of St Andrews, William Lamberton, who actively supported both William Wallace and Robert the Bruce during the Wars of Independence. By then Balliol had been deposed by Edward, yet his blood still carried in it the rightful claim to the throne – William Wallace, after all, did not fight to make himself or Robert the Bruce king, but to restore Balliol. Wanting to be rid of the tainted Balliol claim for good, Lamberton beseeched Duns Scotus for a legal justification that could outweigh the conventions of royal succession. Scotus did not disappoint, telling Lamberton that the true basis of royal authority was not in a king's name or veins, but in the consent bestowed upon him by the people he ruled. If the people no longer felt that a king was worthy of that consent, it could justifiably be withdrawn and the king un-made.[11] The Gaels of Argyll and the Islesmen of the Hebrides had practised a pseudo-meritocracy, but this was the first time that such an idea had been put into writing and applied to the King of Scots.

It is a subtle yet profoundly important distinction that Scotland's king was properly termed the King of Scots, and not the King of Scotland. The emphasis is unequivocally on the role of stewardship and a sort of rudimentary social contract. The *Book of Pluscarden*, composed at the Roman Catholic Benedictine monastery of Pluscarden near Elgin *circa* 1461, summed it up well: 'A ruler is so called from ruling well; for where there is no rule, there is no ruler.'[12] While it would be far too much to say that anything like democracy flourished in Scotland before the modern era, it would not be an overstatement to conclude that the way people thought about power and rule in Early Historic and medieval Scotland was, in fact, distinctive. A major setback to this philosophy came with the Union of Crowns in 1603. Having left Edinburgh to rule in London, James VI and I took the title of 'King of Scotland' for the first time. To his subjects, James was no longer, like his royal predecessors, known as 'our soverane lord'; henceforth, he was 'his sacred majesty'.[13] Only with the return of governance to

Edinburgh with the re-establishment of the Scottish Parliament in 1999 did the damage from this reversal begin to be undone. To this day, inherited power and wealth is both strongly entrenched yet also strongly resented by most Scots. Differences in status, creed, wealth and faith arising from the accident of birth rather than the agency of character are swept aside by the beautiful Scots phrase 'We're all Jock Tamson's bairns' – all people, cut from the same cloth, trying to make our way in the world.

No Man's Lands

Ygritte has a blunt but beautiful way with words that reminds one of the Gavin Douglas quote etched in stone in Edinburgh's Makar's Court, home to the Writers' Museum. A line from Douglas' *Eneados*, a translation of Virgil's *Aeneid* from Latin into Middle Scots, reads, 'Mak it braid and plane / Kepand na sudron bot our awyn langage.' In modern English, that reads as, 'Make it broad and plain / Keeping no southern, but our own language.' It is a statement of linguistic pride encouraging Scots to speak, without flourish or embellishment, in the tongue of their forefathers. In an unapologetic northern brogue, Ygritte never hesitates to point out the injustices and hypocrisies that Jon's southern upbringing represents to her worldview. Obliterating his ideas about feudal ownership in one fell swoop, she decries how:

> 'The gods made the earth for all men t' share. Only when the kings come with their crowns and steel swords, they claimed it was all theirs. My trees, they said, you can't eat them apples. My stream, you can't fish here. My wood, you're not t'hunt. My earth, my water, my castle.'[14]

It's a completely different conception of ownership, one that – like European colonists in relation to the indigenous people of North America – is viewed as barbarous and profane by the supposedly more civilized societies of the world, who enclose property and proclaim ownership of the very land beneath their feet. While private property laws are of course robust in modern Scotland, something of Ygritte's egalitarianism survives in the form of Scotland's 'right to roam'.

Codified into law by the Land Reform (Scotland) Act of 2003, the right to roam is a magnificent extension of the ancient Scottish principle that all people have the right to access and utilize the wonders of the outdoors without restriction. It is an incredibly difficult concept for someone brought up in North America, like myself, to comprehend. All my life I was taught that if a fence cordons off a parcel of land, under no circumstances am I to hop it and commit the crime of trespass. Even after eight years, this deeply engrained conditioning gives me pause whenever I am cycling out to a castle or historic site only to find that a fence encloses the field it stands in or that it falls within the boundaries of some aristocratic estate. There is something about crossing that artificial and ultimately arbitrary boundary that still smacks of transgression; it is incredible how totally that culturally inherited notions of property and land rights can shape how you view the world and what you are permitted do in it. In Scotland, so long as you abide by the Scottish Outdoor Access Code (for instance, you can't damage property by stomping through a farmer's crops and you must leave no trace of your presence behind but your footprints), the land as far as you can behold is truly yours to explore and enjoy. Such freedom irrevocably shifts your perspective; once you have enjoyed Scotland's right to roam, the idea of not being able to go stravaiging in the hills wherever and whenever the mood strikes you is just as outrageous and absurd as Ygritte makes it sound.

If Roman sources can be believed, the ancient Caledonians went even further than this. It was not just the land that was offered freely to any who sought it, but the heart and body, too. Cassius Dio wrote of the Caledonians and neighbouring Maeatae that, 'They ... possess their women in common, and in common rear all their offspring.'[15] He then relates an extraordinary exchange between the Roman empress Julia Domna, the second wife of Emperor Septimius Severus, and the unfortunately unnamed wife of the Caledonian chieftain Argentoxocos. Speaking in not-so-veiled insults while their husbands negotiated a peace along the northern frontier of the empire, Julia Domna must have thought that she put her barbarian counterpart firmly in her place when she noted the 'loose morals' of Caledonian women who took men as lovers wherever and whenever they pleased.[16] Smug in her moral superiority, nothing could have prepared Julia for the Caledonian queen's reply, delivered without missing a beat. It was true, she confessed, that

Caledonian women loved freely, giving themselves openly to the best and mightiest men amongst them, unlike Roman women of ambition who 'let themselves be debauched by the vilest'.[17] If Julia Domna was sipping on wine while basking in what she thought to be her rhetorical victory, the better part of it almost certainly ended up on the ground at that. Yet again, and with inspiring aplomb, Ygritte said it best, broad and plain: 'If someone tried to tell us we couldn't lie down as man and woman we'd shove a spear up his ass.'[18] Jon was right. In life, love, land and war, these were a free folk indeed.

Chapter 20

A Red Wedding and A Black Dinner

'You may be rich and wise and handsome,
But insolence could be your ruin.'
(Common late medieval expression quoted in Childs, 2005, 29)

'And who are you, the proud lord said,
That I must bow so low?
Only a cat of different coat,
That's all the truth I know.
In a coat of gold or a coat of red,
A lion still has claws,
And mine are long and sharp, my lord,
As long and sharp as yours.'

- The Rains of Castamere

George R.R. Martin has confessed that the hardest thing he ever wrote was the Red Wedding. Many readers and viewers of the television show can likely relate, as it was at least as difficult to watch on helplessly as it unfolded. In a story known perhaps best of all for its constant transgressions against expectations and moral certitude, the Red Wedding stands out amongst many atrocities as the most atrocious of them all. Why, in a story that includes flayed men, the burning of innocent Shireen Baratheon, the intolerable cruelties inflicted on Sansa Stark and a thousand other deep cuts, is the Red Wedding considered by many as *the* defining brutal act? This appears to apply not just to us as the audience but to the inhabitants of Westeros, who regularly witness death, destruction, rape and all the horrors of war and tyranny. Yet it is the Red Wedding more than any other event in *A Song of Ice and Fire* that the common folk curse in the ale houses, and it is the Freys rather than the Lannisters who have become the moral lepers of the land. Why? Because the Starks and countless bannermen that they murdered were guests beneath a host's roof.

The law of guest-right in both Scotland and Westeros is ancient. In its barest form, it dictates that shelter cannot be refused to one who seeks it and that once a guest and host have shared food and drink they are solemnly bound to do each other no harm, whatever the circumstances of their relationship may be. In some cultures, bread and salt in particular are taken to symbolize this pact, and indeed the first thing that Catelyn Stark does once her family is within the great hall of the Twins is ask for food as a token of hospitality. Robb goes one step further, specifically asking Walder Frey to serve salt and wine.[1] Walder obliges and proceeds to speak words that formally acknowledge the Starks as his guests: 'My honoured guests. Be welcome within my walls and at my table. I extend to you my hospitality and protection in the light of the Seven.'[2] With those words the Starks are visibly relieved, secure in the knowledge that a hallowed custom now shielded them. In that, they severely underestimated the wretchedness of Lord Frey.

Hospitality even amongst bitter enemies made practical sense, especially in a place like the Scottish Highlands, where proximity bred an often uncomfortable familiarity with neighbouring clans. Adherence to the concept of guest-right is most notable in kin-based societies, especially when combined with harsh climactic conditions such as in Scandinavia and the north of Britain. In one sense, guest-right serves the same sense of self-preservation as the chivalric convention of ransoming, rather than killing, noble enemies after a battle. As a knight, bannerman or representative of a particular noble house, at some point you are likely to find yourself in need of help or mercy from people who do not like you. In such situations, guest-right is like a collective insurance policy – I'll seek your hospitality today, and give you mine tomorrow.

There is also, however, a very powerful moral element to guest-right. To break it was undeniably seen as an even more egregious transgression than mere murder, both in Scotland and Westeros. Maester Yandel, whose perspective George R.R. Martin's *The World of Ice and Fire* is told from, comments that northmen hold the custom of guest-right dearer than any other tradition, and that kinslaying – that other great taboo – is the only crime that is considered equally severe.[3] This is paralleled in medieval Scottish law, which had a special provision for 'murder under trust' which was treated as a particularly grievous form of murder deserving of the harshest sentencing. There are variations on this kind of moral outrage across the world. For instance, Genghis Khan reserved his greatest wrath for those, such as the Sultan of Khwarezm, who harmed or murdered his emissaries in the belief that diplomatic representatives were protected by unspoken laws of hospitality.[4] When these laws were broken, no curse in any tongue would suffice to express the heinousness of the betrayal.

Northern Hospitality

Respect for the laws of hospitality in the North of Westeros goes back to the arrival of the First Men. More than 12,000 years on, the clans of the Northern mountains who are descended from the First Men are still known above all for two things: their endless disputes – in which the Starks periodically have to intervene, to little long-term avail – and their respect for this ancient rite.[5] Like the strongmen of kin-based societies across our own world, the mountain chieftains north of Winterfell go to extreme pains to make their generosity known to all through feasts, gift-giving and the unconditional provision of shelter to those in need[6]. That the givers of this hospitality may well find themselves hacking at the shields of their former guests in open battle on some other day isn't seen as a contradiction, but a necessity borne of the harshness of the land which they all inhabit.

The Wall itself is no obstacle for guest-right. Even thugs such as Craster, who takes his own daughters for wives and sacrifices the male children born to them to the White Walkers, abide by it. When trying to convince Jon to take her away from Craster's Keep, Gilly argued that since Jon did not partake in Craster's offerings of food or shelter, Jon was not duty-bound to him.[7] In a land where an unflinchingly Hobbesian state of nature dominates day-to-day existence, guest-right is respected even by those that civilization deems beyond its remit. At the opposite end of Westeros in King's Landing, the wicked Qyburn, who requires a steady stream of men, women and children on whom to conduct unspeakable experiments in the deepest bowels of the Red Keep, seems to harbour some respect for guest-right. He tells Cersei with a hint of genuine concern that in the city's wine sinks people whisper of the crown's complicity in the Red Wedding, 'an affront to all the laws of gods and men', and that 'those who had a hand in it are damned'.[8] For a man who balks at no evil deed in the pursuit of knowledge, that's a telling admission.

A morbid Westerosi morality tale, told to Bran by Old Nan to sate his appetite for scary stories, reinforces the dire consequences that befall anyone who does not honour guest-right. The Nightfort, one of the largest castles that guard the Wall, is said to be stalked by many terrors, but few are as horrifying as the Rat Cook. Harbouring a grudge against an Andal king of old, the Rat Cook murdered the king's two sons, baked them into a succulent pie and served it to him along with a cup of Dornish red wine. The king even commended the taste of the pie and asked for a second helping. As punishment for this act, the gods changed the cook into a sow-sized white rat, doomed to feast on the flesh of his own children.[9] Ever since, the Rat Cook has roamed the dark corridors of the Nightfort and haunted the nightmares of children across Westeros. Crucially, the gods' curse, Old Nan insists, was not in retribution merely for the cook's act of murder. Were that the case, Westeros would be overrun with Rat Cooks in every corner of the realm. No – what earned the Cook eternal damnation was that he murdered a guest beneath his roof, the one act that gods and men can never forgive.[10]

The Black Dinner

If there's one place in Scotland where the Rat Cook might be found wandering, it is Edinburgh Castle. Casting my gaze up to that precipitous fortress almost daily, I often reflect on the blood shed in its name: the Gododdin riding out from the Rock with forlorn hope to battle the Northumbrians at Catraeth in 600 CE; Thomas Randolph's stealth assault in 1314; the King's Men and the Queen's Men taking pot-shots at each other during the Laing Siege of 1571-73; and an untold number of other violent episodes that unfolded in the brooding castle's halls and prison pits. Yet from amongst a history that spans over 2,000 years, the bloodstain that soaked deepest into Castle Rock is surely that left by the Black Dinner.

The year was 1440, and a boy king sat upon the throne. James II had the crown foisted upon his head at the age of 7 in an environment rife with suspicion and conspiracy. His inheritance came with the shocking murder of his father, James I, three years earlier in St John's Toun of Perth at the hands of his own nobles. Desperate to escape, James I fled into a sewer beneath his lodgings, and there in the mire was stabbed at least sixteen times. His queen, Joan, exacted furious vengeance upon the conspirators afterwards, but the damage was done. James II grew up ever watchful for the emergence of over-mighty earls and prone to see plots in every shadow. Much of his youth was dominated by a tug-of-war between various courtly factions vying to control him, which could only have stoked James' fears and sense of isolation. Depictions of James II, few as they are, are easy to spot. He had a large red birthmark that covered the full left half of his face and flared up in sync with his temper. When 'James of the Fiery Face', as he is known to posterity, lost his temper, the kingdom paid heed.[11]

In this period there were a number of major baronial families in Scotland whose strength, either individually or in concert, could rival or at least significantly threaten the power of the crown. The Sinclairs, MacDonalds, Murrays and Lennox Stewarts were but a few, each with many castles and wealthy estates dotted across the country. None, however, could match the Douglases. Recalling James 'the Black' Douglas, Robert the Bruce's companion and master of unconventional warfare, he and his progeny were amongst the greatest beneficiaries of Bruce's generosity. With major power centres in the Selkirk Forest in the Borders, Galloway in the south-west, Abercorn on the shores of the Firth of Forth only a few hours' ride from Edinburgh, along with many more, the Douglases could field the most potent fighting force in Scotland aside from the king. Such power inevitably attracted resentment, and two men in particular, the Chancellor of Scotland and Keeper of Edinburgh Castle Sir William Crichton and the Guardian Sir Alexander Livingstone, conspired to humble the Douglases. Crichton duly made arrangements for a feast.

At 17 or 18 years old in 1440, William Douglas was only one or two years older than Robb Stark at the time of the Red Wedding. Emboldened by youth and the prestige of the Douglas name, William and his younger brother David, along with Sir Malcolm Fleming of Cumbernauld, departed their heartlands in the south and made their way to Edinburgh. On the way they stopped at Crichton Castle, the Chancellor's ancestral home about 10 miles south of the city, for refreshment before proceeding to the capital, with the great royal castle visible from many miles away.

We will never know exactly what happened next. Accounts of what became known as the Black Dinner were embellished over the decades that followed. All that is known with certainty is that William Douglas and his party entered Edinburgh Castle on 24 November 1440 and would never take another breath beyond its walls. The story told round many a hearth since goes like this. William, David and Malcolm were seated in the castle's Great Hall along with the young king, Chancellor Crichton and attendants from the king's and Crichton's households. All seemed to be going well – William and James struck up what could have blossomed into a friendship had the night not ended in treachery. As French wines flowed and the finest offerings of the land were served on ornate platters, a deep and lonely pipe began to play. We do not know the name of the tune it played, but it cannot have been cheery. The air seemed to vanish from the hall at once, and a servant wordlessly approached Douglas bearing a silver platter. When Douglas saw what it held, he knew he was not long for the world – a black bull's head, a Celtic symbol of impending death. Rising in protest, William, David and Malcolm were seized by Crichton's goons, dragged out before the castle's gates to face a mock trial for treason[12] and soon their heads joined that of the black bull on the platter. Their blood was barely dry before a rhyme spread amongst the common folk of Scotland. As recorded by David Hume of Godscroft, it went:

> 'Edinburgh castle, toun and tour
> God grant you sink for sin
> And that even for the Black Dinner
> Earl Douglas got therein.'[13]

Whether the reality of the Black Dinner was actually as theatrical as all that is very much in doubt. Contemporary accounts are conflicting, yet the bull's head seems to be an addition from the following century at earliest.[14] E.B. Livingston's account in his 1920 work *The Livingstons of Callendar* is considered one of the more reputable versions, and it makes no mention of any mock trial or beheading. The mid-fifteenth-century *Auchinleck Chronicle* gives a frustratingly laconic account, saying only that 'William of Douglas Archebaldis son ... XVIII yeris of age, and his brother David Douglas, was put to deid at Edinburgh. And Malcome Flemyng of Beggar [Biggar] was put to deid in that famyn place within thre days efter.'[15] Most likely, the events of 1440 were conflated with the murder of yet another Douglas earl in the presence of the king little more than a decade latter, a story we will come to shortly.

Contemporary sources also fail to mention one of the more disturbing aspects of the murder of the Sixth Earl at Edinburgh, which is that his own family member was almost certainly in on it. Known to posterity as James 'the Gross' for his tedious inaction and corpulence, he was William's great-uncle. He reaped a considerable boon from the Black Dinner, becoming the Seventh Earl of Douglas and head of the Black Douglas family in the wake of the murder of his grand-nephews – something that would never have happened if either William or David had lived to produce an heir. McGladdery argues convincingly that it is 'stretching the bounds of credulity' to believe that Crichton and Livingston orchestrated the Black Dinner without James the Gross' knowledge and complicity.[16] The *Game of Thrones* equivalent, as if the Red Wedding could possibly be any worse, would be if Brynden 'the Blackfish' Tully had helped to set the trap sprung by the Freys. As usual, Scottish history exceeds even the sometimes cruel machinations of Martin's universe.

Compare the events of 1440 with the proceedings of the Red Wedding as depicted in the television show. Robb and Catelyn Stark, along with Umbers, Tullys and attendant bannermen, warily feasted in the Great Hall of The Twins. Having availed of plenty of food and drink, their anxieties started to ease and relieved smiles even crept across their faces. In the corner of her eye, Catelyn noticed a Frey attendant close and bar the doors of the hall. The band, moments ago playing ribald tunes from a gallery overlooking the festivities, changed their tune to the unmistakable lament of The Rains of Castamere. Outside the castle, Robb's direwolf, Grey Wind, began to fret. Knowing all too well what that wicked tune meant, Catelyn seized Roose Bolton's hand and realized in horror that he was fully armoured underneath his finery. Walder Frey commanded his guests' attention and promised to show them the hospitality they deserved. The band swapped their strings and drums for crossbows and rained death on the Starks below, piercing Robb and Catelyn as Lord Frey grinned. Grey Wind and the King in the North's bannermen were slaughtered in the camp outside the walls, and at last Roose Bolton gave

Robb the Lannisters' regards by burying his sword in the Young Wolf's heart. Robb's head was struck from his body and stitched on that of Grey Wind, in mockery of his moniker and in desecration of all the laws of gods and men. Almost beat for beat, the two harrowing events read the same. Little wonder: Martin has revealed that the Black Dinner of 1440 and the Massacre of Glencoe in 1692 were blended together to create the Red Wedding. The story of the Black Dinner does not end there, however. There was also a part two, though whether Martin was aware of it when writing the Red Wedding is unknown. Prepare to feel a distinct sense of déjà vu.

A Second Helping

The lofty ambitions of Westeros' noble houses are a constant thorn in the side of any who sit upon the Iron Throne. Some kings may rule from its cold embrace with more repose than others, yet none can be entirely comfortable – and if any could, then they are either legends or fools. Few were as ill at ease as the Mad King Aerys. Endless conspiracies and treacheries lurked in the shadows of his twisted mind, though some proved all too real. Tywin Lannister was the subject of Aerys' envy and wrath once it became clear that Tywin, and not he, was the mightiest man in Westeros. The Mad King vented his anger by insulting Tywin's one and only joy in the world, his wife Joanna, during a tournament. If that did not turn Tywin against him, then appointing the young Jaime Lannister to his kingsguard – thereby stripping him of his ability to inherit the seat of House Lannister, Casterly Rock – certainly did.[17] It is said that Aerys' jealous hatred for Tywin ran so deep that, upon the death of Joanna while giving birth to Tyrion, Aerys proclaimed that the gods had 'plucked a fair flower from his hand and given him a monster in her place, to teach him some humility at last'.[18] When he learned that his son had plunged his sword into Aerys' back, I wonder if Tywin hurled the Mad King's words back at him.

In the years after the Black Dinner and the death of James the Gross in 1453, the young and vigorous William Douglas – of the same name as his forebear killed at Edinburgh – became the Eighth Earl and acted immediately to restore the Douglas name to its former prestige. William proved more than capable, if also typically self-confident as a young man with immense power and an axe to grind with it. He launched a two-year campaign against William Crichton, who was widely viewed as the puppet master behind the Black Dinner. This included far-reaching raids on Crichton's lands in Fife and a nine-week siege of Edinburgh Castle in 1445.[19] That William Douglas was able to besiege one of Scotland's mightiest castles is a remarkable testament to Douglas strength, yet it also cannot have failed to be noticed by the maturing James II. If Douglas could invest even Edinburgh, would he reach for the crown next?

By 1452, the boy king had grown into a man, though a hot-tempered and deeply mistrustful one. An all too familiar series of events unfolded. King James invited Douglas to meet with him at Stirling Castle. That the Keeper of Stirling Castle was then none other than William Crichton from the original Black Dinner seems too great a coincidence to entirely ignore. Douglas was rightly suspicious, despite having enjoyed friendly and personal relations with the king for several years. A special assurance was sent out to assuage Douglas' apprehension, which included the king's own privy seal.[20] In retrospect, one wants to reach out through time and shout at Douglas not to follow in the ill-fated footsteps of the Sixth Earl. Yet follow he did.

Meetings were held between Douglas and the king over two days, 21 and 22 February 1452. They would be Douglas' last. It began cordially enough, yet soon – after dinner at seven o'clock, if the *Auchinleck Chronicle* is correct – in a small chamber with a handful of others in attendance, James levelled accusations against Douglas that he was involved in a conspiracy against the crown with John MacDonald, the Earl of Ross, and Alexander Lindsay, Earl of Crawford. This was not entirely unfounded, for Douglas had indeed entered a bond with them regarding the distribution of power in the north of Scotland. Seeing as the Earl of Ross had been in open revolt against the king as recently as 1451, Douglas was in an awkward position. Yet this was a private arrangement, albeit bolder than usual, with no direct reference to the crown.[21] It was enough to turn James' fiery face a seething red, and what happened next was, if anything, even more shocking than the events of 1440. For this time, the king himself struck the first blow.

Douglas refused James' pointed demand to break his bond with the Earls of Ross and Crawford, and in an irrepressible rage the king drew his dagger and plunged it into Douglas' neck. The *Auchinleck Chronicle* recounts the grisly details:

> 'Than the king said, fals tratour sen yow will nocht I sall, and stert sodanly till him with ane knyf, and straik him in at the coler, and down in the body. And thai sayd Patrik Gray straik him nixt the king, with ane poll ax on the hed, and strak out his harnes [brains].'[22]

By the time the king recomposed himself and his henchmen had done their worst, William Douglas' brains and guts were dashed across the floor, his body ridden with twenty-six wounds. His corpse was unceremoniously thrown from a window, and the spot where it landed is still known morbidly as the Douglas Garden.

The king's word was proven worthless that day, for the guest he had invited into his castle with the solemn assurance of his privy seal was now dead by his own hand. A parliamentary inquiry was launched specifically to address this breach of the laws of safe conduct, though its lack of efficacy proved all too familiar: James' feeble defence, worthy of Walder Frey in the wake of the Red Wedding, was simply that Douglas had acted in such a way as to 'have procured and produced the occasion of his death'.[23] With this miscarriage of justice, the king was found guiltless. He soon followed through with what he started in that small chamber in Stirling Castle and went to war against the Black Douglases, using his artillery to smash mighty castles like Threave and utterly root out what had only a few years ago been the most powerful baronial faction in Scotland.

When compiling the gruesome tale of the Black Dinner and all its supposed theatrics, it is likely that chroniclers conflated these two uncannily similar events. We know, for instance, the Eighth Earl dined with James II at Stirling Castle just hours before being murdered by him, whereas it's entirely possible that no dinner was served at all upon the Sixth Earl's arrival at Edinburgh Castle, which is treated in almost every history book as the 'true' Black Dinner. Yet what unfolded in Stirling, culminating with William Douglas' blood feeding the flowers, is arguably the more shocking of the two. Formal assurances of safety were granted, and while the king was in some ways also a victim of the 1440 dinner, his was the hand that stuck the first blow in anger in 1452. Reflecting on what could have changed within the king's heart in the twelve years separating the two events, it all reads as a tragedy. The boy James, manipulated by those who were supposed to ensure his welfare, grew into a man consumed by the same paranoia and covetousness that once oppressed him. George Martin's well-known mantra for creating effective characters is that the only motivation worth writing about is the human heart in conflict with itself – we can only speculate whether, while giving his testimony to parliament with his hands only recently washed of Douglas' blood, some part of James II realized what he had become.

In Cold Blood: The Massacre of Glencoe

The final calamity that Martin rolled into one along with the two Black Dinners has become something of a byword for betrayal and injustice. There are places in Scotland where the events of centuries gone by seem to linger in the air, the weight of them strangely entangled with the beauty of the landscape to give the visitor a profound sense of melancholy. More so than perhaps anywhere else in Scotland, this melancholy echoes through Glencoe.

The Massacre of Glencoe, committed in cold blood in the dark early morning of 13 February 1692, stands out from the Black Dinner as being one of the most exhaustively accounted for episodes in Scotland's story. It has spawned innumerable books, including rigorous non-fiction and historical fiction, and its intricate details – each worth knowing so as to do justice to the victims – have been analyzed by so many eminent historians that they would be impossible to recount fully here. Let's then focus on the aspect of the massacre that surely shook Martin to his core: the most grievous violation of guest-right imaginable.

In 1688, the Protestant William of Orange of the Dutch Republic led an invading army some 30,000-strong across the English Channel and seized the 'vacant' throne in London from King James VII (of Scotland) & II (of England). Heralded by its supporters as a bloodless, 'Glorious Revolution', it was anything but, with widespread fighting and devastation in Ireland and Scotland. So began the long song of the Jacobites, determined to restore James, a Catholic, to the throne usurped by William. Following his defeat of the first Jacobite Rising of 1688-89, King William demanded an oath of allegiance from the Highland chieftains to be made before his officials before the strict deadline of 1 January 1692.

Even before this, some in Scotland had been agitating for bloodshed. John Dalrymple, Master of Stair and Lord Advocate of Scotland, was the thirstiest of them all and eager to please the new king. Directing his ire at the troublesome MacDonalds of Glencoe, it is difficult not to become emotional when reading the letters he sent to colleagues wondering, for instance, whether they 'think that this [the dead of winter] is the proper season to maul them in the cold long nights'.[24] Dalrymple's language echoes the worst sentiments of colonizers, dehumanizing his intended victims and stripping them of any right to existence. '[I]t's a great work of charity to be exact in rooting out that damnable sect,' he wrote. 'God knows whether the 12,000 [pounds] sterling had been better employed to settle the Highlands, or to ravage them.'[25]

The excuse to ravage them came gift-wrapped. The MacDonald chieftain of Glencoe, Alasdair, known as the MacIain, set out in good faith to offer his submission to King William, knowing that to do otherwise would be to invite disaster upon those whose lives he, as the chieftain, was responsible for. Winter storms had battered the Highland passes, which were difficult to traverse at the best of times, slowing his progress considerably. To make matters worse, MacIain mistakenly set out north for Fort William when he was supposed to make his pledge at Inveraray, 60 miles to the south. Arriving in Fort William and being informed of his error, he immediately and with great urgency started south, only to be arrested for twenty-four hours while en route.[26] By the time MacIain arrived in Inveraray and presented himself before the proper officials, it was five days past the 1 January deadline. Undoubtedly the result would have been the same even if MacIain arrived a single minute late, for King William and his agents in Scotland merely sought an excuse to make an example of the MacDonalds. Now they had it.

The document ordering the massacre, signed by King William personally, is oft-quoted with good reason. It is worth reproducing here nearly in full, that we may understand the ruthlessness inflicted on the residents of Glencoe from the highest echelons of power:

> 'You are hereby ordered to fall upon the rebels, the McDonalds of Glencoe, and put all to the sword under seventy. You are to have special care that the old Fox [MacIain] and his sons do upon no account escape your hands, you are to secure all the avenues that no man escape. This you are to put in

execution at five of the clock precisely; and by that time, or very shortly after it, I'll strive to be at you with a stronger party: if I do not come with you at five, you are not to tarry for me, but to fall on. This is by the King's special command, for the good & safety of the Country, that these miscreants be cut off root and branch.'

For their Majesties' service
[signed] Robert Duncanson
To Capt. Robert Campbell of Glenlyon[27]

Robert Campbell of Glenlyon took up this duty with all the enthusiasm that an ageing drunkard could. He had a score to settle with the MacDonalds, they having looted some of his lands and deprived him of income. It should be noted, however, that while the Massacre of Glencoe is commonly presented as the result of the notorious rivalry between the MacDonalds and the Campbells, that is only part of the story. While Glenlyon, leader of the expedition, was a Campbell, many of the soldiers who perpetrated the massacre were not. More significantly, the massacre was not carried out by Campbells acting independently in the manner of the old Highland blood feuds, but rather as a direct order from the king himself, of which Glenlyon was merely an arbiter. To simplify that dark day by presenting it as a continuation of the clans' almost ritualized rivalries is to fundamentally misrepresent the greater power dynamics at play, and to allow those whose authority the massacre was carried out in the name of to escape the judgment of history.

Glenlyon led 130 soldiers into the villages dispersed through Glencoe, including Invercoe, Inveriggan and Achnacon, on 1 February. When we speak of the Massacre of Glencoe, most people likely imagine it occurring in a single cluster of buildings, yet the reality was that it was a far larger operation than that. The original intention was for Glenlyon to be joined by two other divisions, bringing a combined force of around 850 soldiers to bear against a maximum of 100 fighting MacDonalds and around 500 non-combatant residents of the glen.[28] In the end, Glenlyon's force were the sole perpetrators, with the other two held up by the same inhospitable winter conditions that fatefully delayed MacIain on the snowy road to Inveraray. Glenlyon's troops were billeted in the homes of the MacDonalds, who, despite deep suspicions, abided by the ancient custom of guest-right.

Three to five soldiers were stationed in each house, depending on how many future victims lived within.[29] For nearly two weeks they availed of their hosts' hospitality, dining with the families and sleeping under the roofs of their blackhouses. The old rivals Glenlyon and MacIain even reputedly passed the hours – no doubt with simmering tension – by playing cards at MacIain's hearth fire.[30]

At five o'clock in the morning of Saturday, 13 February, with hours of darkness still to come, the killing began. Awoken by a clamour, MacIain rose from his bed and was shot in the back at close range. His elderly wife, clinging to his body, was stripped naked by the redcoats, who pried the rings off her arthritic fingers with their teeth.[31] Families alerted by the sound of gunfire fled their homes in nothing but their bedclothes, with many dying later due to exposure in the bitter cold. Others, unable to escape, were systematically bound, brought outside and executed; one boy of 13 appealed to mercy from Glenlyon but was shot without hesitation by Captain Drummond, Glenlyon's superior officer, who had arrived from Ballachulish.[32]

One story recounts how a soldier was ordered to bayonet a woman who was singing a Gaelic lullaby to her baby:

> 'Cold, cold this night is my bed.
> Cold, cold this night is my child.
> Lasting, lasting this night my sleep.
> I in my shroud and thou in my arm.
> The shadow of death creeps over me.'[33]

Being from the Highlands too, the soldier had heard the same tune as a boy and spared them. Having spent so much time with the people of Glencoe, some soldiers were reluctant to carry out their orders. A Lieutenant Farquhar and Lieutenant Kennedy are mentioned by name as having broken their swords instead of partaking in the massacre. They were subsequently arrested and imprisoned, while others who hesitated were reassured with what we would now recognize as the illegitimate Nuremberg Defence: 'All the blame be on such as gave the Orders; we are free, being bound to obey our Officers.'[34] By the time the late winter sun illuminated the glen, thirty-eight men, women and children lay dead. Perhaps as many again died in the hills as the smoke from the smouldering thatch of their homes, in which their killers warmed themselves only hours ago, bellowed into the crisp morning sky. Indeed, the deadly winter conditions were deliberately weaponized by Dalrymple, Master of Stair, as evidenced by his letter to Sir Thomas Livingstone, which read in part, 'It's true, it's a rigid season for the soldiers to work, but it's the only time that they cannot escape you; for human constitution cannot endure long out of houses.'[35]

Outrage rippled across the land. A desire to avenge the Massacre of Glencoe fired the passions of many Jacobites right up until their last stand at Culloden in 1746. Robert Campbell of Glenlyon, on the other hand, exhibited more than a hint of Walder Frey's moral ambivalence in the weeks after the massacre. Just as Walder openly boasted about his betrayal of the Starks at the Red Wedding to anyone, like Jaime Lannister, who he thought would delight in it, Glenlyon could be found in the ale houses of Edinburgh's High Street showing off the order from King William to any who showed the remotest interest in the recent rumours of bloodshed.[36] While John Dalrymple, Secretary of State for Scotland and author of the ravenous letters described earlier in the lead-up to Glencoe, was stripped of his title, Glenlyon and all other military officers involved continued in their careers unhindered by their complicity. Glenlyon died in 1696, drunk and penniless in a soiled gutter in Bruges.

Scotland has never forgotten Glencoe. In terms of the number of dead, the Massacre of Glencoe was greatly exceeded by several other ignominious episodes in the sixteenth and seventeenth centuries, such as the slaughter of as many as 400 MacDonald civilians at the hands of the MacLeods in a cave on the Isle of Eigg. The reason that the infamy of the Massacre of Glencoe is known throughout the world is not because of the number of innocents killed; such an empirical focus is inherently inadequate when comparing horrors. Glencoe will forever be remembered as the epitome of betrayal because Robert Campbell of Glenlyon and his 130 men were the MacDonalds' guests. They ate their food, they shared the warmth of their fires and they undoubtedly talked and laughed the days and nights away with the very people whom they would later butcher. Though it is now more for tourists than a genuine threat, the Clachaig Inn at Glencoe still displays a sign reading, 'No hawkers or Campbells', more than three centuries after the massacre. Such is the power of stories, the means by which the North does not soon forget.

Endnotes

Preface

1. Martin, George R.R., *Fire and Blood* (London: Harper Voyager, 2018), 391.
2. Martin, George R.R., *On Fantasy* (online, 1996). Available at http://www.georgerrmartin.com/about-george/on-writing-essays/on-fantasy-by-george-r-r-martin/ (accessed 19 September 2019).

PART I

Nature's Crucible: Stirling, The Neck & the Twins

1. Tacitus, Publius Cornelius, *Tacitus: Agricola and Germany* trans. A.R. Birley (New York: Oxford University Press, 1999), 18.
2. Bower, Walter, *Scotichronicon: Vol. 1: Books I and II*, D.E.R. Watt, John Macqueen and Winifred Macqueen (eds) (Edinburgh: The Mercat Press, 1993), 169.
3. Martin, George R.R., García, Elio M., Jr. and Antonsson, Linda, *The World of Ice & Fire: The Untold History of Westeros and the Game of Thrones* (London: Harper Voyager, 2014), 20.
4. Martin, George R.R., *A Game of Thrones* (London: Harper Voyager, 2011), Sansa I, 135.
5. *Game of Thrones: The Complete Third Season* (2014, Blu-ray), Histories and Lore: Season Three: House Reed, narrated by Ellie Kendrick. Written by Bryan Cogman. Warner Home Video.
6. *Game of Thrones: The Complete First Season* (2012, Blu-ray), The Complete Guide to Westeros: The Children of the Forst, the First Men, and the Andals, narrated by Donald Sumpter. Written by Bryan Cogman.

7. *Game of Thrones: The Complete Third Season* (2014, Blu-ray), Histories and Lore: Season Three: House Reed, narrated by Ellie Kendrick. Written by Bryan Cogman. Warner Home Video.
8. A Wiki of Ice and Fire, *Hammer of the Waters* (2018, online). Available at https://awoiaf.westeros.org/index.php/Hammer_of_the_waters (accessed 7 November 2018).
9. Martin, George R.R., *A Game of Thrones* (London: Harper Voyager, 2011), Eddard II, 108.
10. Miles, David, *The Tribes of Britain* (London: Phoenix, 2006), 43.
11. Davies, Norman, *The Isles: A History* (London: Papermac, 2000), 8.
12. Brown, Mike and Mendum, John, *Loch Lomond to Stirling: A Landscape Fashioned by Geology* (Perth: Scottish Natural Heritage & British Geological Survey, 2017), 4.
13. Fawcett, Richard, *The Architectural History of Scotland: Scottish Architecture from the Accession of the Stewarts to the Reformation 1371-1560* (Edinburgh: Edinburgh University Press, 1994), 14.
14. Oliver, Neil, *A History of Scotland* (London: Pheonix, 2010), 110.
15. Martin, George R.R., *A Clash of Kings* (New York: Bantam Books, 2011), Theon II, 395.
16. Martin, George R.R., *A Dance with Dragons* (London: Harper Voyager, 2011), Reek II, 255.
17. Ross, David R., *On the Trail of Robert the Bruce* (Edinburgh: Luath Press Ltd, 1999), 160.
18. *Game of Thrones: The Complete Third Season* (2014, Blu-ray), Histories and Lore: Season Three: House Frey, narrated by Michelle Fairley. Written by Bryan Cogman. Warner Home Video.
19. A Wiki of Ice and Fire, *The Twins* (2018, online). Available at https://awoiaf.westeros.org/index.php/Twins (accessed 4 November 2018).

Rocks of the Ages: Dumbarton & Casterly

1. Davies, Norman, *The Isles: A History* (London: Papermac, 2000), 7.
2. Martin, George R.R., García, Elio M., Jr. and Antonsson, Linda, *The World of Ice & Fire: The Untold History of Westeros and the Game of Thrones* (London: Harper Voyager, 2014), 204.
3. *Ibid.*, 204.
4. *Ibid.*, 205.
5. *Ibid.*, 203.

6. Martin, George R.R., *A Dance with Dragons* (London: Harper Voyager, 2011), Jon I, 59.

7. Davies, Norman, *Vanished Kingdoms: The History of Half-Forgotten Europe* (London: Penguin Books, 2012), 46-47.

8. MacPhail, I.M.M., *Dumbarton Castle* (Edinburgh: John Donald Publishers Ltd, 1979), 7.

9. Davies, Norman, *Vanished Kingdoms: The History of Half-Forgotten Europe* (London: Penguin Books, 2012), 43.

10. MacPhail, I.M.M., *Dumbarton Castle* (Edinburgh: John Donald Publishers Ltd, 1979), 7.

11. *The Annals of Ulster*, Seán Mac Airt and Gearóid Mac Niocaill (eds) (Dublin: Dublin Institute for Advanced Studies, 1983), 327.

12. Davies, Norman, *Vanished Kingdoms: The History of Half-Forgotten Europe* (London: Penguin Books, 2012), 70. Quoting John Davies, *A History of Wales* (1993), 62.

13. MacPhail, I.M.M. *Dumbarton Castle* (Edinburgh: John Donald Publishers Ltd, 1979), 48.

The Isles

1. Ritchie, Anna, *Viking Scotland* (London: B.T. Batsford Ltd, 1993), 10.

2. Davies, Norman, *The Isles: A History* (London: Papermac, 2000), 212.

3. Tolkien, J.R.R., *The Lord of the Rings* (London: BCA, 1991), 45.

4. MacNeil, Ian Roderick, *Castle in the Sea* (New York: Vantage Press, 1975), 11.

5. Samuel Johnson in Black, Ronald (ed.), *To the Hebrides: Samuel Johnson's Journey to the Western Islands of Scotland and James Boswell's Journal of a Tour to the Hebrides* (Edinburgh: Birlinn, 2011), 197.

6. MacNeil, Ian Roderick, *Castle in the Sea* (New York: Vantage Press, 1975), 48.

7. Martin, George R.R., García, Elio M., Jr. and Antonsson, Linda, *The World of Ice & Fire: The Untold History of Westeros and the Game of Thrones* (London: Harper Voyager, 2014), 176.

8. Clements, Jonathan, *A Brief History of the Vikings* (London: Constable & Robertson Ltd, 2005), 7.

9. Martin, George R.R., *A Feast for Crows* (London: Harper Voyager, 2011), The Prophet, 22.

10. Martin, George R.R., *A Clash of Kings* (New York: Bantam Books, 2011), Theon II, 384.

11. *Ibid.*, 22.

12. MacGregor, Martin, 'Warfare in Gaelic Scotland in the Later Middle Ages', in M. Spears, Jeremy A. Crang and Mathew J. Strickland (eds), *A Military History of Scotland* (Edinburgh: Edinburgh University Press, 2014), 212.

13. Martin, George R.R., García, Elio M., Jr. and Antonsson, Linda, *The World of Ice & Fire: The Untold History of Westeros and the Game of Thrones* (London: Harper Voyager, 2014), 176-77.

14. Fisher, Ian, 'Chapter 5: The Heirs of Somerled', in Richard Oram and Geoffrey Stell (eds), *Lordship and Architecture in Medieval and Renaissance Scotland* (Edinburgh: John Donald, 2005), 89.

15. 'The Wars to Come', *Game of Thrones*, Season 5, episode 1 (2015). Directed by Michael Slovis. HBO, 12 April 2015.

16. MacGregor, Martin, 'Warfare in Gaelic Scotland in the Later Middle Ages', in M. Spears, Jeremy A. Crang and Mathew J. Strickland (eds), *A Military History of Scotland* (Edinburgh: Edinburgh University Press, 2014), 213.

17. Martin, George R.R., *A Feast for Crows* (London: Harper Voyager, 2011), The Prophet, 21.

18. Cunningham, Alastair, *A Guide to Dunnottar Castle* (Inverness: Alistair Cunningham, 1998), 3.

19. Canmore, *Dunnicaer* (2018, online). Available at https://canmore.org.uk/site/37001/dunnicaer (accessed 25 November 2018).

20. Martin, George R.R., *Fire and Blood* (London: Harper Voyager, 2018), 243.

21. Martin, George R.R., García, Elio M., Jr. and Antonsson, Linda, *The World of Ice & Fire: The Untold History of Westeros and the Game of Thrones* (London: Harper Voyager, 2014), 176.

22. Dargie, Richard, *Scottish Castles & Fortifications* (Berks: GW Publishing, 2009), 45.

23. Simpson, Douglas W., *The Ancient Stones of Scotland* (London: Robert Hale Limited, 1965), 133.

24. Dargie, Richard, *Scottish Castles & Fortifications* (Berks: GW Publishing, 2009), 45.

North versus South?

1. Ruiter, Brian de, 'A Defense against the "Other"', in Pavlac, Brian A. (ed.), *Game of Thrones Versus History: Written in Blood* (New Jersey: John Wiley & Sons, Inc., 2017), 88-89.
2. Martin, George R.R., *A Game of Thrones* (London: Harper Voyager, 2011), Eddard II, 114.
3. *Ibid.*, 113.
4. 'The Ghost of Harrenhal', *Game of Thrones*, Season 2, episode 5 (2012). Directed by David Petrarka. HBO, 29 April 2012.
5. *Game of Thrones: The Complete Third Season* (2014, Blu-ray), Histories and Lore: Season Three: The North, narrated by Kit Harrington. Written by Bryan Cogman. Warner Home Video.
6. 'Winter is Coming', *Game of Thrones*, Season 1, episode 1 (2011). Directed by Tim Van Patten. HBO, 17 April 2011.
7. Camille, Michael, *Mirror in Parchment: The Luttrell Psalter and the Making of Medieval England* (London: Reaktion Books Ltd, 1998), 179.
8. McDonald, R. Andrew, 'The Western *Gàidhealtachd* in the Middle Ages', in Bob Harris & Alan R. MacDonald (eds), *Making and Unmaking of a Nation* v.1 (2006), 65.
9. Clements, Jonathan, *A Brief History of the Vikings* (London: Constable & Robertson Ltd, 2005) 217.
10. 'A Man Without Honor', *Game of Thrones*, Season 2, episode 7 (2012). Directed by David Nutter. HBO, 13 May 2012.

PART II

No Ruined Stones

1. MacDiarmid, Hugh, *The Hugh MacDiarmid Anthology: Poems in Scots and English*, Michael Grieve and Alexander Scott (eds) (London: Routledge & Kegan Paul, 1972).
2. 'The Ghost of Harrenhal', *Game of Thrones*, Season 2, episode 5 (2012). Directed by David Petrarka. HBO, 29 April 2012.
3. 'The Door', *Game of Thrones*, Season 6, episode 5 (2016). Directed by Jack Bender. HBO, 22 May 2016.
4. Foster, Sally, *Maeshowe and the Heart of Neolithic Orkney* (Edinburgh: Historic Scotland, 2006), 20.
5. Davies, Norman, *The Isles: A History* (London: Papermac, 2000), 17.

6. Noonan, Damien, *Castles & Ancient Monuments of Scotland* (London: Aurum Press, 2000), 13.

7. Martin, George R.R., *A Game of Thrones* (London: Harper Voyager, 2011), Eddard II, 106.

8. Foster, Sally, *Maeshowe and the Heart of Neolithic Orkney* (Edinburgh: Historic Scotland, 2006), 20.

9. Martin, George R.R., *A Storm of Swords* (New York: Bantam Books, 2013), Catelyn V, 625.

10. 'Eastwatch' *Game of Thrones*, Season 7, episode 5 (2017). Directed by Matt Shakman. HBO, 13 August 2017.

11. Webb, Sharon, *In the Footsteps of Kings* (Kilmartin, Argyll: Kilmartin House Trust, 2012), 21.

12. Morris, R.W.B., (1970-71) 'The petroglyphs at Achnabreck, Argyll', in *Proceedings of the Society of Antiquaries of Scotland*, 103, 1974, 53.

13. *Ibid.*, 54.

14. Webb, Sharon, *In the Footsteps of Kings* (Kilmartin, Argyll: Kilmartin House Trust, 2012), 23.

15. *Game of Thrones: The Complete First Season* (2012, Blu-ray), The Complete Guide to Westeros: The Children of the Forst, the First Men and the Andals, narrated by Donald Sumpter. Written by Bryan Cogman.

16. Armit, Ian, *Celtic Scotland* (Edinburgh: Birlinn, 2016), 33.

17. Davies, Norman, *The Isles: A History* (London: Papermac, 2000), 26.

18. Dixon, Nick, *The Crannogs of Perthshire: A Guide* (Perth: Perth and Kinross Heritage Trust), 2.

19. Campsie, Alison, 'Breakthrough in study of Scotland's ancient loch dwellers', *The Scotsman* (online), 30 May 2018. Available at https://www.scotsman.com/lifestyle/breakthrough-in-study-of-scotland-s-ancient-loch-dwellers-1-4747452 (accessed 8 September 2018).

Walls at the Edge of the World

1. Procopius, *History of the Wars*, Books VII and VIII, trans. H.B. Dewing (London: William Heinemann, 1962), 265-67.

2. 'The Climb', *Game of Thrones*, Season 3, episode 6 (2013). Directed by Alik Sakharov. HBO, 5 May 2013.

3. Martin, George R.R., *A Game of Thrones* (London: Harper Voyager, 2011), Jon VI, 503.

4. Gilmore, Mikal, 'George R.R. Martin: The Rolling Stone Interview' (23 April 2014, online), *Rolling Stone*. Available at https://www.rollingstone.com/culture/culture-news/george-r-r-martin-the-rolling-stone-interview-242487/ (accessed 14 September 2018).

5. Oliver, Neil, *A History of Ancient Britain* (London: Phoenix Press, 2012).

6. Kamm, Antony, *The Last Frontier: The Roman Invasions of Scotland* (Stroud: Tempus Publishing Limited, 2004).

7. *Ibid.*, 102.

8. Breeze, David J., *Roman Scotland* (London: B.T. Batsford Ltd & Historic Scotland, 1996), 62.

9. *Ibid.*, 69.

10. Davies, Norman, *The Isles: A History* (London: Papermac, 2000), 108.

11. Breeze, David J., *Roman Scotland* (London: B.T. Batsford Ltd & Historic Scotland, 1996), 63.

12. Martin, George R.R., *A Dance with Dragons* (London: Harper Voyager, 2011), Jon I, 59.

13. Breeze, David J., *Roman Scotland* (London: B.T. Batsford Ltd & Historic Scotland, 1996), 64.

14. Maxwell, Gordon, *A Gathering of Eagles: Scenes from Roman Scotland* (Edinburgh: Birlinn Ltd with Historic Scotland, 2005), 41.

15. Kamm, Antony, *The Last Frontier: The Roman Invasions of Scotland* (Stroud: Tempus Publishing Limited, 2004), 112.

16. Game of Thrones Wiki, *The Wall* (2018, online). Available at https://gameofthrones.fandom.com/wiki/The_Wall (accessed 14 October 2018).

17. Robertson, Anne S., *The Antonine Wall: A handbook to the Roman Wall between Forth and Clyde and a guide to its surviving remains* (Edinburgh: Glasgow Archaeological Society, 1963), 13.

18. Kamm, Antony, *The Last Frontier: The Roman Invasions of Scotland* (Stroud: Tempus Publishing Limited, 2004), 123.

19. Robertson, Anne S., *The Antonine Wall: A handbook to the Roman Wall between Forth and Clyde and a guide to its surviving remains* (Edinburgh: Glasgow Archaeological Society, 1963), 41.

20. 'A Golden Crown', *Game of Thrones*, Season 1, episode 6 (2011). Directed by Daniel Minahan. HBO, 22 May 2011.

21. Davies, Norman, *Vanished Kingdoms: The History of Half-Forgotten Europe* (London: Penguin Books, 2012), 46.

22. *Ibid.*, 46-47.
23. Kamm, Antony, *The Last Frontier: The Roman Invasions of Scotland* (Stroud: Tempus Publishing Limited, 2004), 114.
24. Maxwell, Gordon, *A Gathering of Eagles: Scenes from Roman Scotland* (Edinburgh: Birlinn Ltd with Historic Scotland, 2005), 29.
25. Ross, Stewart, *Scottish Castles* (Moffat, Dumfries and Galloway: Lochar Publishing Ltd, 1990), 13.
26. Breeze, David J., *Roman Scotland* (London: B.T. Batsford Ltd & Historic Scotland, 1996), 117.

Castles: Towers of Power

1. McKean, Charles, *The Scottish Chateau: The Country Houses of Renaissance Scotland* (Thrupp, Oxfordshire: Sutton Publishing Limited, 2001), 43.
2. Martin, George R.R., García, Elio M., Jr. and Antonsson, Linda, *The World of Ice & Fire: The Untold History of Westeros and the Game of Thrones* (London: Harper Voyager, 2014), 38
3. Gies, Joseph and Gies, Francis, *Life in a Medieval Castle* (London: Harper Perennial, 2015), 205.
4. Mackenzie, W. Mackay, *The Mediaeval Castle in Scotland* (New York: Benjamin Blom, Inc., 1972), 6.
5. *Ibid.*, 3.
6. Martin, George R.R., García, Elio M., Jr. and Antonsson, Linda *The World of Ice & Fire: The Untold History of Westeros and the Game of Thrones* (London: Harper Voyager, 2014), 10.
7. Gies, Joseph and Gies, Francis, *Life in a Medieval Castle* (London: Harper Perennial, 2015), 187.
8. Brown, Michael, *The Black Douglases* (East Linton, East Lothian: Tuckwell Press Ltd, 1998), 136-37.
9. Dickinson, W. Croft, Donaldson, Gordon & Milne, Isabel A. (eds), *A Source Book of Scottish History: Volume One: From the Earliest Times to 1424* (Edinburgh: Thomas Nelson and Sons Ltd, 1958), 7.
10. Tabraham, Chris, *Scotland's Castles*, Revised edition (London: B.T. Batsford Ltd & Historic Scotland, 2005), 15.
11. Forder, Simon, *The myth of the motte and bailey castle in Scotland* (online), (accessed 19 October 2018).
12. Tabraham, Chris, *Scotland's Castles*, Revised edition (London: B.T. Batsford Ltd & Historic Scotland, 2005), 18-19.

13. Forder, Simon, *The myth of the motte and bailey castle in Scotland* (online), (accessed 19 October 2018).

14. *Ibid.*

15. Martin, George R.R., *Fire and Blood* (London: Harper Voyager, 2018), 44.

16. Gies, Joseph and Gies, Francis, *Life in a Medieval Castle* (London: Harper Perennial, 2015), 9.

17. Martin, George R.R., *A Clash of Kings* (New York: Bantam Books, 2011), Theon V, 806.

18. Martin, George R.R., *A Storm of Swords* (New York: Bantam Books, 2013), Jon V, 557.

19. Reid, Stuart, *Fortress 46: Castles and Tower Houses of the Scottish Clans 1450-1650* (Oxford: Osprey, 2006), 12.

20. Cruden, Stewart, *The Scottish Castle* (Edinburgh: Nelson, 1960), 145.

21. Martin, George R.R., García, Elio M., Jr. and Antonsson, Linda, *The World of Ice & Fire: The Untold History of Westeros and the Game of Thrones* (London: Harper Voyager, 2014), 151.

22. Martin, George R.R., *A Feast for Crows* (London: Harper Voyager, 2011), Jaime III, 449-50.

23. Durham, Keith, *Fortress 70: Strongholds of the Border Reivers: Fortifications of the Anglo-Scottish Border 1296-1603* (Oxford: Osprey Publishing, 2008), 212.

24. Cruden, Stewart, *The Scottish Castle* (Edinburgh: Nelson, 1960), 83.

25. Brown, Michael, *Fortress 82: Scottish Baronial Castles 1250-1450* (Oxford: Osprey Publishing, 2009), 5.

26. Martin, George R.R., *A Feast for Crows* (London: Harper Voyager, 2011), Jaime III, 451.

27. Martin, George R.R., García, Elio M., Jr. and Antonsson, Linda, *The World of Ice & Fire: The Untold History of Westeros and the Game of Thrones* (London: Harper Voyager, 2014), 37.

28. *Game of Thrones: The Complete Second Season* (2013, Blu-ray), Histories and Lore: Season Two: Harrenhal, narrated by Michelle Fairley. Written by Dave Hill. Warner Home Video.

29. Ascherson, Neil, *Stone Voices: The Search for Scotland* (London: Granta Books, 2003), 8.

30. Martin, George R.R., García, Elio M., Jr. and Antonsson, Linda, *The World of Ice & Fire: The Untold History of Westeros and the Game of Thrones* (London: Harper Voyager, 2014), 143.

31. *Ibid.*, 143.
32. Martin, George R.R., *A Storm of Swords* (New York: Bantam Books, 2013), Sansa VII, 1,102.
33. Martin, George R.R., García, Elio M., Jr. and Antonsson, Linda, *The World of Ice & Fire: The Untold History of Westeros and the Game of Thrones* (London: Harper Voyager, 2014), 142.
34. *Game of Thrones: The Complete Fifth Season* (2016, Blu-ray), Histories and Lore: Season Five: Winterfell, narrated by Michael McElhatton. Writen by Dave Hill. Waner Home Video.
35. Martin, George R.R., García, Elio M., Jr. and Antonsson, Linda, *The World of Ice & Fire: The Untold History of Westeros and the Game of Thrones* (London: Harper Voyager, 2014), 143.
36. Martin, George R.R., *A Game of Thrones* (London: Harper Voyager, 2011), Bran II, 77.
37. Lindsay, Maurice, *The Castles of Scotland: A Constable Guide* (London: Constable, 1986), 163.
38. Tabraham, Chris, *Craigmillar Castle* (Edinburgh: Historic Scotland, 2007), 17.
39. Fawcett, Richard, *The Architectural History of Scotland: Scottish Architecture from the Accession of the Stewarts to the Reformation 1371-1560* (Edinburgh: Edinburgh University Press, 1994), 274.

PART III

The Sea Kings: Islesmen and Ironborn

1. Martin, George R.R., García, Elio M., Jr. and Antonsson, Linda, *The World of Ice & Fire: The Untold History of Westeros and the Game of Thrones* (London: Harper Voyager, 2014), 182.
2. Martin, George R.R., *A Feast for Crows* (London: Harper Voyager, 2011), The iron Captain, 289-90.
3. Clements, Jonathan, *A Brief History of the Vikings* (London: Constable & Robertson Ltd, 2005), 216.
4. *Orkneyinga Saga: The History of the Earls of Orkney*, trans. Hermann Pálsson and Paul Edwards (London: Penguin Books, 1978), 215.
5. Davies, Norman, *The Isles: A History* (London: Papermac, 2000), 209.
6. Clarkson, Tim, *The Picts: A History* (Edinburgh: Birlinn, 2017), 169.
7. Driscoll, Stephen, *Alba: The Gaelic Kingdom of Scotland AD 800–1124* (Edinburgh: Birlinn, 2002), 32.

8. Ritchie, Anna, *Viking Scotland* (London: B.T. Batsford Ltd, 1993), 13.

9. MacPhee, Kathleen, *Somerled: Hammer of the Norse* (Glasgow: NWP, 2004), 129.

10. *Game of Thrones: The Complete Sixth Season* (2016, Blu-ray), Histories and Lore: Season Six: The Old Way, narrated by Pilou Asbæk. Written by Dave Hill. Warner Home Video.

11. Martin, George R.R., García, Elio M., Jr. and Antonsson, Linda, *The World of Ice & Fire: The Untold History of Westeros and the Game of Thrones* (London: Harper Voyager, 2014), 90.

12. Brown, Michael, *The Wars of Scotland 1214-1371: Vol.4* (Edinburgh: Edinburgh University Press, 2004), 82.

13. Clements, Jonathan, *A Brief History of the Vikings* (London: Constable & Robertson Ltd, 2005), 217.

14. Marsden, John, *Somerled and the Emergence of Gaelic Scotland* (East Linton, East Lothian: Tuckwell Press, 2000), 23.

15. Paterson, Raymond Campbell, *The Lords of the Isles: A History of Clan Donald* (Edinburgh: Birlinn, 2001), 5.

16. *Ibid.*, 6.

17. McDonald, R. Andrew, 'Rebels without a Cause? The Relations of Fergus of Galloway and Somerled of Argyll with the Scottish Kings, 1153-1164', in E.J.Cowan and R. Andrew McDonald (eds), *Alba: Celtic Scotland in the Medieval Era* (Edinburgh: John Donald, 2005), 169.

18. Paterson, Raymond Campbell, *The Lords of the Isles: A History of Clan Donald* (Edinburgh: Birlinn, 2001), 9.

19. Tabraham, Chris, *Castles of Scotland: A Voyage Through the Centuries* (London: B.T. Batsford, 2005), 68.

20. Barrow, G.W.S., *Kingship and Unity* (Edinburgh: Edinburgh University Press, 2003), 140.

21. Bower, Walter, *Scotichronicon: Vol. 1: Books I and II*, D.E.R. Watt, John Macqueen and Winifred Macqueen (eds) (Edinburgh: The Mercat Press, 1993), 253.

22. Casey, Dan, *Finlaggan and the Lordship* (online). Available at https://www.islayinfo.com/finlaggan_clan_donald.html (accessed 18 November 2018).

23. McDonald, R. Andrew, 'The Western *Gàidhealtachd* in the Middle Ages', in Bob Harris & Alan R. MacDonald (eds), *Making and Unmaking of a Nation* v.1 (2006), 66.

24. Martin, George R.R., García, Elio M., Jr. and Antonsson, Linda *The World of Ice & Fire: The Untold History of Westeros and the Game of Thrones* (London: Harper Voyager, 2014), 191.
25. *Ibid.*, 131.
26. *Ibid.*, 193.
27. MacDougall, Norman, 'Achilles' Heel? The Earldom of Ross, the Lordship of the Isles, and the Stewart Kings, 1449-1507', in E.J.Cowan and R. Andrew McDonald (eds), *Alba: Celtic Scotland in the Medieval Era* (Edinburgh: John Donald, 2005), 249.
28. *Ibid.*
29. Paterson, Raymond Campbell, *The Lords of the Isles: A History of Clan Donald* (Edinburgh: Birlinn, 2001), 48.
30. Dickinson, W. Croft, Donaldson, Gordon & Milne, Isabel A. (eds), *A Source Book of Scottish History: Volume Two: From 1424 to 1567* (Edinburgh: Thomas Nelson and Sons Ltd, 1958), 54.
31. MacDougall, Norman, 'Achilles' Heel? The Earldom of Ross, the Lordship of the Isles, and the Stewart Kings, 1449-1507', in E.J.Cowan and R. Andrew McDonald (eds), *Alba: Celtic Scotland in the Medieval Era* (Edinburgh: John Donald, 2005), 260.
32. *Ibid.*, 262.
33. 'Lord Snow', *Game of Thrones*, Season 1, episode 3. Directed by Brian Kirk. HBO, 1 May 2011.
34. MacGregor, Martin, 'Warfare in Gaelic Scotland in the Later Middle Ages', in M. Spears, Jeremy A. Crang and Mathew J. Strickland (eds), *A Military History of Scotland* (Edinburgh: Edinburgh University Press, 2014), 216.
35. *Ibid.*
36. Brown, Michael, *The Wars of Scotland 1214-1371: Vol.4* (Edinburgh: Edinburgh University Press, 2004), 72.
37. MacGregor, Martin, 'Warfare in Gaelic Scotland in the Later Middle Ages', in M. Spears, Jeremy A. Crang and Mathew J. Strickland (eds), *A Military History of Scotland* (Edinburgh: Edinburgh University Press, 2014), 218.
38. *Game of Thrones: The Complete Second Season* (2013, Blu-ray), Histories and Lore: Season Two: Greyjoy Rebellion, narrated by Stephen Dillane. Written by Dave Hill. Warner Home Video.
39. Larrington, Carolyne, *Winter is Coming: The Medieval World of Game of Thrones* (London: I.B. Tauris & Co. Ltd, 2016), 71.

40. *Urquhart Castle*, (Edinburgh: Historic Scotland, 2012), 43.

41. MacPhee, Kathleen, *Somerled: Hammer of the Norse* (Glasgow: NWP, 2004), 110.

42. Brown, Michael, *The Wars of Scotland 1214-1371: Vol.4* (Edinburgh: Edinburgh University Press, 2010), 72.

43. Martin, George R.R., García, Elio M., Jr. and Antonsson, Linda, *The World of Ice & Fire: The Untold History of Westeros and the Game of Thrones* (London: Harper Voyager, 2014), 192-93.

44. Miket, Roger and Roberts, David L., *The Mediaeval Castles of Skye and Lochalsh* (Edinburgh: Birlinn, 2007), xiii.

45. Martin, George R.R., *A Feast for Crows* (London: Harper Voyager, 2011), The Kraken's Daughter, 181.

46. Black, Ronald (ed.), *To the Hebrides: Samuel Johnson's Journey to the Western Islands of Scotland and James Boswell's Journal of a Tour to the Hebrides* (Edinburgh: Birlinn, 2011), 121.

47. Osborne, Brian D., Armstrong, Ronald and Renton, Ronald (eds), *Cradle of the Scots: An Argyll Anthology* (Edinburgh: Birlinn, 2000), 181-83.

48. Simpson, Douglas W., *The Ancient Stones of Scotland* (London: Robert Hale Limited, 1965), 127.

49. MacPhee, Kathleen, *Somerled: Hammer of the Norse* (Glasgow: NWP, 2004), 159-60.

50. McDonald, R. Andrew, 'The Western *Gàidhealtachd* in the Middle Ages', in Bob Harris & Alan R. MacDonald (eds), *Making and Unmaking of a Nation* v.1, 2006, 79.

51. Paterson, Raymond Campbell, *The Lords of the Isles: A History of Clan Donald* (Edinburgh: Birlinn, 2001), viii.

52. Martin, George R.R., *A Feast for Crows* (London: Harper Voyager, 2011), The Kraken's Daughter, 184-85.

Barbarians at the Gates: Caledonians & Wildlings

1. Hodgman, John. Radio interview with George R.R. Martin, *The Sound of Young America*, 19 September 2011 (online). Available at: http://www.maximumfun.org/sound-young-america/george-r-r-martin-author-song-ice-and-fire-series-interview-sound-young-america (accessed 3 October 2018).

2. Goring, Rosemary (ed.), *Scotland: The Autobiography* (London: Penguin Books, 2014), 21.

3. Camille, Michael, *Mirror in Parchment: The Luttrell Psalter and the Making of Medieval England* (London: Reaktion Books Ltd, 1998), 286.

4. Bower, Walter, *Scotichronicon: Vol. 1: Books I and II*, D.E.R. Watt, John Macqueen and Winifred Macqueen (eds) (Edinburgh: The Mercat Press, 1993), 185.

5. Martin, George R.R., *A Game of Thrones* (London: Harper Voyager, 2011), Bran I, 11.

6. Martin, George R.R., García, Elio M., Jr. and Antonsson, Linda, *The World of Ice & Fire: The Untold History of Westeros and the Game of Thrones*. (London: Harper Voyager, 2014), 139.

7. 'The Wars to Come', *Game of Thrones*, Season 5, episode 1 (2015). Directed by Michael Slovis. HBO, 12 April 2015.

8. Clarkson, Tim, *The Picts: A History* (Edinburgh: Birlinn, 2017), 202.

9. Oliver, Neil, *A History of Ancient Britain* (London: Phoenix Press, 2012), 410.

10. Haywood, John, *The Historical Atlas of the Celtic World* (London: Thames & Hudson, 2015), 86.

11. Tacitus, Publius Cornelius, *Tacitus: Agricola and Germany,* trans. A.R. Birley (New York: Oxford University Press, 1999), 10.

12. *Ibid.*, 12.

13. Clarkson, Tim, *The Picts: A History* (Edinburgh: Birlinn, 2017), 202.

14. National Museums Scotland, *Deskford Carnyx* (2018, online). Available at https://www.nms.ac.uk/explore-our-collections/stories/scottish-history-and-archaeology/deskford-carnyx/ (accessed 2 December 2018).

15. Armit, Ian, *Celtic Scotland* (Edinburgh: Birlinn, 2016), 53.

16. National Museums Scotland, *Reconstruction of the Deskford carnyx (80-200 AD), in bronze and brass with wooden tongue and enamel eye inserts, by Dr Purser and John Creed, Glasgow, 1992* (2018, online),. Available at https://www.nms.ac.uk/explore-our-collections/collection-search-results/?item_id=384359 (accessed 2 December 2018).

17. Tacitus, Publius Cornelius, *Tacitus: Agricola and Germany*, trans. A.R. Birley (New York: Oxford University Press, 1999), 10.

18. Kamm, Antony, *The Last Frontier: The Roman Invasions of Scotland* (Stroud: Tempus Publishing Limited, 2004), 82.

19. 'Dark Wings, Dark Words', *Game of Thrones*, Season 3, episode 2 (2013). Directed by Daniel Minahan. HBO, 7 April 2013.

20. Kamm, Antony, *The Last Frontier: The Roman Invasions of Scotland* (Stroud: Tempus Publishing Limited, 2004), 65.

21. Fraser, James E., *The Roman Conquest of Scotland: The Battle of Mons Graupius AD 84* (Stroud: Tempus Publishing Limited, 2005), 85.

22. Kamm, Antony, *The Last Frontier: The Roman Invasions of Scotland* (Stroud: Tempus Publishing Limited, 2004), 65; Breeze, David J., *Roman Scotland* (London: B.T. Batsford Ltd & Historic Scotland, 1996); Fraser, James E., *The Roman Conquest of Scotland: The Battle of Mons Graupius AD 84* (Stroud: Tempus Publishing Limited, 2005), 85.

23. Breeze, David J., *Roman Scotland* (London: B.T. Batsford Ltd & Historic Scotland, 1996), 46.

24. Tacitus, Publius Cornelius, *Tacitus: Agricola and Germany*, trans. A.R. Birley (New York: Oxford University Press, 1999), 21.

25. Forder, Simon, *The myth of the motte and bailey castle in Scotland* (2014, online). Available at: https://thecastleguy.co.uk/wp-content/uploads/2014/04/The-myth-of-the-motte-and-bailey-castle-in-Scotland.pdf (accessed 19 October 2018).

26. Fraser, James E., *The Roman Conquest of Scotland: The Battle of Mons Graupius AD 84* (Stroud: Tempus Publishing Limited, 2005), 85.

27. *Ibid.*, 86.

28. Breeze, David J., *Roman Scotland* (London: B.T. Batsford Ltd & Historic Scotland, 1996), 50.

29. Tacitus, Publius Cornelius, *Tacitus: Agricola and Germany* trans. A.R. Birley (New York: Oxford University Press, 1999), 25.

30. *Ibid.*, 21-22.

31. Martin, George R.R., *A Storm of Swords* (New York: Bantam Books, 2013), Jon X, 1,022.

32. 'The Bear and the Maiden Fair', *Game of Thrones*, Season 3, episode 7 (2013). Directed by Michelle MacLaren. HBO, 12 May 2013.

33. Martin, George R.R., *A Storm of Swords* (New York: Bantam Books, 2013), Jon VIII, 876.

34. Tacitus, Publius Cornelius, *Tacitus: Agricola and Germany* trans. A.R. Birley (New York: Oxford University Press, 1999), 27.

35. *Ibid.*, 28.

36. Martin, George R.R., *A Storm of Swords* (New York: Bantam Books, 2013), Jon VIII, 878.

The King Who Knelt

1. Martin, George R.R., *A Game of Thrones* (London: Harper Voyager, 2011), Sansa Arya III, 339.
2. Martin, George R.R., García, Elio M., Jr. and Antonsson, Linda, *The World of Ice & Fire: The Untold History of Westeros and the Game of Thrones* (London: Harper Voyager, 2014), 42.
3. *Game of Thrones: The Complete Second Season* (2013, Blu-ray), Histories and Lore: Season Two: Greyjoy Rebellion, narrated by Alfie Allen. Written by Dave Hill. Warner Home Video.
4. *The Anglo-Saxon Chronicles*, trans. Michael Swanton (ed.) (London: Phoenix Press, 2000), 201.
5. Walker, Ian W., *Lords of Alba: The Making of Scotland* (Stroud: Sutton Publishing Limited, 2006), 156.
6. *The Anglo-Saxon Chronicles*, trans. Michael Swanton (ed.) (London: Phoenix Press, 2000), 208.
7. *Ibid.*.
8. Barrow, G.W.S., *Robert Bruce and the Community of the Realm of Scotland* (Edinburgh: Edinburgh University Press, 2013), 16.
9. Walker, Ian W., *Lords of Alba: The Making of Scotland* (Stroud: Sutton Publishing Limited, 2006), 165.
10. Barrow, G.W.S., *Robert Bruce and the Community of the Realm of Scotland* (Edinburgh: Edinburgh University Press, 2013), 16.
11. Strickland, Matthew J., 'The King of Scots at War, c. 1093-1286', in Edward M. Spiers, Jeremy A. Crang and Mathew J. Strickland, *A Military History of Scotland* (Edinburgh: Edinburgh University Press, 2014), 94.

The Lion and His Claws: Edward I & Tywin Lannister

1. Santiuste, David, *The Hammer of the Scots: Edward I and the Scottish Wars of Independence* (Barnsley: Pen & Sword, 2015), 13-14.
2. *Ibid*.
3. Martin, George R.R., García, Elio M., Jr. and Antonsson, Linda, *The World of Ice & Fire: The Untold History of Westeros and the Game of Thrones* (London: Harper Voyager, 2014), 114.
4. *The Chronicle of Lanercost: Volume 2* (1913), trans. Sir Herbert Maxwell (Cribyn, Ceredigion: Llanerch Press, 2001), 182.
5. 'Valar Dohaeris', *Game of Thrones*, Season 3, episode 1. Directed by Daniel Minahan. HBO, 31 March 2013.

6. *Vita Edwardi Secundi,* trans. Wendy R. Childs (ed.) (Oxford: Oxford University Press, 2005), 5.

7. 'Breaker of Chains', *Game of Thrones*, Season 4, episode 3. Directed by Alex Graves. HBO, 20 April 2014.

8. *Vita Edwardi Secundi*, trans. Wendy R. Childs (ed.) (Oxford: Oxford University Press, 2005), 69.

9. *Ibid.*, xlix.

10. Tacitus, Publius Cornelius, *Tacitus: Agricola and Germany*, trans. A.R. Birley (New York: Oxford University Press, 1999), 20.

11. *Game of Thrones: The Complete First Season* (2012, Blu-ray), The Complete Guide to Westeros: The Sack of King's Landing, narrated by Donald Sumpter. Written by Bryan Cogman.

12. Davies, Norman, *The Isles: A History* (London: Papermac, 2000), 318.

13. *Ibid.*, 314.

14. Santiuste, David, *The Hammer of the Scots: Edward I and the Scottish Wars of Independence* (Barnsley: Pen & Sword, 2015), 90.

15. *Ibid.*, 54.

16. *The Chronicle of Lanercost: Volume 2* (1913), trans. Sir Herbert Maxwell (Cribyn, Ceredigion: Llanerch Press, 2001), 115.

17. Bower, Walter, *Scotichronicon: Vol. 4: Book XI*, D.E.R. Watt (ed.) (Edinburgh: The Mercat Press, 1998), 59.

18. Barrow, G.W.S., *Robert Bruce and the Community of the Realm of Scotland* (Edinburgh: Edinburgh University Press, 2013), 273.

19. *Ibid.*, 92-93.

20. Machiavelli, Niccolò, *The Prince* (London: William Collins, 2018), Chapter VIII, 40.

21. *Ibid.*, Chapter III, 9

22. *Ibid.*, Chapter XV.

23. Martin, George R.R., García, Elio M., Jr. and Antonsson, Linda, *The World of Ice & Fire: The Untold History of Westeros and the Game of Thrones* (London: Harper Voyager, 2014), 114.

24. 'You Win or You Die', *Game of Thrones*, Season 1, episode 7. Directed by Daniel Minahan. HBO, 29 May 2011.

25. Moffat, Alistair, *The Borders* (Edinburgh: Birlinn, 2007), 308.

26. Martin, George R.R., *A Feast for Crows* (London: Harper Voyager, 2011), Jaime I, 133.

27. Martin, George R.R., *A Feast for Crows* (London: Harper Voyager, 2011), Cersei II, 114.
28. Machiavelli, Niccolò, *The Prince* (London: William Collins, 2018), Chapter XVII, 74.

The Banner with the Bloody Heart

1. *John of Fordun's Chronicle of the Scottish Nation: Volume 2*, W.F. Skene (ed.), facsimile reprint (Cribyn, Ceredigion: Llanerch Publishers, 1993), 346.
2. Brown, Michael, *The Black Douglases* (East Linton, East Lothian: Tuckwell Press Ltd, 1998), 19.
3. Ross, David R., *James The Good: The Black Douglas* (Edinburgh: Luath Press, 2008), 96.
4. Barbour, John, *The Bruce*, trans. A.A.H. Douglas (Glasgow: William Maclellan, 1964), 31.
5. *Ibid.*, 467.
6. *Ibid.*, 316.
7. Tabraham, Chris, *Clan and Castle* (Edinburgh: Historic Scotland, 2008), 29.
8. Bower, Walter, *Scotichronicon: Vol. 7: Books XIII and XIV*, D.E.R. Watt, A.B. Scott, Ulrike Morét and Norman F. Shead (eds) (Edinburgh: The Mercat Press, 1996), 71.
9. *Froissart's Chronicles*, trans. Jon Jolliffe (ed.) (London: Penguin Books, 1967), 45.
10. *Ibid.*, 47.
11. Scott, Sir Walter, *Tales of a Grandfather: First Series*, J. Hutchison (ed.) (London: MacMillan and Co., Limited, 1908), 37-38.
12. Ross, David R., *On the Trail of Robert the Bruce* (Edinburgh: Luath Press Ltd, 1999), 141.
13. Barbour, John, *The Bruce*, trans. A.A.H. Douglas (Glasgow: William Maclellan, 1964), 468.

A Tale of Two Roberts: Bruce and Baratheon

1. Penman, Michael, *Robert the Bruce: King of the Scots* (London: Yale University Press, 2014), 310.
2. Whitman, James Q., *The Verdict of Battle: The Law of Victory and the Making of Modern War* (London: Harvard University Press, 2012), 52.

3. Clarkson, Tim, *The Picts: A History* (Edinburgh: Birlinn, 2017), 81.
4. Brown, Chris, *King and Outlaw: The Real Robert the Bruce* (Stroud: The History Press, 2018), 171.
5. Barrow, G.W.S., *Robert Bruce and the Community of the Realm of Scotland* (Edinburgh: Edinburgh University Press, 2013), 303.
6. *The Chronicle of Lanercost: Volume 2*, trans. Sir Herbert Maxwell (Cribyn, Ceredigion: Llanerch Press, 2010), 210.
7. Martin, George R.R., *A Game of Thrones* (London: Harper Voyager, 2011), Eddard VII, 299.
8. *The Book of Pluscarden: Vol. II.*, Felix J.H. Skene (ed.) (Edinburgh: William Paterson, 1880), 195.
9. Martin, George R.R., *A Game of Thrones* (London: Harper Voyager, 2011), Eddard II, 107.
10. *Ibid.*, Eddard I, 41.
11. Santiuste, David, *The Hammer of the Scots: Edward I and the Scottish Wars of Independence* (Barnsley: Pen & Sword, 2015), 181.
12. Barbour, John, *The Bruce*, trans. A.A.H. Douglas (Glasgow: William Maclellan, 1964), 281.
13. *Vita Edwardi Secundi*, trans. Wendy R. Childs (ed.) (Oxford: Oxford University Press, 2005), 89.
14. Barrow, G.W.S., *Robert Bruce and the Community of the Realm of Scotland* (Edinburgh: Edinburgh University Press, 2013), 285.
15. 'Fire and Blood', *Game of Thrones*, Season 1, episode 10. Directed by Alan Taylor. HBO, 19 June 2011.
16. Barrow, G.W.S., *Robert Bruce and the Community of the Realm of Scotland* (Edinburgh: Edinburgh University Press, 2013), 341.
17. Barbour, John, *The Bruce*, trans. A.A.H. Douglas (Glasgow: William Maclellan, 1964), 314.
18. Martin, George R.R., García, Elio M., Jr. and Antonsson, Linda, *The World of Ice & Fire: The Untold History of Westeros and the Game of Thrones* (London: Harper Voyager, 2014), 129.
19. Martin, George R.R., *A Game of Thrones* (London: Harper Voyager, 2011), Eddard VIII, 488.
20. *Froissart's Chronicles*, trans. Jon Jolliffe (ed.) (London: Penguin Books, 1967), 45.

PART IV

A Steamroller of Spears: Schiltrons & Battle Of The Bastards

1. *Vita Edwardi Secundi*, trans. Wendy R. Childs (ed.) (Oxford: Oxford University Press, 2005).
2. Barrow, G.W.S., *Robert Bruce and the Community of the Realm of Scotland* (Edinburgh: Edinburgh University Press, 2013), 271.
3. *Ibid.*, 268.
4. *Vita Edwardi Secundi*, trans. Wendy R. Childs (ed.) (Oxford: Oxford University Press, 2005), 91.
5. 'Battle of the Bastards', *Game of Thrones*, Season 6, episode 9. Directed by Miguel Sapochnik. HBO, 19 June 2016.
6. Moffat, Alistair, *Scotland: A History from Earliest Times* (Edinburgh: Birlinn, 2015), 167.
7. Barbour, John, *The Bruce*, trans. A.A.H. Douglas (Glasgow: William Maclellan, 1964), 277.
8. *Vita Edwardi Secundi*, trans. Wendy R. Childs (ed.) (Oxford: Oxford University Press, 2005), 5.
9. *The Chronicle of Lanercost: Volume 2*, trans. Sir Herbert Maxwell (Cribyn, Ceredigion: Llanerch Press, 2001), 208.
10. Barrow, G.W.S., *Robert Bruce and the Community of the Realm of Scotland* (Edinburgh: Edinburgh University Press, 2013), 298.
11. Barbour, John, *The Bruce*, trans. A.A.H. Douglas (Glasgow: William Maclellan, 1964), 202.
12. *Ibid.*, 308.

Under Siege

1. 'The Pointy End', *Game of Thrones*, Season 1, episode 8. Directed by Daniel Minahan. HBO, 5 June 2011.
2. Tabraham, Chris, *Scotland's Castles*, revised edition (London: B.T. Batsford Ltd & Historic Scotland, 2005), 26.
3. Barbour, John, *The Bruce*, trans. A.A.H. Douglas (Glasgow: William Maclellan, 1964), 250.
4. Martin, George R.R., *A Feast for Crows* (London: Harper Voyager, 2011), 599.
5. Tabraham, Chris, *Scotland's Castles* (London: B.T. Batsford Ltd & Historic Scotland, 1997), 109.

6. Brown, Michael, *Fortress 82: Scottish Baronial Castles 1250-1450* (Oxford: Osprey Publishing, 2009), 36.

7. Dargie, Richard, *Scottish Castles & Fortifications* (Berks: G.W. Publishing, 2009), 24.

8. 'The Broken Man', *Game of Thrones*, Season 6, episode 7. Directed by Mark Mylod. HBO, 5 June 2016.

9. Tabraham, Chris, *Bothwell* Castle (Edinburgh: Historic Scotland, 2009), 3.

10. Rutherford, Allan and Malcolm, John, '"*That stalwart toure*": Bothwell Castle in the Thirteenth and Early Fourteenth Centuries', in Dakin, A., Glendinning, M. & MacKechnie, A. (eds), *Scotland's Castle Culture* (Edinburgh: John Donald, 2011), 192.

11. *Ibid.*, 193.

12. Lindsay, Maurice, *The Castles of Scotland: A Constable Guide* (London: Constable, 1986), 90.

13. Dargie, Richard, *Scottish Castles & Fortifications* (Berks: G.W. Publishing, 2009), 59.

14. Tranter, Nigel, *The Story of Scotland* (Glasgow: Neil Wilson Publishing, 1987), 80-81.

15. *Game of Thrones: The Complete Sixth Season* (2016, Blu-ray), Histories and Lore: Season Six: Riverrun, narrated by Clive Russell. Written by Dave Hill. Warner Home Video.

16. *Ibid.*

17. Martin, George R.R., *A Dance with Dragons* (London: Harper Voyager, 2011), Jon IV, 226.

18. Brown, Michael, *Fortress 82: Scottish Baronial Castles 1250-1450* (Oxford: Osprey Publishing, 2009), 33.

19. Santiuste, David, *The Hammer of the Scots: Edward I and the Scottish Wars of Independence* (Barnsley: Pen & Sword, 2015), 126.

20. Brown, Michael, *Fortress 82: Scottish Baronial Castles 1250-1450* (Oxford: Osprey Publishing, 2009), 31.

21. *The Siege of Caerlaverock*, trans. C.W. Scott-Giles (online). Available at https://www.theheraldrysociety.com/articles/the-siege-of-caerlaverock/ (accessed 31 October 2018).

22. Dargie, Richard, *Scottish Castles & Fortifications* (Berks: G.W. Publishing, 2009), 26.

23. *The Siege of Caerlaverock*, trans. C.W. Scott-Giles (online). Available at https://www.theheraldrysociety.com/articles/the-siege-of-caerlaverock/ (accessed 31 October 2018).
24. Santiuste, David, *The Hammer of the Scots: Edward I and the Scottish Wars of Independence* (Barnsley: Pen & Sword, 2015), 128.

Raiders in the Riverlands

1. Brown, Michael, *The Black Douglases* (East Linton, East Lothian: Tuckwell Press Ltd, 1998), 134.
2. Barrow, G.W.S., *Robert Bruce and the Community of the Realm of Scotland* (Edinburgh: Edinburgh University Press, 2013), 305.
3. 'Fire and Blood', *Game of Thrones*, Season 1, episode 10. Directed by Alan Taylor. HBO, 19 June 2011.
4. Fawcett, Richard, *The Architectural History of Scotland: Scottish Architecture from the Accession of the Stewarts to the Reformation 1371-1560* (Edinburgh: Edinburgh University Press, 1994), 236.
5. Moffat, Alistair, *The Borders* (Edinburgh: Birlinn, 2007), 315.
6. Dickinson, W. Croft, Donaldson, Gordon & Milne, Isabel A. (eds), *A Source Book of Scottish History: Volume Two: From 1424 to 1567* (Edinburgh: Thomas Nelson and Sons Ltd, 1958), 133.
7. Moffat, Alistair, *The Borders* (Edinburgh: Birlinn, 2007), 317.
8. Moffat, Alistair, *Scotland: A History from Earliest Times* (Edinburgh: Birlinn, 2015), 197.
9. Durham, Keith, *Warrior 154: Border Reiver 1513-1603* (Oxford: Osprey Publishing, 2011), 20.
10. Santiuste, David, *The Hammer of the Scots: Edward I and the Scottish Wars of Independence* (Barnsley: Pen & Sword, 2015), 16.
11. Fraser, George MacDonald, *The Steel Bonnets: The Story of the Anglo-Scottish Border Reivers* (London: Harvill, 1989), 65.
12. Durham, Keith, *Warrior 154: Border Reiver 1513-1603* (Oxford: Osprey Publishing, 2011), 7.
13. Moffat, Alistair, *The Borders* (Edinburgh: Birlinn, 2007), 334.
14. *Ibid.*, 334.
15. Durham, Keith, *Warrior 154: Border Reiver 1513-1603* (Oxford: Osprey Publishing, 2011), 7.
16. Fraser, George MacDonald, *The Steel Bonnets: The Story of the Anglo-Scottish Border Reivers* (London: Harvill, 1989), 57-64.

17. Martin, George R.R., *A Feast for Crows* (London: Harper Voyager, 2011), The Reaver, 480.

18. Fraser, George MacDonald, *The Steel Bonnets: The Story of the Anglo-Scottish Border Reivers* (London: Harvill, 1989), 192.

19. Durham, Keith, *Warrior 154: Border Reiver 1513-1603* (Oxford: Osprey Publishing, 2011), 16.

20. Moffat, Alistair, *The Borders* (Edinburgh: Birlinn, 2007), 324-25.

21. Durham, Keith, *Warrior 154: Border Reiver 1513-1603* (Oxford: Osprey Publishing, 2011), 50.

22. *Froissart's Chronicles*, trans. Jon Jolliffe (ed.) (London: Penguin Books, 1967), 29.

23. *Ibid.*, 30.

24. Brown, Michael, *The Black Douglases* (East Linton, East Lothian: Tuckwell Press Ltd, 1998), 139.

25. Moffat, Alistair, *The Borders* (Edinburgh: Birlinn, 2007), 325.

26. Glozier, Matthew, 'The Wars of Mary and James VI and I, 1560-1625', in Edward M. Spiers, Jeremy A. Crang and Mathew J. Strickland (eds), *A Military History of Scotland* (Edinburgh: Edinburgh University Press, 2014), 241.

27. Durham, Keith, *Warrior 154: Border Reiver 1513-1603* (Oxford: Osprey Publishing, 2011), 14.

28. Glozier, Matthew, 'The Wars of Mary and James VI and I, 1560-1625', in Edward M. Spiers, Jeremy A. Crang and Mathew J. Strickland (eds), *A Military History of Scotland* (Edinburgh: Edinburgh University Press, 2014),. 241.

29. *Ibid.*, 241-42.

30. Goodare, Julian, 'Scottish politics in the reign of James VI', in Bob Harris and Alan R. MacDonald (eds), *Scotland: The Making and Unmaking of the Nation c.1500-1707: Volume 4: Readings: c.1500-1707* (Dundee: Dundee University Press & The Open University in Scotland, 2007), 32.

31. Moffat, Alistair, *The Borders* (Edinburgh: Birlinn, 2007), 354.

Firepower: Guns & Dragons

1. 'A Man Without Honor', *Game of Thrones*, Season 2, episode 7. Directed by David Nutter. HBO, 13 May 2012.

2. Lewtas, Ian, McAlister, Rachael, Wallis, Adam, Woodley, Clive and Cullis, Ian, 'The ballistic performance of the bombard Mons Meg',

in *Defence Technology* 12 (2), 2016, pp. 59-68 (online) (accessed 6 August 2018).

3. Cruden, Stewart, *The Scottish Castle* (Edinburgh: Nelson, 1960), 198.

4. Reid, Stuart, *Fortress 46: Castles and Tower Houses of the Scottish Clans 1450-1650* (Oxford: Osprey Publishing, 2006), 32.

5. Cruden, Stewart, *The Scottish Castle* (Edinburgh: Nelson, 1960), 219.

6. Martin, George R.R., *Fire and Blood* (London: Harper Voyager, 2018), 246-51.

7. *The Auchinleck Chronicle: Ane Schort Memoriale of the Scottis Corniklis for Addicioun* (Edinburgh: Thomas Thomson, Esq., 1818), 57.

8. Cruden, Stewart, *The Scottish Castle* (Edinburgh: Nelson, 1960), 205.

9. Moffat, Alistair, *The Borders* (Edinburgh: Birlinn, 2007), 309.

10. Philips, Gervase, 'Scotland in the Age of the Military Revolution, 1488-1560', in Edward M. Spiers, Jeremy A. Crang and Mathew J. Strickland (eds), *A Military History of Scotland* (Edinburgh: Edinburgh University Press, 2012), 188.

11. Cruden, Stewart, *The Scottish Castle* (Edinburgh: Nelson, 1960), 203.

12. Tabraham, Chris, *Tantallon Castle* (Edinburgh: Historic Scotland, 2007), 23.

13. Brown, Michael, *Fortress 82: Scottish Baronial Castles 1250-1450* (Oxford: Osprey Publishing, 2009), 57.

14. Philips, Gervase, 'Scotland in the Age of the Military Revolution, 1488-1560', in Edward M. Spiers, Jeremy A. Crang and Mathew J. Strickland (eds), *A Military History of Scotland* (Edinburgh: Edinburgh University Press, 2012), 187.

15. Glozier, Matthew, 'The Wars of Mary and James VI and I, 1560-1625', in Edward M. Spiers, Jeremy A. Crang and Mathew J. Strickland (eds), *A Military History of Scotland* (Edinburgh: Edinburgh University Press, 2014), pp. 242-43.

16. Tabraham, Chris and Grove, Doreen, *Fortress Scotland and the Jacobites* (London: B.T. Batsford & Historic Scotland, 2001), 18.

17. Gies, Joseph and Gies, Francis, *Life in a Medieval Castle* (London: Harper Perennial, 2015), 219.

PART V

Gods and Monsters

1. Westwood, Jennifer and Kingshill, Sophia, *The Lore of Scotland: A guide to Scottish legends* (London: Arrow Books, 2011), 223.
2. Connor, Robert, *Jesus the Sorcerer: Exorcist and Prophet of the Apocalypse* (Oxford: Mandrake of Oxford, 2006), 97.
3. Martin, George R.R., *A Dance with Dragons* (London: Harper Voyager, 2011), Bran III, 453.
4. Martin, George R.R., *A Storm of Swords* (New York: Bantam Books, 2013), Jon II, 213.
5. Bower, Walter, *Scotichronicon: Vol. 1: Books I and II*, D.E.R. Watt, John Macqueen and Winifred Macqueen (eds) (Edinburgh: The Mercat Press, 1993), 169.
6. Geoffrey of Monmouth, *The History of the Kings of Britain*, trans. Lewis Thorpe (London: Penguin Books, 1966), 72.
7. *Ibid.*
8. Westwood, Jennifer and Kingshill, Sophia, *The Lore of Scotland: A guide to Scottish legends* (London: Arrow Books, 2011), 21.
9. Martin, George R.R., García, Elio M., Jr. and Antonsson, Linda, *The World of Ice & Fire: The Untold History of Westeros and the Game of Thrones* (London: Harper Voyager, 2014), 5.
10. *Game of Thrones: The Complete Fourth Season.* (2015, Blu-ray), Histories and Lore: Season Four: The Nations of the North, narrated by Kristofer Hivju. Written by Dave Hill. Warner Home Video.
11. Mackenzie, W. Mackay, *The Mediaeval Castle in Scotland* (New York: Benjamin Blom, Inc., 1972), 92.
12. Westwood, Jennifer and Kingshill, Sophia, *The Lore of Scotland: A guide to Scottish legends* (London: Arrow Books, 2011), 469.
13. *Ibid.*, 352.
14. Mackenzie, W. Mackay, *The Mediaeval Castle in Scotland* (New York: Benjamin Blom, Inc., 1972), 92.
15. Game of Thrones Wiki, *Night's Queen* (online, 2018). Available at (https://gameofthrones.fandom.com/wiki/Night%27s_Queen (accessed 2 November 2018).
16. Martin, George R.R., García, Elio M., Jr. and Antonsson, Linda, *The World of Ice & Fire: The Untold History of Westeros and the Game of Thrones* (London: Harper Voyager, 2014), 145.

17. *Ibid.*
18. Westwood, Jennifer and Kingshill, Sophia, *The Lore of Scotland: A guide to Scottish legends* (London: Arrow Books, 2011), 353.
19. Martin, George R.R., *A Game of Thrones* (London: Harper Voyager, 2011), Bran VII, 714.
20. Armit, Ian, *Celtic Scotland* (Edinburgh: Birlinn, 2016), 104.
21. Dig It! TV, *Dunino Den: Scotland's Saga* (online video, 2016), presented by Saga Torquil Crawford. Available at www.youtube.com/watch?time_continue=172&v=xu1sD8xCyZM (accessed 14 December 2016).
22. Moffat, Alistair, *The Sea Kingdoms: The History of Celtic Britain and Ireland* (Edinburgh: Birlinn, 2017), 21.
23. Dig It! TV, *Dunino Den: Scotland's Saga* (online video, 2016), presented by Saga Torquil Crawford. Available at www.youtube.com/watch?time_continue=172&v=xu1sD8xCyZM (accessed 14 December 2016).
24. Clasby, Daniel J., 'Coexistence and Conflict in the Religions of Game of Thrones', in Brian A. Pavlac (ed.), *Game of Thrones Versus History: Written in Blood* (New Jersey: John Wiley & Sons, Inc., 2017), 198.
25. Larrington, Carolyne, *Winter is Coming: The Medieval World of Game of Thrones* (London: I.B. Tauris & Co. Ltd, 2016), 93.
26. Moffat, Alistair, *The Sea Kingdoms: The History of Celtic Britain and Ireland* (Edinburgh: Birlinn, 2017), 93.
27. Martin, George R.R., *A Game of Thrones* (London: Harper Voyager, 2011), Catelyn I, 20.
28. Game of Thrones Wiki, *Weirwood* (online, 2018). Available at https://gameofthrones.fandom.com/wiki/Night%27s_Queen (accessed 1 November 2018).
29. 'Winter is Coming', *Game of Thrones*, Season 1, episode 1. Directed by Tim Van Patten. HBO, 17 April 2011.
30. Armit, Ian, *Celtic Scotland* (Edinburgh: Birlinn, 2016), 102.
31. Christison, Sir Robert, 'On an ancient wooden image, found in November last at Ballachulish peat-moss', in *Proceedings of the Society of Antiquaries of Scotland* (15), 1881, 160.
32. National Museums Scotland, *Ballachulish figure* (online). Available at https://www.nms.ac.uk/ballachulishfigure (accessed 10 November 2018).
33. Armit, Ian, *Celtic Scotland* (Edinburgh: Birlinn, 2016), 103.

The Last of the Free

1. Barbour, John, *The Bruce*, trans. A.A.H. Douglas (Glasgow: William Maclellan, 1964), 53.

2. 'The Broken Man', *Game of Thrones*, Season 6, episode 7. Directed by Mark Mylod. HBO, 5 June 2016.

3. Tacitus, Publius Cornelius, *Tacitus: Agricola and Germany*, trans. A.R. Birley (New York: Oxford University Press, 1999), 21-22.

4. *Game of Thrones: The Complete Second Season* (2013), Histories and Lore: Season Two: The Free Folk, narrated by Rose Leslie. Written by Dave Hill. Warner Home Video.

5. Davies, Norman, *The Isles: A History* (London: Papermac, 2000), 161.

6. Clarkson, Tim, *The Picts: A History* (Edinburgh: Birlinn, 2017), 81.

7. Martin, George R.R., *A Storm of Swords* (New York: Bantam Books, 2013), Jon I, 92.

8. Fry, Michael, *Edinburgh: A History of the City* (London: Pan Books, 2010), 56.

9. *Ibid.*, 56-57.

10. Barrow, G.W.S., *Robert Bruce and the Community of the Realm of Scotland* (Edinburgh: Edinburgh University Press, 2013), 398.

11. Oliver, Neil, *A History of Scotland* (London: Phoenix, 2010), 126-27.

12. *The Book of Pluscarden: Vol. II*, Felix J.H. Skene (ed.) (Edinburgh: William Paterson, 1880), 81.

13. Wormald, Jenny, 'The Reign of James VI: 1537-1625', in Bob Harris and Alan R. MacDonald (eds), *Scotland: The Making and Unmaking of the Nations c.1100-1707. Volume 2: Early Modern Scotland: c.1500-1707* (Dundee: Dundee University Press & The Open University, 2007), 31.

14. Martin, George R.R., *A Storm of Swords* (New York: Bantam Books, 2013), Jon V, 558.

15. Ruiter, Brian de, 'A Defense against the "Other"', in Pavlac, Brian A. (ed.), *Game of Thrones Versus History: Written in Blood* (New Jersey: John Wiley & Sons, Inc., 2017), 90.

16. Clarkson, Tim, *The Picts: A History* (Edinburgh: Birlinn, 2017), 25.

17. *Ibid.*

18. 'A Man Without Honor', *Game of Thrones*, Season 2, episode 7. Directed by David Nutter. HBO, 13 May 2012.

A Red Wedding and a Black Dinner

1. Martin, George R.R., *A Storm of Swords* (New York: Bantam Books, 2013), Catelyn VI, 679.
2. 'The Rains of Castamere', *Game of Thrones*, Season 3, episode 9. Directed by David Nutter. HBO, 2 June 2013.
3. Martin, George R.R., García, Elio M., Jr. and Antonsson, Linda, *The World of Ice & Fire: The Untold History of Westeros and the Game of Thrones* (London: Harper Voyager, 2014), 136.
4. Weatherford, Jack, *Genghis Khan and the Making of the Modern World* (New York: Three Rivers Press, 2004), 106.
5. Martin, George R.R., García, Elio M., Jr. and Antonsson, Linda, *The World of Ice & Fire: The Untold History of Westeros and the Game of Thrones* (London: Harper Voyager, 2014), 139.
6. Martin, George R.R., *A Dance with Dragons* (London: Harper Voyager, 2011), 231.
7. Martin, George R.R., *A Clash of Kings* (New York: Bantam Books, 2011), Jon III, 369.
8. Martin, George R.R., *A Feast for Crows* (London: Harper Voyager, 2011), Cersei IV, 276.
9. Martin, George R.R., García, Elio M., Jr. and Antonsson, Linda, *The World of Ice & Fire: The Untold History of Westeros and the Game of Thrones* (London: Harper Voyager, 2014), 136.
10. Martin, George R.R., *A Storm of Swords* (New York: Bantam Books, 2013), Bran IV, 764.
11. Lynch, Michael, *Scotland: A New History* (London: Pimlico, 1992), 148.
12. Brown, Michael, *The Black Douglases* (East Linton, East Lothian: Tuckwell Press Ltd, 1998), 261.
13. *Ibid.*, 260.
14. McGladdery, Christine, *James II* (Edinburgh: John Donald, 2015), 30.
15. *The Auchinleck Chronicle: Ane Schort Memoriale of the Scottis Corniklis for Addicioun* (Edinburgh: Thomas Thomson, Esq., 1818), 35.
16. McGladdery, Christine, *James II* (Edinburgh: John Donald, 2015), 30-31.
17. Martin, George R.R., García, Elio M., Jr. and Antonsson, Linda, *The World of Ice & Fire: The Untold History of Westeros and the Game of Thrones* (London: Harper Voyager, 2014), 116.

18. *Ibid.*
19. Brown, Michael, *The Black Douglases* (East Linton, East Lothian: Tuckwell Press Ltd, 1998), 272-74.
20. *The Auchinleck Chronicle: Ane Schort Memoriale of the Scottis Corniklis for Addicioun* (Edinburgh: Thomas Thomson, Esq., 1818), 46.
21. McGladdery, Christine, *James II* (Edinburgh: John Donald, 2015), 115.
22. *The Auchinleck Chronicle: Ane Schort Memoriale of the Scottis Corniklis for Addicioun* (Edinburgh: Thomas Thomson, Esq., 1818), 46-47.
23. McGladdery, Christine, *James II* (Edinburgh: John Donald, 2015), 117.
24. Goring, Rosemary (ed.), *Scotland: The Autobiography* (London: Penguin Books, 2014), 97.
25. *Ibid.*
26. Lynch, Michael, *Scotland: A New History* (London: Pimlico, 1992), 306.
27. Moffat, Alistair, *Scotland: A History from Earliest Times* (Edinburgh: Birlinn, 2015).
28. Lynch, Michael, *Scotland: A New History* (London: Pimlico, 1992), 305.
29. Goring, Rosemary (ed.), *Scotland: The Autobiography* (London: Penguin Books, 2014), 100.
30. Moffat, Alistair, *Scotland: A History from Earliest Times* (Edinburgh: Birlinn, 2015), 281.
31. *Ibid.*
32. Linklater, Magnus, *Massacre: The Story of Glencoe* (Glasgow: William Collins Sons and Company Limited, 1982), 119.
33. *Ibid.*, 123.
34. Goring, Rosemary (ed.), *Scotland: The Autobiography* (London: Penguin Books, 2014), 102.
35. Linklater, Magnus, *Massacre: The Story of Glencoe* (Glasgow: William Collins Sons and Company Limited, 1982), 101.
36. Moffat, Alistair, *Scotland: A History from Earliest Times* (Edinburgh: Birlinn, 2015), 282.

Bibliography

'A Golden Crown', *Game of Thrones*, Season 1, episode 6. Directed by Daniel Minahan. HBO, 22 May 2011.

'A Man Without Honor', *Game of Thrones*, Season 2, episode 7. Directed by David Nutter. HBO, 13 May 2012.

A Wiki of Ice and Fire (2018), *Hammer of the Waters* (online). Available at https://awoiaf.westeros.org/index.php/Hammer_of_ the_waters (accessed 7 November 2018).

A Wiki of Ice and Fire (2018), *The Twins* (online). Available at https://awoiaf.westeros.org/index.php/Twins (accessed 4 November 2018).

Armit, Ian, *Celtic Scotland* (Edinburgh: Birlinn, 2016).

Ascherson, Neil, *Stone Voices: The Search for Scotland* (London: Granta Books, 2003).

Barbour, John, *The Bruce*, trans. A.A.H. Douglas (Glasgow: William Maclellan, 1964).

Barbour, John, *The Bruce*, trans. A.A.M. Duncan (Edinburgh: Canongate Books Limited, 1997).

Barrow, G.W.S., *Kingship and Unity* (Edinburgh: Edinburgh University Press, 2003).

Barrow, G.W.S., *Robert Bruce and the Community of the Realm of Scotland* (Edinburgh: Edinburgh University Press, 2013).

'Battle of the Bastards', *Game of Thrones*, Season 6, episode 9. Directed by Miguel Sapochnik. HBO, 19 June 2016.

Black, Ronald (ed.), *To the Hebrides: Samuel Johnson's Journey to the Western Islands of Scotland and James Boswell's Journal of a Tour to the Hebrides* (Edinburgh: Birlinn, 2011).

Bower, Walter, *Scotichronicon: Vol. 1: Books I and II*, D.E.R. Watt, John Macqueen and Winifred Macqueen (eds) (Edinburgh: The Mercat Press, 1993).

Bower, Walter, *Scotichronicon: Vol. 4: Book XI*, D.E.R. Watt (ed.) (Edinburgh: The Mercat Press, 1998).

Bower, Walter, *Scotichronicon: Vol. 6: Books XI and XII*, D.E.R. Watt, Norman F. Shead, Wendy B. Stevenson, Alan Borthwick, R.E. Latham, J.R.S. Phillips and Martin S. Smith (eds) (Aberdeen: Aberdeen University Press, 1991).

Bower, Walter, *Scotichronicon: Vol. 7: Books XIII and XIV*, D.E.R. Watt, A.B. Scott, Ulrike Morét and Norman F. Shead (eds) (Edinburgh: The Mercat Press, 1996).

'Breaker of Chains', *Game of Thrones*, Season 4, episode 3. Directed by Alex Graves. HBO, 20 April 2014.

Breeze, David J., *Roman Scotland* (London: B.T. Batsford Ltd & Historic Scotland, 1996)

Brown, Chris, *King and Outlaw: The Real Robert the Bruce* (Stroud: The History Press, 2018).

Brown, Michael, *The Black Douglases* (East Linton, East Lothian: Tuckwell Press Ltd, 1998).

Brown, Michael, *Fortress 82: Scottish Baronial Castles 1250-1450* (Oxford: Osprey, 2009).

Brown, Michael, *The Wars of Scotland 1214-1371: Vol.4* (Edinburgh: Edinburgh University Press, 2010).

Brown, Mike and Mendum, John, *Loch Lomond to Stirling: A Landscape Fashioned by Geology* (Perth: Scottish Natural Heritage & British Geological Survey, 2017).

Buick, John Blackburn, *Abernethy Round Tower: A Full Visitor's Guide* (Newtyle, 2003).

Caldwell, David H. (ed.), *Scottish Weapons & Fortifications 1100-1800* (Edinburgh: John Donald Publishers Ltd, 1981).

Camille, Michael, *Mirror in Parchment: The Luttrell Psalter and the Making of Medieval England* (London: Reaktion Books Ltd, 1998).

Campsie, Alison, 'Breakthrough in study of Scotland's ancient loch dwellers', *The Scotsman* (online), 30 May 2018. Available at https://www.scotsman.com/lifestyle/breakthrough-in-study-of-scotland-s-ancient-loch-dwellers-1-4747452 (accessed 8 September 2018).

Canmore, *Dunnicaer* (online, 2018). Available at https://canmore.org.uk/site/37001/dunnicaer (accessed 25 November 2018).

Casey, Dan, *Finlaggan and the Lordship* (online). Available at https://www.islayinfo.com/finlaggan_clan_donald.html (accessed 18 November 2018).

Christison, Sir Robert, 'On an ancient wooden image, found in November last at Ballachulish peat-moss', in *Proceedings of the Society of Antiquaries of Scotland* (15), 1881, pp.158-78.

Clarkson, Tim, *The Picts: A History* (Edinburgh: Birlinn, 2017).

Clasby, Daniel J., 'Coexistence and Conflict in the Religions of Game of Thrones', in Brian A. Pavlac (ed.), *Game of Thrones Versus History: Written in Blood* (New Jersey: John Wiley & Sons, Inc, 2017).

Clements, Jonathan, *A Brief History of the Vikings* (London: Constable & Robertson Ltd, 2005).

Connor, Robert, *Jesus the Sorcerer: Exorcist and Prophet of the Apocalypse* (Oxford: Mandrake of Oxford, 2006).

Cowan, E.J. and McDonald, R. Andrew (eds), *Alba: Celtic Scotland in the Medieval Era* (East Linton, East Lothian: Tuckwell Press Ltd, 2000).

Crawford, Barbara E., *The Northern Earldoms: Orkney and Caithness from Ad 870 to 1470* (Edinburgh: John Donald, 2013).

Cruden, Stewart, *The Scottish Castle* (Edinburgh: Nelson, 1960).

Cunningham, Alastair, *A Guide to Dunnottar Castle* (Inverness: Alistair Cunningham, 1998).

Dakin, Audrey, Glendinning, Miles and MacKechnie, Aonghus (eds), *Scotland's Castle Culture* (Edinburgh: John Donald, 2011).

Dargie, Richard, *Scottish Castles & Fortifications* (Berks: GW Publishing, 2009).

'Dark Wings, Dark Words', *Game of Thrones*, Season 3, episode 2. Directed by Daniel Minahan. HBO, 7 April 2013.

Davies, Norman, *The Isles: A History* (London: Papermac, 2000).

Davies, Norman, *Vanished Kingdoms: The History of Half-Forgotten Europe* (London: Penguin Books, 2012).

Dickinson, W. Croft, Donaldson, Gordon and Milne, Isabel A. (eds), *A Source Book of Scottish History: Volume One: From the Earliest Times to 1424* (Edinburgh: Thomas Nelson and Sons Ltd, 1958).

Dickinson, W. Croft, Donaldson, Gordon and Milne, Isabel A. (eds), *A Source Book of Scottish History: Volume Two: From 1424 to 1567* (Edinburgh: Thomas Nelson and Sons Ltd, 1958).

Dig It! TV, *Dunino Den: Scotland's Saga* (online video, 2016). Presented by Saga Torquil Crawford. Available at www.youtube.

com/watch?time_continue=172&v=xu1sD8xCyZM   (accessed 14 December 2016).

Dixon, Nick, *The Crannogs of Perthshire: A Guide* (Perth and Kinross Heritage Trust).

Driscoll, Stephen, *Alba: The Gaelic Kingdom of Scotland AD 800–1124* (Edinburgh: Birlinn, 2002).

Durham, Keith, *Fortress 70: Strongholds of the Border Reivers: Fortifications of the Anglo-Scottish Border 1296-1603* (Oxford: Osprey Publishing, 2008).

Durham, Keith, *Warrior 154: Border Reiver 1513-1603* (Oxford: Osprey Publishing, 2011).

'Eastwatch', *Game of Thrones*, Season 7, episode 5. Directed by Matt Shakman. HBO, 13 August 2017.

Erskine, Caroline, MacDonald, Alan R. and Penman, Michael (eds), *Scotland: The Making and Unmaking of the Nation c.1100-1707 Volume 5* (Dundee: Dundee University Press & The Open University in Scotland, 2007).

Fawcett, Richard, *The Architectural History of Scotland: Scottish Architecture from the Accession of the Stewarts to the Reformation 1371-1560* (Edinburgh: Edinburgh University Press, 1994).

'Fire and Blood', *Game of Thrones*, Season 1, episode 10. Directed by Alan Taylor. HBO, 19 June 2011.

Fisher, Ian., 'Chapter 5: The Heirs of Somerled', in Richard Oram and Geoffrey Stell (eds), *Lordship and Architecture in Medieval and Renaissance Scotland* (Edinburgh: John Donald, 2005), pp.84-95.

Forder, Simon, *The myth of the motte and bailey castle in Scotland* (online, 2014). Available at: https://thecastleguy.co.uk/wp-content/uploads/2014/04/The-myth-of-the-motte-and-bailey-castle-in-Scotland.pdf (accessed 19 October 2018).

Foster, Sally, *Maeshowe and the Heart of Neolithic Orkney* (Edinburgh: Historic Scotland, 2006).

Fraser, George MacDonald, *The Steel Bonnets: The Story of the Anglo-Scottish Border Reivers* (London: Harvill, 1989).

Fraser, James E., *The Roman Conquest of Scotland: The Battle of Mons Graupius AD 84* (Stroud: Tempus Publishing Limited, 2005).

Froissart's Chronicles, trans. Jon Jolliffe (ed.) (London: Penguin Books, 1967).

Fry, Michael, *Edinburgh: A History of the City* (London: Pan Books, 2010).

Game of Thrones: The Complete First Season (2012, Blu-ray). The Complete Guide to Westeros: The Children of the Forest, the First Men and the Andals, narrated by Donald Sumpter. Written by Bryan Cogman.

Game of Thrones: The Complete First Season (2012, Blu-ray). The Complete Guide to Westeros: The Sack of King's Landing, narrated by Donald Sumpter. Written by Bryan Cogman.

Game of Thrones: The Complete Second Season (2013, Blu-ray). Histories and Lore: Season Two: Harrenhal, narrated by Michelle Fairley. Written by Dave Hill. Warner Home Video.

Game of Thrones: The Complete Second Season (2013, Blu-ray). Histories and Lore: Season Two: Greyjoy Rebellion, narrated by Alfie Allen. Written by Dave Hill. Warner Home Video.

Game of Thrones: The Complete Second Season (2013, Blu-ray). Histories and Lore: Season Two: Greyjoy Rebellion, narrated by Stephen Dillane. Written by Dave Hill. Warner Home Video.

Game of Thrones: The Complete Second Season (2013, Blu-ray). Histories and Lore: Season Two: The Free Folk, narrated by Rose Leslie. Written by Dave Hill. Warner Home Video.

Game of Thrones: The Complete Third Season (2014, Blu-ray). Histories and Lore: Season Three: House Frey, narrated by Michelle Fairley. Written by Dave Hill. Warner Home Video.

Game of Thrones: The Complete Third Season (2014, Blu-ray). Histories and Lore: Season Three: House Reed, narrated by Ellie Kendrick. Written by Bryan Cogman. Warner Home Video.

Game of Thrones: The Complete Third Season (2014, Blu-ray). Histories and Lore: Season Three: The North, narrated by Kit Harrington. Written by Bryan Cogman. Warner Home Video.

Game of Thrones: The Complete Fourth Season (2015, Blu-ray). Histories and Lore: Season Four: The Nations of the North, narrated by Kristofer Hivju. Written by Dave Hill. Warner Home Video.

Game of Thrones: The Complete Fifth Season (2016, Blu-ray). Histories and Lore: Season Five: Winterfell, narrated by Michael McElhatton. Writen by Dave Hill. Waner Home Video.

Game of Thrones: The Complete Sixth Season (2016, Blu-ray). Histories and Lore: Season Six: Riverrun, narrated by Clive Russell. Written by Dave Hill. Warner Home Video.

Bibliography

Game of Thrones: The Complete Sixth Season (2016, Blu-ray). Histories and Lore: Season Six: The Old Way, narrated by Pilou Asbæk. Written by Dave Hill. Warner Home Video.

Game of Thrones Wiki, *Night's Queen* (online, 2018). Available at (https://gameofthrones.fandom.com/wiki/Night%27s_Queen (accessed 2 November 2018).

Game of Thrones Wiki, *The Wall* (online, 2018). Available at https://gameofthrones.fandom.com/wiki/The_Wall (accessed 14 October 2018).

Game of Thrones Wiki *Weirwood* (online, 2018). Available at https://gameofthrones.fandom.com/wiki/Night%27s_Queen (accessed 1 November 2018).

Geoffrey of Monmouth, *The History of the Kings of Britain*, trans. Lewis Thorpe (London: Penguin Books, 1966).

Gies, Joseph and Gies, Francis, *Life in a Medieval Castle* (London: Harper Perennial, 2015).

Gilmore, Mikal, 'George R.R. Martin: The Rolling Stone Interview' (online, 23 April 2014), *Rolling Stone*. Available at https://www.rollingstone.com/culture/culture-news/george-r-r-martin-the-rolling-stone-interview-242487/ (accessed 14 September 2018).

Glozier, Matthew, 'The Wars of Mary and James VI and I, 1560-1625', in Edward M. Spiers, Jeremy A. Crang and Mathew J. Strickland (eds), *A Military History of Scotland* (Edinburgh: Edinburgh University Press, 2014), pp.235-47.

Goodare, Julian, 'Scottish politics in the reign of James VI', in Bob Harris and Alan R. MacDonald (eds), *Scotland: The Making and Unmaking of the Nation c.1500-1707: Volume 4: Readings: c.1500-1707* (Dundee: Dundee University Press & The Open University in Scotland, 2007), pp.20-40.

Goring, Rosemary (ed.), *Scotland: The Autobiography* (London: Penguin Books, 2014).

Grey, Thomas, *Scalacronica: A Chronicle of England and Scotland* (Edinburgh: The Maitland Club, 1836).

Harris, Bob and MacDonald, Alan R. (eds), *Scotland: The Making and Unmaking of the Nation c.1100-1707 Volume 1* (Dundee: Dundee University Press & The Open University in Scotland, 2006).

Haywood, John, *The Historical Atlas of the Celtic World* (London: Thames & Hudson, 2015).

Hodgman, John, radio interview with George R.R. Martin, *The Sound of Young America* (online, 19 September 2011). Available at: http://www. maximumfun.org/sound-young-america/george-r-r-martin-author-song-ice-and-fire-series-interview-sound-young-america (accessed 3 October 2018).

John of Fordun's Chronicle of the Scottish Nation: Volume 1, W.F. Skene (ed.), Facsimile reprint (Cribyn, Ceredigion: Llanerch Publishers, 1993).

John of Fordun's Chronicle of the Scottish Nation: Volume 2, W.F. Skene (ed.), Facsimile reprint (Cribyn, Ceredigion: Llanerch Publishers, 1993).

Kamm, Antony, *The Last Frontier: The Roman Invasions of Scotland* (Stroud: Tempus Publishing Limited, 2004).

Larrington, Carolyne, *Winter is Coming: The Medieval World of Game of Thrones* (London: I.B. Tauris & Co. Ltd, 2016).

Lewtas, Ian, McAlister, Rachael, Wallis, Adam, Woodley, Clive and Cullis, Ian, 'The ballistic performance of the bombard Mons Meg,' in *Defence Technology* 12 (2), 2016, pp.59-68 (online). Available at: https://www. sciencedirect.com/science/article/pii/S2214914715000835 (accessed 6 August 2018).

Lindsay, Maurice, *The Castles of Scotland: A Constable Guide* (London: Constable, 1986).

Linklater, Magnus, *Massacre: The Story of Glencoe* (Glasgow: William Collins Sons and Company Limited, 1982).

'Lord Snow', *Game of Thrones*, Season 1, episode 3. HBO. Directed by Brian Kirk. 1 May 2011.

Lowder, James (ed.), *Beyond the Wall: Exploring George R.R. Martin's A Song of Ice and Fire* (Dallas: BenBella Books, Inc, 2012).

Lynch, Michael, *Scotland: A New History* (London: Pimlico, 1992).

MacDiarmid, Hugh, *The Hugh MacDiarmid Anthology: Poems in Scots and English*, Michael Grieve and Alexander Scott (eds) (London: Routledge & Kegan Paul, 1972).

MacDougall, Norman, 'Achilles' Heel? The Earldom of Ross, the Lordship of the Isles, and the Stewart Kings, 1449-1507', in E.J.Cowan and R. Andrew McDonald (eds), *Alba: Celtic Scotland in the Medieval Era* (Edinburgh: John Donald, 2005), pp.248-75.

MacGregor, Martin, 'Warfare in Gaelic Scotland in the Later Middle Ages', in M. Spears, Jeremy A. Crang and Mathew J. Strickland (eds), *A Military History of Scotland* (Edinburgh: Edinburgh University Press, 2014), pp.209-34.

Machiavelli, Niccolò, *The Prince* (London: William Collins, 2018).

Mackenzie, Donald Alexander, *Wonder Tales from Scottish Myth and Legend* (Glasgow: Blackie and Son Limited, 1917).

Mackenzie, W. Mackay, *The Mediaeval Castle in Scotland* (New York: Benjamin Blom, Inc, 1972).

MacNeil, Ian Roderick, *Castle in the Sea* (New York: Vantage Press, 1975).

MacPhail, I.M.M., *Dumbarton Castle* (Edinburgh: John Donald Publishers Ltd, 1979).

MacPhee, Kathleen, *Somerled: Hammer of the Norse* (Glasgow: NWP, 2004).

Marsden, John, *Somerled and the Emergence of Gaelic Scotland* (East Linton, East Lothian: Tuckwell Press, 2000).

Martin, George R.R., *A Clash of Kings* (New York: Bantam Books, 2011).

Martin, George R.R., *A Game of Thrones* (London: Harper Voyager, 2011).

Martin, George R.R., *A Dance with Dragons* (London: Harper Voyager, 2011).

Martin, George R.R., *A Feast for Crows* (London: Harper Voyager, 2011).

Martin, George R.R., *A Storm of Swords* (New York: Bantam Books, 2013).

Martin, George R. R., *Fire and Blood* (London: Harper Voyager, 2018).

Martin, George R.R., *On Fantasy* (online, 1996). Available at http://www.georgerrmartin.com/about-george/on-writing-essays/on-fantasy-by-george-r-r-martin/ (accessed 19 September 2019).

Martin, George R.R., interviewed by Jamie Sims for *The New York Times*, 16 October 2018. Available at: https://www.nytimes.com/2018/10/16/t-magazine/george-rr-martin-qanda-game-of-thrones.html (accessed 12 November 2018).

Martin, George R.R., García, Elio M., Jr. and Antonsson, Linda, *The World of Ice & Fire: The Untold History of Westeros and the Game of Thrones* London: Harper Voyager, 2014).

Maxwell, Gordon, *A Gathering of Eagles: Scenes from Roman Scotland* (Edinburgh: Birlinn Ltd, with Historic Scotland, 2005).

McDonald, R. Andrew, 'Rebels without a Cause? The Relations of Fergus of Galloway and Somerled of Argyll with the Scottish Kings, 1153-1164', in E.J. Cowan and R. Andrew McDonald (eds), *Alba: Celtic Scotland in the Medieval Era* (Edinburgh: John Donald, 2005), pp.166-86.

McDonald, R. Andrew, 'The Western *Gàidhealtachd* in the Middle Ages', in Bob Harris and Alan R. MacDonald (eds), *Making and Unmaking of a Nation* v.1 (2006), pp.65-89.

McGladdery, Christine, *James II* (Edinburgh: John Donald, 2015).

McKean, Charles, *The Scottish Chateau: The Country Houses of Renaissance Scotland* (Thrupp: Sutton Publishing Limited, 2001).

Miket, Roger and Roberts, David L., *The Mediaeval Castles of Skye and Lochalsh* (Edinburgh: Birlinn, 2007).

Miles, David, *The Tribes of Britain* (London: Phoenix, 2006).

Moffat, Alistair, *Scotland: A History from Earliest Times* (Edinburgh: Birlinn, 2015).

Moffat, Alistair, *The Borders* (Edinburgh: Birlinn, 2007).

Moffat, Alistair, *The Sea Kingdoms: The History of Celtic Britain and Ireland* (Edinburgh: Birlinn, 2017).

Morris, R.W.B., 'The petroglyphs at Achnabreck, Argyll', in *Proceedings of the Society of Antiquaries of Scotland* 103 (1974), pp.33-56.

National Museums Scotland, *Deskford Carnyx* (online, 2018). Available at https://www.nms.ac.uk/explore-our-collections/stories/scottish-history-and-archaeology/deskford-carnyx/ (accessed 2 December 2018).

National Museums Scotland, *Reconstruction of the Deskford carnyx (80-200 AD), in bronze and brass with wooden tongue and enamel eye inserts, by Dr Purser and John Creed, Glasgow, 1992* (online, 2018). Available at https://www.nms.ac.uk/explore-our-collections/collection-search-results/?item_id=384359 (accessed 2 December 2018).

Noonan, Damien, *Castles & Ancient Monuments of Scotland* (London: Aurum Press, 2000).

Oliver, Neil, *A History of Ancient Britain* (London: Phoenix Press, 2012).

Oliver, Neil, *A History of Scotland* (London: Phoenix, 2010).

Orkneyinga Saga: The History of the Earls of Orkney, trans. Hermann Pálsson and Paul Edwards (London: Penguin Books, 1978).

Osborne, Brian D., Armstrong, Ronald and Renton, Ronald (eds), *Cradle of the Scots: An Argyll Anthology* (Edinburgh: Birlinn, 2000).

Paterson, Raymond Campbell, *The Lords of the Isles: A History of Clan Donald* (Edinburgh: Birlinn, 2001).

Pavlac, Brian A. (ed.), *Game of Thrones Versus History: Written in Blood* (New Jersey: John Wiley & Sons, Inc, 2017).

Penman, Michael, *Robert the Bruce: King of the Scots* (London: Yale University Press, 2014).

Philips, Gervase, 'Scotland in the Age of the Military Revolution, 1488-1560', in Edward M. Spiers, Jeremy A. Crang and Mathew J. Strickland (eds), *A Military History of Scotland* (Edinburgh: Edinburgh University Press, 2012), pp.182-208.

Procopius, *History of the Wars: Books VII & VIII*, trans. H.B. Dewing (London: William Heinemann, 1962).

Reid, Stuart, *Fortress 46: Castles and Tower Houses of the Scottish Clans 1450-1650* (Oxford: Osprey, 2006).

Ritchie, Anna, *Viking Scotland* (London: B.T. Batsford Ltd, 1993).

Robertson, Anne S., *The Antonine Wall: A handbook to the Roman Wall between Forth and Clyde and a guide to its surviving remains* (Edinburgh: Glasgow Archaeological Society, 1963).

Ross, David R., *James The Good: The Black Douglas* (Edinburgh: Luath Press, 2008).

Ross, David R., *On the Trail of Robert the Bruce* (Edinburgh: Luath Press Ltd, 1999).

Ross, Stewart, *Scottish Castles* (Moffat, Dumfries and Galloway: Lochar Publishing Ltd, 1990).

Ruiter, Brian de, 'A Defense against the "Other"', in Pavlac, Brian A. (ed.), *Game of Thrones Versus History: Written in Blood* (New Jersey: John Wiley & Sons, Inc, 2017), pp.85-96.

Rutherford, Allan and Malcolm, John, '"*That stalwart toure*": Bothwell Castle in the Thirteenth and Early Fourteenth Centuries', in: Dakin, A., Glendinning, M. and MacKechnie, A. (eds), *Scotland's Castle Culture* (Edinburgh: John Donald, 2011), pp.189-98.

Santiuste, David, *The Hammer of the Scots: Edward I and the Scottish Wars of Independence* (Barnsley: Pen & Sword, 2015).

Scott, Sir Walter, *Tales of a Grandfather: First Series*, ed. J. Hutchison (London: MacMillan and Co., Limited, 1908).

Simpson, Douglas W., *The Ancient Stones of Scotland* (London: Robert Hale Limited, 1965).

Strickland, Matthew J., 'The King of Scots at War, *c.* 1093-1286', in Edward M. Spiers, Jeremy A. Crang and Mathew J. Strickland, *A Military History of Scotland* (Edinburgh: Edinburgh University Press, 2014), pp.94-132.

Tabraham, Chris, *Bothwell Castle* (Edinburgh: Historic Scotland, 2009).

Tabraham, Chris, *Castles of Scotland: A Voyage Through the Centuries* (London: B.T. Batsford, 2005).

Tabraham, Chris, *Clan and Castle* (Edinburgh: Historic Scotland, 2008).

Tabraham, Chris, *Craigmillar Castle* (Edinburgh: Historic Scotland, 2007).

Tabraham, Chris, *Edinburgh Castle* (Edinburgh: Historic Scotland, 2008).

Tabraham, Chris, *Scotland's Castles* (London: B.T. Batsford Ltd and Historic Scotland, 1997).

Tabraham, Chris, *Scotland's Castles*, Revised edition (London: B.T. Batsford Ltd and Historic Scotland, 2005).

Tabraham, Chris, *Tantallon Castle* (Edinburgh: Historic Scotland, 2007).

Tabraham, Chris and Grove, Doreen, *Fortress Scotland and the Jacobites*. (London: B.T. Batsford and Historic Scotland, 2001).

Tacitus, Publius Cornelius, *Tacitus: Agricola and Germany*, trans. A.R. Birley (New York: Oxford University Press, 1999).

The Anglo-Saxon Chronicles, trans. Michael Swanton (ed.) (London: Phoenix Press, 2000).

The Annals of Ulster, Seán Mac Airt and Gearóid Mac Niocaill (eds) (Dublin: Dublin Institute for Advanced Studies, 1983).

The Auchinleck Chronicle: Ane Schort Memoriale of the Scottis Corniklis for Addicioun (Edinburgh: Thomas Thomson, Esq., 1818).

'The Bear and the Maiden Fair', *Game of Thrones*, Season 3, episode 7. Directed by Michelle MacLaren. HBO, 12 May 2013.

The Book of Pluscarden: Vol. II, Felix J.H. Skene (ed.) (Edinburgh: William Paterson, 1880).

'The Broken Man', *Game of Thrones*, Season 6, episode 7. Directed by Mark Mylod. HBO, 5 June 2016.

The Chronicle of Lanercost: Volume 1, trans. Sir Herbert Maxwell (Cribyn,Ceredigion: Llanerch Press, 2001).

The Chronicle of Lanercost: Volume 2, trans. Sir Herbert Maxwell (Cribyn, Ceredigion: Llanerch Press, 2001).

'The Climb', *Game of Thrones*, Season 3, episode 6. Directed by Alik Sakharov. HBO, 5 May 2013.

'The Door', *Game of Thrones*, Season 6, episode 5. Directed by Jack Bender. HBO, 22 May 2016.

'The Ghost of Harrenhal', *Game of Thrones*, Season 2, episode 5. Directed by David Petrarka. HBO, 29 April 2012.

'The Pointy End', *Game of Thrones*, Season 1, episode 8. Directed by Daniel Minahan. HBO, 5 June 2011.

'The Rains of Castamere', *Game of Thrones*, Season 3, episode 9. Directed by David Nutter. HBO, 2 June 2013.

The Siege of Caerlaverock, trans. C.W. Scott-Giles (online, 2018). Available at https://www.theheraldrysociety.com/articles/the-siege-of-caerlaverock/ (accessed 31 October 2018).

'The Wars to Come', *Game of Thrones*, Season 5, episode 1. Directed by Michael Slovis. HBO, 12 April 2015.

Tolkien, J.R.R. *The Lord of the Rings* (London: BCA, 1991).

Tranter, Nigel, *The Story of Scotland* (Glasgow: Neil Wilson Publishing, 1987).

Urquhart Castle (Edinburgh: Historic Scotland, 2012).

'Valar Dohaeris', *Game of Thrones*, Season 3, episode 1. Directed by Daniel Minahan. HBO, 31 March 2013.

Vita Edwardi Secundi, trans. Wendy R. Childs (ed.) (Oxford: Oxford University Press, 2005).

Walker, Ian W., *Lords of Alba: The Making of Scotland* (Stroud: Sutton Publishing Limited, 2006).

Watson, Fiona J., 'Adapting Tradition? The Earldom of Strathearn, 1114-1296', in Richard Oram and Geoffrey Stell (eds), *Lordship and Architecture in Medieval and Renaissance Scotland* (Edinburgh: John Donald, 2005), pp.26-43.

Weatherford, Jack, *Genghis Khan and the Making of the Modern World* (New York: Three Rivers Press, 2004).

Webb, Sharon, *In the Footsteps of Kings* (Kilmartin, Argyll: Kilmartin House Trust, 2012).

Westwood, Jennifer and Kingshill, Sophia, *The Lore of Scotland: A guide to Scottish legends* (London: Arrow Books, 2011).

Whitman, James Q., *The Verdict of Battle: The Law of Victory and the Making of Modern War* (London: Harvard University Press, 2012).

'Winter is Coming', *Game of Thrones*, Season 1, episode 1. Directed by Tim Van Patten. HBO, 17 April 2011.

Wormald, Jenny, 'The Reign of James VI: 1537-1625', in Bob Harris and Alan R. MacDonald (eds), *Scotland: The Making and Unmaking of the Nations c.1100-1707. Volume 2: Early Modern Scotland: c.1500-1707* (Dundee: Dundee University Press and The Open University, 2007), pp.18-35.

'You Win or You Die', *Game of Thrones*, Season 1, episode 7. Directed by Daniel Minahan. HBO, 29 May 2011.

Acknowledgements

A writer in isolation is as likely to thrive as Jon Snow on his first expedition beyond the Wall, and so I find myself indebted to many individuals and organisations who supported the writing process and made the idea possible in the first place. I would also like to absolve them of any responsibility for misinterpretations, errors or omissions within this book, which are entirely my own.

I am sincerely thankful to the editing and publishing team at Pen & Sword Books, who bravely took on a first-time author and saw me through the countless questions, addendums and alterations that I threw their way. I am also grateful to individual creatives, including Bob Marshall who illustrated the wonderful map that does so much to merge Scotland's history with Martin's fantasy atmosphere.

Several of the publications that I write for have graciously helped with promoting the book, not to mention serving as a honing ground for my writing and storytelling. My thanks to *The Scots Magazine* and *History Scotland* magazine in particular. I also owe a debt of gratitude to the Society of Antiquaries of Scotland and their public awareness arm Dig It!, with whom I have worked for several years and who offered support at every turn.

Much of this book was written in the cafes of the National Museum of Scotland and the National Library of Scotland, as well as within the Edinburgh and Scottish Collection of the Central Library. Essential research was also carried out at these institutions. I count myself incredibly fortunate to have access to such places, for libraries and museums are a wellspring not just for inspiration but also for individual and communal wellbeing. We should all frequent them more.

Thanks to my friends who put up with my frequent absenteeism and provided essential feedback on chapter drafts, in particular Bryce and

Acknowledgements

Erika Cleborne-Berube, Samantha Myers and Sarah Cockburn. Above all, thanks to my partner, Ana Soldatenko, who not only put up heroically with my mercurial process for many months but also made invaluable contributions to the book's concept and design.

Of course, this book would not exist if not for the imagination of George R.R. Martin and the other writers of fantasy, non-fiction and historical fiction who contributed in a thousand small ways to my life-long fascination with history. Nor would it exist without the filmmakers and television producers who bring history off the page and onto screen. I can only hope that this book does some justice to their visions and insights, and that it inspires you, the reader, to use their stories as a lens through which our own world becomes just a little more magical.

February 2019
Edinburgh